READINGS

in Archaeology, Ethnohistory, *and* Ethnography

Feffer & Simons, Inc. *London and Amsterdam*

The
North Mexican
Frontier

EDITED BY
Basil C. Hedrick
J. Charles Kelley
Carroll L. Riley

Southern Illinois University Press

Carbondale and Edwardsville

TO
Anne
Ellen
Brent

CONTENTS

INTRODUCTION

WITHIN the last twenty years, the area of the north and west of Mexico has attracted increasing attention from specialists in a variety of fields—archaeology, cultural geography, ethnology, ethnohistory, and history. This is, in part, due to the fact that relatively little work has been done in this area and that work has tended to be very spotty; a series of special investigations of particular problems, but with relatively little attempt at synthesis. This is all the more surprising, because the northern Mexican area was of very great importance as a transmitter of culture from the civilization of Mesoamerica to the Puebloan area of the southwest United States.

At present, extensive work in northern Mexico is being done, especially in archaeology, but also in all of the other fields mentioned above. Because of this rising interest, we feel that now is the time to republish some of the more difficult-to-obtain studies of the past. The papers reproduced here include some of the earliest systematic archaeological work done in northwest Mexico, a selection of oft-quoted materials from documentary sources, plus older ethnological papers, and articles in archaeology and ethnology that have had relatively little circulation. Also included is a valuable short synthesis of a large area within north Mexico, and one of a single important group within north Mexico. We have also included one general theoretical work, the application of which goes beyond our area, but which uses a major speech family within the area as an example of how one may do culture history.

For convenience and readability, type has been set on all papers and we have translated the various Spanish documents into English. The translations of the articles, originally published in Spanish, may represent the first printing of those items in English. Editing has been minimal and confined mainly to removing incidental references to illustrations which have not been used. As an editorial policy we have decided to delete virtually all illustrations. In fact, only three papers, those of Gamio, Batres, and Hrdlička, are heavily illustrated. Even so we realize that our illustration policy may lessen, somewhat, the value of the volume. However, all three of the extensively illustrated works are reasonably easy to obtain for the specialist who really wishes to check out a point that involves illustration. Our volume, then, is intended for specialists in various disciplines who will have quick, ready-at-hand reference to a variety of papers, some of which he will most probably not have on his shelf. It should also be very useful to students who are specializing in north Mexican studies.

We acknowledge with gratitude the following people who have helped in one phase or another of this project: Mr. Dale R. Whiteside, especially for his work on the translation of the Batres article; Mrs. Ellen A. Kelley, who helped in various aspects of the work; Mrs. Geraldine Kelley, for her supervision of the manuscript production; Mr. Louis Cadkin, for his reproduction of the Berghes map. Also, our thanks to Donna Kathleen Abbass, Toni Coleman, Judy Grimes, Theresa Page, Carla Jones, Pamela Rendleman, and Charlotte Jones for their help in working with the manuscript.

SPECIAL ACKNOWLEDGMENT is made for permission to reprint the following works. "Notes on the Geography and Archaeology of Zape, Durango" by Donald D. Brand, from *So Live the Works of Men* (Albuquerque: University of New Mexico Press, 1939). Reprinted by permission of the author.

"Navacoyan: A Preliminary Survey" by Agnes M. Howard, from *Bulletin of the Texas Archaeological Society*, 28 (Austin, 1957). Reprinted by permission of the Texas Archaeological Society.

"Late Archaeological Sites in Durango, Mexico, from Chalchihuites to Zape" by J. Alden Mason, from *Twenty-Fifth Anniversary Studies, Publications of the Philadelphia Anthropological Society*, 1 (1937). Reprinted by permission of the University of Pennsylvania Press.

"A Brief and Succinct Account of the Events of the War with the Tepehuanes, Government of Nueva Vizcaya, from November 15, 1616 to May 16, 1618," from *Historical Documents Relating to New Mexico, Nueva Vizcaya, and Approaches Thereto, to 1773* (1923), ed. Charles Wilson Hackett. Reprinted by permission of the Carnegie Institution of Washington.

"The Opata: An Inland Tribe of Sonora" by Jean B. Johnson, from University of New Mexico Publications in Anthropology, No. 6 (1950). Reprinted by permission of the University of New Mexico Press.

"The Hunting-Gathering People of North Mexico" by Paul Kirch-hoff, from *El Norte de México y el Sur de Estados Unidos* (Mexico, 1943). Reprinted by permission of the author.

"The Tepehuán of Northern Mexico" by J. Alden Mason, from *Amerikanistische Miszellen*, 25 (Hamburg, 1959). Reprinted by permission of the Hamburgisches Museum für Völkerkunde und Vorgeschichte.

"The Genetic Model and Uto-Aztecan Time Perspective" by A. Kimball Romney, from *Davidson Journal of Anthropology*, 3, No. 2 (Winter 1957). Reprinted by permission of the author.

> Basil C. Hedrick
>
> J. Charles Kelley
>
> Carroll L. Riley

Carbondale, Illinois
January 1971

The North Mexican Frontier

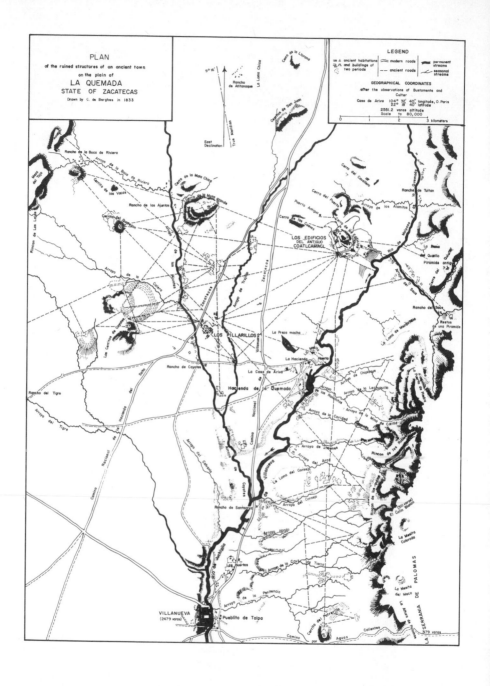

PLAN
of the ruined structures of an ancient town
on the plain of
LA QUEMADA
STATE OF ZACATECAS
Drawn by C. de Berghes in 1833

LEGEND

⌂ ancient habitations and buildings of two periods
═══ modern roads
--- ancient roads
permanent streams
seasonal streams

GEOGRAPHICAL COORDINATES
after the observations of Bustamante and Cutier
Casa de Ariva 104° 32' 40" longitude, O. Paris
22° 18' 40" latitude
2551.2 varas altitude
Scale to 80,000

0   1   2   3 kilometers

THE C. DE BERGHES MAP OF 1833

THE BERGHES MAP of the La Quemada area is perhaps the most important single source for the archaeology of the region, although not specifically for La Quemada itself. De Berghes was a German mining engineer at the mine Veta Grande in Zacatecas, who was commissioned by the governor of the state in 1831 to make the La Quemada survey. A portion of the map showing the area around La Quemada was published by Carlos Nebel (1836 [French edition]), 1840, in *Viaje Pintoresco y Arqueológico Sobre la Parte Más Interesante de la República Mexicana*, and republished in Mexico in 1963 by Librería de Manuel Porrua, S.A. (cf. plate 23 and text on pp. 18 and 19). The entire map was published in Batres's *Visit to the Archaeological Remains of La Quemada, Zacatecas, Mexico* (1903), while Noguera in 1960 published a very poor reproduction of the map. The present reproduction is based on a draftsman's copy of the Berghes map, derived from one in the possession of Mr. Federico Sesscosse of Zacatecas.

When Berghes made his survey of the area, many of the smaller archaeological sites of the Rio Malpaso valley were still easily visible, as were the innumerable artificial roadways which linked the villages to each other and to La Quemada. His map shows thirteen roadways extending out from La Quemada, while many others connect the villages to each other or run to uncertain destinations. Several of these roadways can still be identified in the field; one exposed in an erosional cross section was constructed by building parallel masonry walls and filling between them with rubble to form a high, broad, stone paved roadway similar to the *sacbes* of the Maya. While engaged in field work at La Quemada on a Southern Illinois University research project in 1963, Pedro Armillas said (1963, p. 17, present translation by Kelley):

In all of the sections investigated these roads were paved strips several meters in width; in part they are veritable causeways formed by lateral walls, constructed with large boulders, filled between with dry stones and paved with cobblestones. These routes extended for several kilometers and led to the rural population centers.

The fortresslike nature of La Quemada itself, veritably a castle-stronghold, its situation directly on the northern ecological-ethnic frontier, taken together with the network of villages and roads effectively blocking the passage of the northern Chichimecs down the open valley of the Rios Malpaso-Jerez, an avenue leading deep into Mesoamerica in the Tarascan area, suggest that the city and the village-roadway network were organized and constructed deliberately to defend the northern frontier of a long extinct and historically unknown Mesoamerican political entity.

In addition to presenting evidence for hypotheses such as that given above, the map has real utility for archaeological work in the field. It is an extremely valuable basic source, especially because of the early date of the survey.

J. C. K.

Visit to the Archaeological Remains of La Quemada, Zacatecas, Mexico

Leopoldo Batres

Fray Antonio Tello described the great ruin of La Quemada, or Tuitlan, (known locally and certainly erroneously as "Chicomostoc") as early as 1650 (Tello, 1650, quoted in Noguera, 1960, p. 23); Berghes mapped the Rio Malpaso valley with its ruins, including La Quemada, and the innumerable constructed roadways which join the many village sites to each other and to La Quemade (see elsewhere in this volume) in 1833; his map of La Quemada itself was included in Carlos Nebel's description of the site (Nebel, 1840). In 1866 a detailed map of La Quemada was made by Tarayre (Tarayre, 1869); this map has served as a basis for many later maps. Batres did not visit the site until 1903 and his article, translated here into English for the first time, is not especcially outstanding. Nevertheless, the article does provide a good description of the site early in this century and in addition describes and illustrates part of a collection of artifacts in the nearby Hacienda La Quemada which purportedly had been found at the site. This collection, it is said, was later destroyed in a fire. Included in the Batres report was the Berghes map of 1833, reproduced in this volume.

If the Hacienda La Quemada collection did indeed come from La Quemada, the site was occupied earlier than other evidence has indicated. Porter (1956) has noted that two of the pottery vessels from this collection illustrated by Batres are Chupicuaro types. This would place the beginnings of La Quemada at least as early as the end of the Late Pre-Classic. I know of no other evidence that supports such an early date for La Quemada. Three published radiocarbon dates for La Quemada (Michigan 430, 431, 432; Crane and Griffin, 1958 a and b) are A.D. 890, 780, and 1210, with a total range including probable error from A.D.

540 to 1370. A series of radiocarbon dates obtained more recently by Pedro Armillas fall into the same pattern, with a concentration in the tenth and eleventh centuries A.D. Culturally, La Quemada resembles most closely, especially in ceramics, other sites to the south and west, along the Rio Juchipila and the Rio Bolaños. All of these sites share negative painted and paint cloisonné ceramic wares together with some incised or engraved wares and varying red-on-brown wares; plus much polished red, polished black, and plain and textured brown utility wares. There are also some ties with the Chalchihuites Culture to the northwest, but the latter appears to be essentially a separate line of development. Both Chalchihuites sites and La Quemada have halls-of-columns and the much smaller Chalchihuites site of Cerro de Moctehuma architecturally resembles La Quemada quite closely.

One correction of Batres's description of La Quemada is in order. He identifies one large high-walled room on the so-called "acropolis" as a ball court. Here he must have been referring to a handball court, not to the ball courts traditionally a part of Mesoamerican culture. There is a true Mesoamerican ball court at La Quemada, however. It is a very large capital I-shaped court lying on the lower level of the main site between the hall of columns and the "votive pyramid." Batres, like most other observers, early and late, also failed to note the presence of an apparent corbelled arch in a tunnel or large drain at one corner of the hall of columns.

Regardless of some questions regarding the provenience of the artifacts which Batres attributes to La Quemada, this article is not only of historic interest but is an important early and basic source for students of La Quemada archaeology.

J. C. K.

HAVING been commissioned by the Office of Justice and Public Instruction to visit the archaeological monuments known as Chicomostoc, ruins of structures located on the Hacienda La Quemada, (Zacatecas) and also to appoint a caretaker to oversee their conservation, I arrived at that hacienda accompanied by my son, Salvador. We were received with open and loyal hospitality by the farm owner, Mr. Ildefonso Franco, his good wife, and distinguished son, Juan, who outfitted me with whatever provisions I needed to fulfill the purpose of my visit.

We left [the hacienda of] La Quemada, and after walking for forty minutes northward across work land we arrived at the foot of the hill on which the buildings were situated. At that point I began to discover that those colossal constructions synthesized the grandeur of a people who, following the custom of primitive peoples, raised daring structures worthy of the majesty of their gods. Those peoples, who did not believe in the unity of a Supreme Being, had to multiply their efforts in order to satisfy each of the many deities who constituted their Olympus. The ruins on La Quemada meet this exigency, since they contain not only one temple, but many.

The walls, today bare of facing, but formerly covered with the finest of stucco-plaster work, product of the expertise of those fanatic workmen and artists in their attempts to please their idols and to attain to that much-desired good fortune in the world of darkness, must have presented an imposing aspect, fantastic and grandiose when they were at their apogee.

The climb to the buildings is truly difficult, one can say dangerous, because the stairs which led to the platforms upon which the temples and habitations rest are nearly destroyed; the places where once there were balustrades are now like landslides on which one climbs only by means of gymnastic effort. One marvels upon considering how the builders of that city could construct the extensive and lofty curtains of defense which form at the same time the foundation walls of the broad platforms at the shoulder of the hill. Where did those aerial masons support and secure their scaffolds? And I say aerial because they had to have been suspended on ropes to do such difficult work.

The curtains to which I referred rise at the edge of the precipices to a height of eighty meters above the ground.

Getting on with my observations, my eyes fixed on the interstices in the rocks of the ancient construction, seeking the famous rattlesnakes, of which we hear so much from the visitors to those ruins, assuring us that they had to wait until the winter season to risk the visit, claiming moreover that winter is the only possible season by virtue of the fact that the reptiles are dormant in their dens permitting the traveler to walk around in such dangerous places. That advice became widespread, to the extent that some visitors, fearful of perishing as victims of some of those terrible descendants of the seducer of Eve, were satisfied simply to admire the monuments from the foot of the little mountain on which they stand.

For my part, I must avow that, although I ascended and descended in and about the old constructions, I did not see any snakes, or even a sign that they might exist in that place. I talked with the *vaqueros* that look after cows that graze on the hill where the structures are and they told me: "No, sir, there are no snakes here; we have been watching cows here for many years, every day on this hill, and we can assure you that, if we see one snake in a year, that is a great many." How human fantasy conjures up images! Unfortunately, everything which has been told about these monuments is as fantastic as the exaggerated eruption of snakes.

To guess the antiquity of those stone testimonies is impossible; let us satisfy ourselves, therefore, with the ability to determine who were the founders.

The two tasks outlined by the order from my superior were completed: I visited the ruins and I appointed the caretaker who guards them today.

Mexico, April of 1903.

L. B.

Historical Description

THE LA QUEMADA ruins have been known for many years among scholars and even among laymen. They have been the object of strange conjectures, and they have been pointed up as the separation place of the famous seven tribes; but, to tell the truth, they have not been studied scientifically, but rather have served only as a topic which helps give flight to the imagination of visitors to the site.

Referring to the immigration of the four or nine tribes which came from the north, leaving many of their number at home, Torquemada, in his *Monarquía Indiana* (vol. 1, col. 1, p. 81) says: "they departed, leaving behind some of the old and some of the young for some reason; there are many traces of this in all these regions; in the northern parts, seven leagues south of Zacatecas, I saw some buildings and ruins of ancient populations, ruins of the largest imaginable dimensions."

The Franciscan chronicler tells us clearly that in his judgment those buildings were the work of the immigrants, and, judging by the locality in which Torquemada places them in relation to Zacatecas, it is clear that the site he refers to is the La Quemada ruins. Since there is no other group of Pre-Columbian buildings worthy of Torquemada's description, "more pompous than one can imagine," located that distance and in that direction from the capital of the state, it is certain that those ruins are none other than those which motivate the present volume.

In book 2, part 1, page 78 of *Monarquía Indiana*, referring to the immigrant tribes, Torquemada states: "but although they were all of a common generation and lineage, they did not comprise a single family; the first was called Mexicana; the second, Tlacoxcalca; the third, Chalmeca and the fourth, Calpico." Others claim that there were nine; the names may be of interest: Chalca, Matlatzin, Tepaneca, Malinalca, Xochimilca, Cuitlahuaca, Chichimeca, Mixquica and México.

If the La Quemada ruins are the same as those referred to by the historian quoted above, which, for reasons already stated, we believe to be the case, and if he attributes them to one of the immigrant tribes, then it follows that these ruins are the relics they left behind, and that the features of the buildings and the objects found within them would have to belong to one of the four or nine tribes. If this is not the case, then the objects found in the monuments and the type of architecture and construction materials belong to the Tarascan civilization, and the Tarascans are not included in any of the four or nine immigrant tribes. As a result, the group of ancient monuments at La Quemada could not have been the work of the tribes cited by history, but would have to be attributed to Chicomostoc origin.

Other historians have tried to build into these ruins the famous Chicomostoc of the divine flint legend; but this manner of judging them has been arbitrary, since in the opinion of the old historians, Torquemada included, *Chicomostoc* means "place of seven caves"; however, in the hill there is not one cave, to say nothing of seven. The only feature which they call cave, and unjustly so, is situated on the eastern portion of the hill, a recession in the wall into which two men can barely squeeze, if they remain standing.

Mr. Guillemin Tarayre, a member of the French scientific expedition, has published an illustrated report concerning the La Quemada ruins, and it is a truly brilliant work. The plans which he drew of the buildings and of the hill are very exact; I checked them and consequently used them to aid my memory.

Nebel published a plan and a perspective of the La Quemada ruins; the perspective is accurate enough, but the plan abounds in significant errors.

The famous Jalisco historian, Dr. Agustín Rivera, wrote a pamphlet on the subject, entitled *Chicomostoc*, and the *Museo mexicano*, a periodical published in Mexico, carried the following official documents concerning the monuments in question (vol. 1, p. 184); since they are of importance, I do not hesitate to quote them.

Since 1831, when we visited the famous ruins shown in the accompanying sketch, we have never been able to efface the profound impression made on our souls by the sight of those monuments. They are so ancient, their origin and their aim so obscure; so grandiose was the plan needed to construct those works, that no one can visit them without experiencing a sense of admiration and also sadness upon seeing how the monuments of national power and glory are destroyed not only by time, but also by the barbarity of men.

Unfortunately, the only time we looked at those ruins we were not able to examine them as carefully as we wished; nevertheless, we inspected them sufficiently to preserve a clear idea of that beautiful grouping of monuments, some demolished, others fallen in ruins and yet others nearly intact, as shown with total accuracy in the adjacent sketch. This sketch has been scrupulously copied from the work of Mr. Nebel and reduced to a smaller scale. We adopted this view for the cover of the article, because we are certain of the fidelity with which the ruins are represented in it.

Clavijero made a fleeting reference to the existence of some ancient buildings which can be no other than the ones we are discussing. Mr. Francisco García, Governor of the State of Zacatecas in 1830, charged Mr. Marcos Esparza during his trip to the provinces of Juchipila, Tlaltenango and Villanueva with the task of making such investigations as were possible into the vestiges of antiquity which were said to be found in those provinces, and to inform the Governor of the findings of his inquiries and searches. Mr. Esparza was not able to examine the La Quemada ruins, owing as much to the many tasks which occupied him on his trip as to the snakes which thronged the debris of those monuments—places which can be examined carefully only in the winter, when those reptiles are dormant. All the same, Mr. Esparza obtained information which was generally correct, and the publication of it greatly excited the curiosity of those enamored of a study of antiquity. The résumé which he wrote of the accounts is as follows:

In order to satisfy the wishes of the Government on this point it would have been necessary to dedicate the entire trip to seeking monuments discussed in this article, thereby obtaining a level of erudition worthy of our illustrious Government. Nevertheless, wishing to present

to Your Excellency a report of the status of the ruined structures called
La Quemada, which I mentioned in the respective place, I copied here
the account of a local man, Pedro Rivera. By virtue of his frequent
visits to the ruins, sometimes alone, sometimes in the company of his
father, the former Count of Santiago, his account deserves full credence; this is supported, in that his facts conform to those of the many
persons with whom I spoke in Villanueva on this subject. The report is
as follows:

"To the north of Villanueva, within the holdings of the Hacienda
La Quemada, are found some isolated hills of slight elevation. On the
principal hill, commonly called that of the "Buildings," there stand
some buildings which are said to have been constructed by the *indios*
during pagan times. From the brow of the hill along the road which
leads from the house at La Quemada one begins to perceive some
ruins, some of them half-demolished, others entirely demolished, and
only through careful scrutiny can one distinguish their foundations.
Most of them are small and positioned without any order whatsoever,
from which one infers that they were not occupied by anyone. Along
the same brow of the hill, prior to arriving at the roughest point, one
finds a quadrangular pyramid, very well constructed, the height of
which is about seven or eight yards, and the length of the sides at the
base are four to four and one-half yards. It is now truncated; but it
still bears marks which indicate that it formerly terminated in a vertex.
Standing atop the pyramid one can see clearly three roads straight as
stretched cords, four or five yards wide: one leads to the east, ending in
the Palomas range on a little hill named Cuisillo situated in the highest
part of the mountains; the second points toward the south-west, traversing the Coyotes ranch which belongs to the hacienda of the same name;
the third heads south-east, passing the principal houses on that
hacienda. The terminating points of the second and third roads are
obscured by long disuse and by the fact that they disappear into plowed
fields, so extensively has the land been tilled in those areas. Continuing
along the road, at a distance of fifty or sixty yards, the hill levels off
into a small plain in which there stands a large edifice approximately
thirty-five to forty yards long with a width of slightly less, so that at
first glance it appears to be square. The construction indicates that it
was surely a place where some lord gave audience to his vassals, or
doubtless where the more powerful gathered to deliberate on the most
weighty matters. It is not known what sort of roof the building had,
but it is believed to have been some beautiful beams, considering that
the walls bear not the slightest indication of pilasters from which could
spring the arches necessary to form that immense vault. A short distance from this palace is another magnificent structure fifty to sixty
yards long and wide, the walls of which still stand at a height of eight
or nine yards: in the interior are arranged two rows of five beautiful
columns each, perfectly cylindrical and equal in height to the walls and

one and one-half to two yards in diameter. On the west side there are still signs of steps, from which we infer that it was the location of an altar, which suggests that the building was a great temple; immediately adjacent, and on that wall are the ruins of a perfectly circular figure, six or seven yards in diameter, approachable via five or six stairsteps. There are five cavities in which it is supposed that the nobles made their sacrifices. At the summit of the hill stand several rooms, some of which are nearly destroyed, in which it is suspected that the petty king or governing personage lived. On the north-east side of the hill is a pyramid like the one described above, although not so tall. It, too, serves as the terminus of a road, the other end of which is situated on one of the San Juan Hills to the west of the road to Zacatecas. All around the top of the hill one observes vestiges of other buildings, although less splendid than those described. All are constructed of very smooth flagstone two or three inches thick and a very hard red mortar. The mortar adheres to the stones so well that, despite the passage of so many years since the construction, a considerable effort is required to break the joints loose."

To the west of that hill is a cave to the bottom of which no one has allegedly attained; however, Count Santa Rosa, with whom I spoke, made a special point personally to ascertain where the cave ended. The populace is convinced that there remain portions of the riches left by the *indios* at the time of their flight, but this belief has no basis in fact. At the east foot of the hill next to the road to Juitan, the Malpaso Ranch, stands a beautiful circular stone figure commonly known by the name of *Monarca* because of sculpted figures of a foot and a hand. The dimensions of it are three or four yards in diameter and one yard thick, and it appears in color and substance very much like those aligned in the portico of the Cathedral of Mexico. Some of the older residents on the Hacienda La Quemada, who were present at the time when Juan Manuel de la Bárcena bought this farm, assured me that all the rock used in the construction of the hacienda buildings was taken from that hill—taken from a great variety of buildings which the owner ordered razed for the purpose. Of this there seems no doubt, if one stops to notice that all the stone of the farm buildings is the same as that of the structures already mentioned.

Mr. García in the memoirs which he presented to the Congress of Zacatecas in 1831, called attention to the La Quemada ruins in the following terms:

On the evidence of historical monuments remaining from antiquity and those later discovered among the ruins on the La Quemada hacienda, commonly called Los Edificios, there is no doubt that a part of the state territory was inhabited by Aztecs on their long pilgrimage from the north to the south. The great extensiveness of the ruins mentioned and of many others discovered in the environs, along with the considerable number of roads on which there was travel from one site to another, proves incontestably that the nation which effected those works remained for some time in that place. It proves additionally that the nation was large and powerful and that it had arrived at a certain level of civilization. But above all, the works of fortification which are still to be seen on the hill where the structures are found [are] larger than any others of that sort found in the Republic, and astoundingly solid. [They] prove incontestably that the country was inhabited by some terrible nation, no doubt the *cascanes* who later gave the Spaniards considerable trouble. This was apparently the status of things until 1535, when the first Viceroy of Mexico conquered the whole territory by means of brilliant victories over the indigenous peoples in the province of Juchipila.

We have quoted this paragraph from the memoirs of Mr. García in the conviction that it is always creditable for a government to fix its attention on scientific matters, regardless of the gravity of the circumstances which surround it. It is also to the honor of the Congress of Zacatecas to have decreed and sanctioned the authorization of the Government to collect and preserve the antiquities of that country. We include that decree next, diverging for a moment from the principal objective of this article.

SECRETARIAT

OF THE

CONGRESS OF THE FREE STATE OF ZACATECAS.

Your Excellency:

The Honorable Congress, having taken into consideration the contents of Your Excellency's official letter of March twenty-seventh past, and in which were enclosed two pieces of pottery previously sent to Your Excellency by the interim parish priest of the town of Juchipila, and which were found in some excavations made in an ancient structure, the following has been resolved:

1]   It is granted to the Government that, when the status of public funds allows, it may make expenditures required for the conservation of ancient buildings of Juchipila and others of this type; to make excavations there and in other sites in the state with the object of seeking antiquities; to make plans and sketches of said buildings;

and to buy antiquities of all kinds found within the territory of the state.

2]   The pieces of ancient pottery which have been found in Juchipila and all the other antiquities of this type which may be found will be deposited in the public library until such time as a sufficient number is collected to form a museum of antiquities in the capital of the state.

This we communicate to Your Excellency for purposes of information and consequent action.

God and Liberty.   Zacatecas, April fourteenth, 1831.

Justo Hermosillo, *Deputy Secretary.*
Miguel Román, *Deputy Secretary.*
His Excellency the Governor of this State.

The Reverend Father Fray Francisco Frejes, in his excellent account of the Conquest of Zacatecas, gives his opinions on the origin and meaning of the La Quemada monuments as follows:

Concerning the religion of our *indios*, we have, very near our capital, authentic monuments in the form of the structures called La Quemada. To the north of Villanueva, on a hill of modest size one can observe ruins of various habitations, of a quadrangular pyramid; of a hall twenty-five yards square; and finally, of three roads six yards wide which run to the south in diverging lines some leagues until lost from view. This extraordinary amphitheater could not have taken form without a great massing of peoples, who had to come together at some point in time without mutual harassment, without any restraint on sacrifices, adorations and respects which they offered to their gods. According to the author of *The Conquest of New Galicia*, the *indio* Pantecal stated that the Chichimecas had three principal idols: the first was named Teopilzintli, god of the seasons; the second, called Herí, was god of the sciences; and the third, Nayarit, was the god of war. He states also that the Valley of Teul took its name from the great Teoul, or the temple which the *indios* had erected on it. Such was the respect and veneration on the part of the indigenous peoples that they came from all corners of the empire to worship it and to offer up sacrifices to it. He goes on to affirm that in the Valley of Teoul was founded Villanueva. Therefore, recognizing the fact that at that time the Nayarits held sway (as Padre Fluvia, author of the book *Afanes apostólicos*, says) up to the region of Mazapil, and since the inhabitants of the surrounding mountains so called themselves, it may be inferred without doubt that these buildings were the great Teoul dedicated to the god, Nayarit; and that the three roads which adorn it were two feasible adits for other nations or belligerent parties to use, without danger of being divided, for establishing peace or declaring war. The structure manifested in this edifice is evident proof of the entry of Israelites into this empire, since it bears a more than careful instruction in the architecture of temples, added to the fact that the language of all the indigenous nations has incorporated the Hebrew word *Teos* for naming God or the things of God.

There are other ruins of a temple and dwellings, not far from the present town of San Juan Teul. In view of features which it borrows from the *indios'* principal temple to the idol Nayarit (described by Mr. Mota Padilla, author of manuscripts which are in my possession), it appears that there was an attempt to improve construction by taking advantage of existing architectural competence. Since the Nayaristas dominated all this territory as far as Mazapil, it is not surprising that there were bloody pre-conquest wars between the Cascanes and the Nayaristas, the former defeating the latter and reducing their realm to that of the *sierra* which bears their name. In the opinion of Father Fluvia, the foregoing deserves credence, as well as the fact that the Cascanes would have constructed a temple, since the first was destroyed. In addition to the foregoing, this theory has two bases: first, when the Zacatecan chiefs invited all the Comarcan nations to join them in combatting the Spaniards, there was no mention of the Nayaristas; second, when Pedro Chirino first entered Zacatecan territory in company with the Spanish, the Cascanes were not yet at war with the Guachichiles, who had been taken for Nayaristas. For that reason the *indios*, of whom there were two hundred accompanying the Spaniards, did not continue with the expedition, but went as far as Jerez, then returned to Zacatecas, as the history was written.

From the foregoing writings we get an inkling of other monuments which exist in the [Valley of] Teul, and we wish for their examination. In the absence of such study these venerable vestiges of antiquity will be destroyed in one manner or another; whereas we ought to preserve even the debris as a proof of civilization and out of the interest which we take in the advancement of the sciences.

It has been believed, with reason, that Clavijero referred to the La Quemada monuments, when, speaking of the migration of the Aztecs, he says:

Walking many days from Hucicolhuacan toward the east, they arrived at Chicomostoc, where they stopped. Up to that point the seven tribes of Nahuatlaques had traveled together, but there they divided. The Mexicanos remained there *with their idol*, while the Tepaneques, the Colhuis, the Chalqueses, the Tlahuiques and the Tlaxcaleses went on. The Mexicanos say that the separation took place under the express mandate of their god; however, the probable truth is that it occurred as a result of some discord aroused among the several tribes. The location of Chicomostoc, where the Mexicanos resided for nine years, is not

known; nevertheless, I believe that it had to be twenty miles south of
Zacatecas where today are seen the ruins of a great building, no doubt
the work of the Mexicanos during their wandering. Taking into account
the tradition of the Zacatecas, ancient inhabitants of that country who
were completely barbaric, had no houses or knowledge of house construction, one has no choice but to attribute to the Aztecs this great
construction discovered by the Spaniards. The attrition of their numbers resulting from the separation is doubtless the reason why they did
not build additional structures on the remainder of their long walk.

In our concept, the most notable feature of the beautiful ruins of
La Quemada is the extensive rampart which extends from south to
north, retaining in some places, when we saw it, a height of five to six
yards and a thickness of more than ten. On seeing it we estimated that
two coaches (abreast) could travel on it comfortably for a considerable
piece. The hill on which these monuments are constructed is not of
great height, but it inspires awe in that its entire southern brow has
been fortified with a type of masonry which is preserved in large part
today, and which must have covered the entire hill in ancient times.
One must have been able to see none of the natural rock of the hill
itself, for everywhere one looks now one discovers remnants of that
masonry. The drawings which we include represent only the monuments which stand at the summit of the hill. For that reason they contain neither the rampart nor a lovely pyramid which we saw standing
nearly intact after so many centuries among other, smaller ones at the
foot of the hill on the east side.

All these monuments were constructed of a stone which is known
by the name of *laja*, a kind of flagstone, held together by a red clay
mixed with herbage. Within this mortar we found corncob which we
could pulverize with a mere touch. Such is the consistency of the mortar, and so well constructed are the structures that they were doubtless
nearly intact when the Spaniards discovered them. And there had to be
a barbarity among the first who colonized those districts to allow for
the purposeful destruction of such grand monuments, with the object
of creating animal pens and making barns of the materials which they
extracted from those monuments. In the structures one can not fail to
recognize the characteristics of Aztec architecture, and the fact that
among these ruins there are no inscriptions, hieroglyphics, or sculptures
of any sort is attributable to various causes. First, the material used in
the construction of those edifices does not lend itself to any kind of
sculture; flagstones are formed of very thin layers of sandy composition

which crumbles easily. It will be noted that the sketch reproduces perfectly the aspect which those flat stones, thin and superimposed, give to the monuments. The Aztecs did not inhabit that district sufficiently long to construct luxurious works; everything they built there was necessary; all their works there are large, but of simple construction; and finally, their life there probably included a continual battle with the tribes which inhabited the country prior to the arrival of the *Nahuatlaques*. Therefore, it is not strange that we find no sculpture in the monuments. The only article found was a stone turtle, probably of serpentine; we did not have the opportunity to see it; but, we were assured that on the lower side of it is sculpted a reed (*caña*) which is the symbol for *acatl* on the Mexican calendar. Perhaps it has characters which fix not only the year, but also the century in which they resided there, since that turtle (symbol of quietude) must signify that they suspended their peregrination in that place for some time.

Although we can say nothing assertively about those monuments and the reasons why they were constructed, we shall make a succinct statement of opinion. It is not wished that the terms in which we couch our opinions give rise to any notion that we are satisfied with their validity. The structures of La Quemada are the ruins of the ancient city and fortification of Chicomostoc. This city was constructed by the Aztecs and by the other tribes which formed the nation of Nahuatlaque during their peregrination to the country of Anáhuac. These edifices were constructed near the end of the twelfth century of the Christian Era; they must therefore have an age of approximately seven hundred years. The city of Chicomostoc consisted principally of a large village for habitation by the people, of some large buildings for the chiefs, of a great hall . . . which has annexed rooms for living quarters for some person. In this hall are found the beautiful cylindrical columns which we saw, also formed of flagstones and without bases or capitals. These columns supported the stringers on which rested the roof beams. The truncated pyramid seen at the bottom of the drawing was erected to Huitzilopoztli; atop it was fixed the timber statue of that god, which, according to Clavijero, the Mexicanos carried with them on their trek. The type of altar seen at the foot of the pyramid was designated for sacrifices. The Aztecs fortified themselves in this place to resist the savage tribes which surrounded them; to this end, and to avoid assault, they covered the slopes of the hill with masonry; and at other points they ringed it with a rampart which, in every way, is similar to

those seen in the ruins called Casas Grandes. The Aztecs were not able
to endure long periods in Chicomostoc, primarily due to the scarcity of
water on the site where they established themselves. We did not see a
single spring on the entire hill. The elevated position does not preclude
the possibility of springs, for they are abundant on the principal hill at
the Pinos Mine and on the mountain at the Bufa de Zacatecas. The
scarcity of rain and the frequent frosts of that district must have destroyed the corn crops of the Aztecs many times, and they doubtless
cultivated that plant on the adjacent prairie. The savages vied with
them for hunting rights and made their existence precarious. Thus they
had to abandon Chicomostoc, and they left it without destroying its
buildings, which subsequently even the savages respected. This state
persisted until some Spanish colonists destroyed works which would
have withstood natural deterioration for at least fifteen hundred years.
Clavijero was mistaken only in the distance from the monuments to
the capital of Zacatecas, a stretch of twelve or thirteen leagues. The
pyramids standing at the foot of the hill were probably erected to the
sun and the moon. As we have said, these pyramids do not appear in
the drawing. The La Quemada monuments record one of the principal
events in the history of Mexico: the separation of the tribes, which was
probably represented by the Mexicanos in paintings to which perhaps
a very different interpretation has been given. When the Aztecs departed from Chicomostoc, some families remained in those districts,
founding villages in the regions of Teul, Chalchihuites, Mazapil and
Sombrerete, and also near Juchipila, Jalpa, Tabasco, and Nochistlán.
Regardless of what we have done to give an exact idea of the importance, origin and antiquity of the La Quemada monuments, it is impossible to form a complete concept of them without comparing this
article with the work of Mr. Nebel, especially his plan of the ruins and
the general view of them. By virtue of our careful and curious examination of the Chicomostoc monuments, albeit cursory, we are certain of
the precision with which Mr. Nebel has represented them in his drawings, although we are not in complete agreement with some of his
explanations of the ruins.

Description of the Structures

THE CONSTRUCTIONS begin to manifest themselves on the brows of the
hill. On the south side there rises an ample platform which supports

the hall of columns and the terrace which is to the west of the hall entrance. The terrace measures 74.15 meters on the southwest side and 68.20 meters on the northeast. The hall of columns measures 40.40 meters on the east side and 31.20 meters on the south. The walls of this spacious room are largely destroyed, but the best preserved pieces reach a height of 4 meters.

Climbing the hill northward, after walking but a short way, one finds the second group of monuments, composed of a small basement for a *teocalli* (sacrificial mound), a terrace and two dwellings, all arranged on the high platform constructed on the slope of the hill, affecting the form of a scarp. In the central part of the hill, at the same height as the group mentioned above, there is a rectangular patio surrounded by a sidewalk which borders the east, west, and south sides. In the center of the patio are the remains of a basement which probably sustained the indispensible *texcatl* (sacrificial stone). To the north of that patio rises a truncated pyramid the stair of which looks to the south.

On the west side of the galleries which encircle the patio are the vestiges of a dwelling composed of five adjoining rooms, the entrance to the first of which is a narrow door located in the west gallery of the patio.

In order to ascend to this second level of the hill it was necessary to mount the stair situated on the south side of the platform which sustains these constructions. The height of the platform, i.e., of the walls which form it, is 6.80 meters. The face of these is inclined, and the slope is so steep as to make them inaccessible. At the same level are found other patios or terraces in which stand two *teocallis* and the base of a stair which leads to the third group of monuments. The floor which I have just described has an altitude of 2,350 meters above sea level and 62 meters above the lowest point in the contiguous terrain.

Taking advantage of the little *Talberg* [-e; draws or gulleys] of the hill, on the western slope they constructed the drainage system for the entire upper portion of the platform.

A short distance to the north of the truncated pyramid rises a terrace, the west and south sides of which form a right angle; the east side has a stone staircase leading up to the *teocalli* which is situated in the angle formed by the south and east walls of the scarp of the third platform.

Ascending to the third platform is a narrow passage formed by the

walls which border the galleries located to the south of the construction; these galleries form two irregular geometric figures. The west gallery has its entrance on the north, and the east gallery is entered on the
west, very near to the top step of the stone stairway.

Following the passage toward the north, with a slight deviation to
the west, one arrives at a sidewalk which surrounds the patio, the patio
being 60 centimeters lower than the walk; descending to the patio are
three pieces of stairstep, one in the center of the south walk, another in
the center of the east walk, and the third in the northeast corner.

The platform which supports the structures of this third group is
composed of three staggered parts with sloping faces. The first component constitutes the base of support. It measures 8.23 meters high. The
second is 1.55 meters high, and the third, 4.45 meters. Since the west
sides of these platforms are built on the slopes of the hill, the *indios*
made good use of the abutments to form truly unimpugnable fortifications. The great patio situated to the east of the walk, with its principal entrance on the west and the smallest on the north, affects the
form of a rectangular parallelogram, the sides of which measure: north
and south, 22 meters; east and west, 30 meters. In the northeast corner
is found another construction formed of three walls in parallelogram
corresponding to compass points North, East, and West, and it is open
on the south in order to communicate with the place I am describing.
The wall height of this large hall is 8 meters, and the thickness is 2.50
meters. I call this place the *frontón*, for I believe that the game of
pelota was played here. In the center of the patio with walkways, are
seen traces of the location of the *texcatl* (sacrificial stone).

A short distance to the north is found a nicely preserved *teocalli*
base, composed of five tiered components from larger to smaller, measuring (at the base in each case) 11.70 meters, 9.90 meters, 7.80 meters,
4.40 meters, and 4 meters. One climbs to the last tier by means of a
stone stair located at the south of the monument. The height of each
of these tiers is as follows: The uppermost, 77 centimeters; the second,
1.10 meters; the third, 80 centimeters; the fourth, 42 centimeters; the
fifth, 1.10 meters; and each tier has a slope of 39 centimeters. The
outer surfaces of these tiers are inclined.

The steps leading to the first landing on the way to the ample
staircase of the fourth level are located to the north of the east walk of
the patio. On the west side of the patio are other constructions. The
barometric height of this level is 2,390 meters above sea level.

The fourth level of the hill has, in its center, an outcropping of fair height and width, naturally formed, around the base of which extends a series of structures, such as temples, esplanades and galleries.

Following the undulations of the hill, there occur other edifices defended by extensive walls 6 meters thick. These walls occupy the summit of the hill and run from north to south in the same way as all the structures of La Quemada.

To the west of the structures on the fourth level of the hill are four platforms with ruins. Being staggered or terraced, these are at various heights from the brow down to a near joining with the bottom of the upper platform support walls. To the east of these esplanades is the only stone which has inscriptions, the Stone of the Snakes.

One of the most interesting monuments of the La Quemada ruins is the votive pyramid. This structure is the first of its kind, to my knowledge, in American antiquities.

Geological Study of the Terrain Where Stand the Ruins of La Quemada

FOLLOWING is the geological classification of the terrain, prepared by Mr. E. Guillemin Tarayre, a member of the Mexico scientific expedition sent by Napoleon III.

The hill of the structures, like the hills which surround it and the higher ones which dominate the valley to the east and west, belongs to the geologic level which crowns the great mesas of Mexico from Lake Chapala to the Río del Norte (Río Grande). This level is formed of feldspar tufa in pseudosedimentary stratification in various stages of metamorphosis, or porphyries of various composition. The rock structure of the hill is formed of thin granulated layers, slightly crystalline. The outcropping took place toward the northwest, so that the west side is defined by a vertical fifteen to twenty meter high scarp, and on the east there are irregular declivities, according to dip.

The rock is disposed in regular layers which are not very adherent; one can lift easily stones four to six centimeters thick and whatever lateral dimension is desired.

These are the materials which were used by the builders of those edifices.

The Tarascans

THIS TRIBE, belonging to the yellow family, spread itself over a large part of the Mexican territory; I have found traces of it in the states of Puebla, Tlaxcala, Guanajuato, Querétaro, Michoacán, Jalisco, Colima, Guerrero, Zacatecas and Durango.

In my opinion, the Tarascans are one of the American peoples most worthy of study. The artifacts which we have from them reveal a high culture, and, though their sculpture was defective, their metallurgy was very strong. In the collection of Padre Don Francisco Plancarte, I have seen gold-plated copper. Their bone objects are true jewels; and their musical instruments possess an ordered and uniform progression of pitches, ascending and descending. The present bishop of Cuernavaca, Dr. Don Francisco Plancarte, has knowledge of how the scales are obtained on these small musical instruments. It is truly disgruntling that this tribe is not better known. Sculptures of representative human bodies nearly always possess genital organs without cover.

Among the gods of Tarascan mythology figured the god Caimán. Let us hear the words of the *Relación de Michoacán*, [Account of Michoacán], pp. 67 and 75: "A fisherman on a float, fishing with a hook, caught a large *bagre* (kind of delicious fish), and an alligator came from the river and dragged the fisherman to the bottom of the waters, etc., etc." The alligator which is included was given to me as a gift by Mr. Elían Amador. It was found near La Quemada.

The Tarascans were robust, well formed, valiant, and bellicose, great spanners of the bow, skillful in the use of arms. They dressed in a manner similar to that of the *mexica* tribe. Some members of higher status wore a kind of long tunic which hung midway between knee and ankle; the square blanket or mantel was knotted over one of the shoulders; *cactli*, or leather sandals, retained with thongs, knotted at the ankle. The common people used the *maxtlatl* or loincloth to cover their genitals, along with blankets of coarse threads. Men of rank and women wore their hair high, tied around the head, forming braids and interlacings with cotton cords of various colors. The remainder of the common folk wore their hair loose, with one or more feathers. They wove their material of cotton, some white, some black, as well as several beautiful colors. They adorned them with threads of rabbit hair in a very curious fashion.

The anthropological type of the Tarascans is shown on sheet no. 26, a representation of two Tarascans from Lake Pátzcuaro. Using the analogy method, I classified their physiognomy between that of the present-day *indios* and that of the sculptures of their predecessors. As will be seen, there is a total similarity between the one and the others, and since it was the Tarascans who built the La Quemada monuments, this is without doubt the type of the constructors of La Quemada.

The Architecture
of the La Quemada Archaeological Monuments

THE CONSTRUCTION with which we are concerned has, by no means, the architectonic importance of that of the Mayas, the Zapotecs, or the Toltecs. In this architecture one sees only the superhuman force required to make gigantic and daring walls; but there is nothing beautiful or artistic in these works. Even when, among primitive peoples, we find an activity which, by virtue of awareness, differentiates itself from that of animals, one can speak of architecture only in that instance where a higher civilization has given rise to problems of this nature. But the development of culture was never equal among all the peoples who comprise mankind; the most necessary conditions for its existence were not to be found everywhere; thus we can speak of civilization and of architecture of peoples who flourished many thousands of years before our era, while others who still exist scarcely show the most rudimentary elements of them.

A formal law of articulation which is repeated universally is the division of each component into three parts. The central, or principal, part manifests the function; the lower part, or foot, shows its relation to the base or foundation; and the upper part, the transition to the pinnacle of the work. This, according to the same law, and in all nations, the body of the edifice is divided into socle, stories, and cornice (architrave); each column into base, fust, and capital. Now, the ruins of La Quemada, which are inferior constructions, omit one of these parts and interrupt the rigorous and natural order. The story of these edifices has no socle, only walls without architrave; the columns lack base and capital, containing only the fust. Despite the fact that those monuments have substantial construction defects, they deeply impress the spirit of him who regards them. The originality of these ruins consists in the principal grouping of the components.

The character, or perhaps the conjoining of distinctive features, is greatly analogous to the original type of the Tarascans of Michoacán; and as a means of comparison, I am submitting to the press a Tarascan crypt discovered in Tzintzuntzan. The mortar used to lay the stones has the reddish yellow color so peculiar to the architecture of Michoacán.

It has often been said that the architecture of every age is the most accurate reflection of that age, because both the materialistic and idealistic sides of each civilization would appear to be symbolized and expressed in the architectural works of that civilization. The ruins of La Quemada do not belong to their own time, but are a good indicator of the type of civilization to which La Quemada belongs.

2

NOTES ON THE

Geography and Archaeology of Zape, Durango

Donald D. Brand

Donald Brand's article is a detailed study of the archaeology and geography of the area around Zape, in northwestern Durango, based on field work carried out in 1936. Both field work and article overlap somewhat with Mason's slightly earlier field work and publication, reproduced elsewhere in this volume. Mason's work was a general survey of the entire Chalchihuites Culture and area in Durango and Zacatecas, while Brand's work represents a thorough study of one small part of that area and culture.

The region around Zape is archaeologically rich and important. This area represents the northernmost extension of the Chalchihuites Culture (and Mesoamerican culture in general) in northern Mexico. We now know that three principal archaeological components are present at Zape. These are 1] a well developed Archaic, or Desert Culture, tradition, represented principally in rock shelter sites, which included some agriculture in its basic economy; 2] an extremely well developed Loma San Gabriel occupance, probably extending from the first centuries of the Christian Era into virtually historic times; 3] either a late and restricted Chalchihuites Culture occupance of the area, principally at the site of Santa Ana or, alternatively, late acculturation of the Loma San Gabriel occupance by the Chalchihuites Culture, essentially during the late Las Joyas and Rio Tunal phases, with some Calera Phase materials represented. The ceramics described in this article by Brand include a mixture of Chalchihuites and Loma San Gabriel types, including specimens transitional between the two ceramic traditions. Unknowingly, Brand at Zape had encountered an extremely involved cultural contact situation.

Brand's careful analysis of the geography of the Zape area led other workers, including the present writer (Kelley, 1956) to the discovery that the Chalchihuites Culture had expanded northward in Durango along a very narrow and restricted ecological strip paralleling the eastern foothills of the Sierra Madre Occidental. Because of its thoroughgoing analysis of both archaeology and geography—as well as its excellent summary of early historical and archaeological sources for the Zape area—the Brand article is truly a landmark in the history of archaeological research in the Durango area, and remains a basic source for anyone working in the area.

J. C. K.

A TOWN which has entered frequently into the literature of north Mexican archaeology and history during the past three hundred years is Zape,[1] in northwestern Durango. Nevertheless, despite dozens of mentions, very little definite information has been available concerning this supposed northern outpost of Central Mexican culture.[2] The following notes represent the gleanings from several years of random library research, and observations made during a brief visit in the summer of 1936.

By automobile, the road from Chihuahua City to El Zape is three hundred miles, driving through Camargo, up the Florido tributary of the Conchos, past the famous old mining town of Santa María del Oro, down to the Cofradía ford of the Rio del Oro (Rio Sestín, Sextín, or Sestin), and over an exceedingly rough forty miles to Zape, on the right bank of a river by the same name. This trip can be shortened thirty miles in distance and several hours in time by taking the road that parallels the power line between the Avalos smelter and Las Boquillas dam, and then on, via Parral and Villa Ocampo, to El Oro. The last portion of the road is feasible only for a powerful car with a high clearance, as the road (little more than a wagon trace in places) climbs more than 2,200 feet in seventeen miles from the ford (1,650 m.) to the first crest of the Sierra de Canoas (2,380 m.), then dips steeply and climbs abruptly for six tortuous miles over this deeply canyoned eastern spur of the Sierra Madre Occidental before descending the comparatively gentle western slope to Zape (1,970 m.). Minimum driving time over the forty-four miles between Zape and El Oro is about four hours.

The pueblo of Zape is sprawled over the rocky ledges which outcrop from the base of the rhyolitic Cerro de la Cruz down to the brink of the river. The hummocky surfaces of these ledges of pinkish gray rhyolitic tuff serve as foundations for the houses, and as an everlasting pavement for the streets. Opposite the central part of town the river has been dammed, forming a large but shallow pond bordered by occasional poplars and willows. An unforgettable scene here was that of a crimson sun sinking behind the distant sierras, the towered church outlined against the darkening western horizon, and lowing cattle laboriously plowing through the waters of the pond as they sought their stables in the pueblo. The pond is fed by the ever-flowing waters of the Rio del Zape, and by the constant hot springs which gush out of the rocks at the margin of town and pond. These hot springs (about 30° C.) are among the five most important in the state, and are famed for their medicinal properties far beyond the borders of Durango.

Natural Landscape

THE VALLEY of El Zape occupies a NNW-SSE structural depression near the eastern margin of the Sierra Madre Occidental. In this general area, once covered by a Cretaceous sea, there was a Tertiary development of andesites and related rocks that completely obscured the Cretaceous limestone plinth. Upon the andesites, probably in late Tertiary time, was deposited a mantle of rhyolites, rhyolitic tuffs, and tuffs—presumably from fissure vulcanism. These rhyolites and tuffs constitute the country rock wherever it is visible in the Zape area. It is only farther to the north, around the *mineral* of Guaceví, that the older ore-bearing rocks are exposed. Into the Zape depression, partly filled with rhyolites and tuffs, quaternary streams brought a varied debris which filled the basin to a point at least one hundred feet higher than the present elevation of the *talweg*. This denudational debris was converted, in part, into conglomerates, which now constitute the low *lomas*, that extend from the western mountain chain down to the left bank of the river. The right bank of the Rio del Zape is made up principally of rhyolitic exposures which range, in form, from low shelves to abrupt cliffs several hundreds of feet in height.

The through-flowing Rio Zape, whose waters are permanent, has its origin a few miles above El Zape in the Ciénega de Escobar. This river is considered to be one of the two headwaters of the Rio Nazas. The name changes involved are as follows: Originates as Rio de Santa Ana, takes the name of Rio Zape from the town of that name, breaks east and then south around the north spur of the Sierra de Canoas to become the Rio Sextín or Sestín, flows by Santa María del Oro to be named Rio del Oro, and finally joins the Rio Ramos (made up of the Tepehuanes and Santiago Papasquiaro rivers) to become the Rio Nazas. In the sector between Zape and Santa Ana there is evidence of a rather recent erosional activity, especially in the lower reaches of the short tributaries that flow down from the western *lomas*. These affluents carry water only during the rainy seasons.

In climate and vegetation, the Zape area partakes of both the meso-thermal savannah (*Cw*) and the hot steppe (*BSh*). An elevation of approximately 6,400 feet, together with Sierra Madre ridges (which rise above 7,800 feet) on the east, west, and south, provide cool, highland conditions. However, location in 25°43′ north latitude, and within a depression that connects with the great arid basin of eastern Durango, allows a tongue of steppe climate and vegetation to advance along the river bottoms as far as Hacienda Santa Ana. No thermopluviometric records have been kept at El Zape, but approximations can be obtained from the short period records at Guanacevi (130 m. higher) and El Oro (140 m. lower). The annual mean temperature is 16° C., with absolute extremes of 34° C. and −7° C. Normally, June and July are the hottest months, and December and January are the coldest. Strong and constant winds blow from the south and southwest during the period January to April. These winds are essentially geostrophic. From June to September, the winds tend to be from the general direction of the Gulf of Mexico, to the east and south. Often these summer winds are locally deflected so that they blow up the Zape Valley, from the north. Between 70 and 90 percent of the precipitation comes during the months of June, July, August, and September. The summer rainstorms are usually of convectional origin, and are frequently accompanied by thunder, lightning, and some hail. A minor precipitation period occurs during December, at which time snow may mantle the surrounding mountains for several days at a time. The total annual precipitation is in excess of 700 mm. Mexican climatologists place the Zape area on the border between the "Altura extremoso" and "Templado de Montaña" climates; or, within the "Zona de los Valles," bordered by the "Zona de las Cumbres de la Sierra."[3]

Upon the surrounding mountain heights, and extending down to within a mile or two of the *talweg*, is an open forest formation which is dominated by a pine-oak association. Other elements within this association are pinyon, juniper, cypress, madroño, manzanilla, and several grasses. Bear, deer, mountain lions, Mexican wolf, tree squirrels, woodrats, wild turkey, pigeons, jays, woodpeckers, and parrots are fairly common in the forested area. Some trout exist in the permanent streams. Extending up the river valley, especially on the lower foothills, *lomas*, and knolls, is a xerophytic vegetation of mesquite *(Prosopis juliflora)*, *huizaches (Acacia sp.)* agaves (not numerous), cacti (mainly opuntias), and grasses (chiefly *Bouteloua, Paspalum, Muhlenbergia, Stipa, Hilaria, and Aristida)*. Along the river and near springs are many poplars and willows. Inhabiting both valley and woodland regions are coyotes, foxes, jack rabbits, cottontail rabbits, doves, blackbirds, crows, eagles, hawks, buzzards, owls, lizards, and a few snakes. Despite the reputation that the state of Durango has for many and venomous scorpions, the *alacrán* [scorpion] is not common in the Zape area.

Resources and Economy

THE ZAPE or southern district of the *municipio* of Guanaceví is essentially agricultural. The geologic formation here (as mentioned above) does not contain the silver-gold ores that have made the northern area around Guanaceví and San Pedro famous for more than three hundred and fifty years. However, a fairly good soil, an abundance of water, and situation within five hours' walking distance from the downstream mining district, united to attract crop farmers and raisers of livestock.

Agriculture   The cultivated lands lie immediately around the pueblo of Zape and the ranchos of Santa Ana (four miles upstream) and Zape Chico (three miles downstream). There are only a few isolated farmsteads. Land holdings are indicated usually by *mojoneras* or stone cornermarkers, occasionally by stone or adobe walls, or by pole and brush fences. Most of the farmers own the fields that they cultivate; but *ejidos*, from part of the former Hacienda Santa Ana, have been granted in recent years to agrarians, and the remainder of the Santa Ana lands is leased by a citizen of Zape. Farming is carried on entirely by manual and animal labor. The main crop, in acreage and income, is maize. The growth noted during the summer of 1936 seemed quite poor; but it is amazing that the soil should yield at all, since these fields have been cultivated for more than three hundred years with no rotation of crops, or fertilization. Kidney beans rank as a poor second to maize. There is some cultivation, in very small plots, of wheat, chile peppers, onions, pumpkins, potatoes, and tobacco. All crops are raised on both irrigated (*regadas*) and nonirrigated (*temporales*) lands, but the five last mentioned are usually irrigated. Water for irrigation is obtained directly from springs, and also from the river. Chickens, sheep, cattle, goats, geese, horses, pigs, and donkeys are of numerical importance in approximately the order named. Chickens and geese provide eggs; the cows and goats afford a little milk; and occasionally sheep, cattle, goats, and pigs are slaughtered for meat. While we were in Zape there was no meat available, a deficiency which was made up by serving eggs three times a day. Seemingly, there cannot be much agricultural surplus for sale to the mining districts.

Other activities   There are no formalized industries in Zape, with the exception of a meager "tourist trade" that has developed in connection with the medicinal hot springs. One of these springs is covered by a bathhouse. A few cottage industries do exist, such as the making of cheese, weaving of woolen cloth, working of leather and wood, etc., but these are all on a very minor scale. The most common fuel is oak and pinyon wood, brought into town in faggot form, tied on the backs of donkeys and horses. Some charcoal is made from the limbs and roots of oaks, mesquite, and acacias. Very little trade is carried on in the few small general stores, since the population is small, poor, and with but few needs that cannot be supplied in the home or from the farm. Sugar, coffee, salt, cotton goods, and hardware are the chief commodities of exterior origin. As yet there are neither numerous enough automobiles owned locally nor sufficient through travel to justify garage or service station.

Communication   In the days of Porfirio Díaz, a stagecoach, or *diligencia*, road passed through Zape from Durango and Tepehuanes on the south to Villa Ocampo and Parral to the north. Now there remains of this vehicular road only a section, some twenty miles long, between Santa Ana and Guanaceví. The only wheel trace out of the Guanaceví-Zape area at present is the road over the Sierra de Canoas to Santa María del Oro. This road has been feasible for automobiles only during the last three or four years. For many years there has been projected a railroad that would follow approximately the old *diligencia* highway and connect the present railheads at Tepehuanes and Estación Rosario (near Villa Ocampo), but nothing has been done since the initial survey was made. There is a post office in Zape, but the mail connections with the outside are somewhat irregular.

Population and housing   According to the census of 1930, the population of El Zape is 366 (184 males, 182 females), of Santa Ana is 141 (75, 66), and of Zape Chico 132 (72, 60)—a total for the area of 639. This gives a density of about 20 to the square mile, since the inhabited area is approximately ten miles long and three miles wide. The census of 1921 gave values as follows: El Zape 428, Santa Ana 235, Zape Chico 105—a total for the Zape area of 768. These losses probably represent, in part, the effect of the decline in mining subsequent to the depression that began a year before the census was taken. The loss in the agricultural Zape area was a trifle less than 17 percent. It is doubtful if the present (1936) actual population equals the figures of the 1930 census.

There is no evident plan to the pueblo of Zape. The highway drops down from the eastern slopes to the river ford, and this road constitutes the main street. Narrow rocky streets angle off the main street in the triangle between it and the river. Haphazard cross streets (little more than alleys littered with rubbish and inhabited by a variety of livestock) divide the town into irregular blocks. The houses are commonly of one story, built in the form of compounds, and constructed of roughly quarried rhyolitic tuff. A few houses are of adobe, or of adobe and river pebbles. Flat roofs, of dirt or tile over poles or planks laid on round or roughly hewn *vigas* [stringers], predominate. The exteriors have, in time past, been plastered or stuccoed, but there has been little attempt to maintain appearances.

European History

RECORDED HISTORY, in this region, began with the founding of the *mineral* [mine] of Indé, in 1563,[4] by one of Ibarra's lieutenants. Within the next thirty years mining camps were established farther up the valley at Santa María del Oro, Sestín, and Guanaceví (founded, certainly, before 1597). These Spanish mining settlements were on the eastern fringe of the forested and broken Sierra Madre country occupied by the Tepehuán Indians. The Company of Jesus, which had entered Nueva Vizcaya in 1589, undertook the conversion of the Tepehuanes and their

western neighbors, the Acaxee. After the conversion of many Tepehuanes, in the mountain country between Indé and Topia, Father
Gerónimo Ramírez persuaded them to settle in the Zape Valley, at the
foot of a high rock.[5] This Tepehuán settlement in the Zape Valley took
place in 1604.[6] A few years later, probably in 1612, a mission church
was erected and dedicated to San Ignacio, by Father Diego Larios.[7] By
this time, San Ignacio del Zape had become one of the three Jesuit mission *cabeceras* ["capitals" or centers] in the Tepehuán country.[8] In the
Valley of Zape, in addition, there were also ranchos and haciendas that
produced supplies for the mines at Guanaceví and elsewhere in the area.

In November of 1616, the Tepehuán nation was stirred to rebellion
by shamans (*hechiceros*) who were jealous of the missionaries. This
most sanguinary of Tepehuán revolts (1616–18), incidentally, made
Zape famous throughout Mexico. Nearly the entire Christian population of the Zape area, including a number of Spanish miners and ranch-
ers from Guanaceví, had gathered on November 18 at the mission
church at San Ignacio del Zape to celebrate the installation (scheduled
for November 21) of an image of the Holy Virgin Mother, which had
been obtained from Mexico City by the miners of Guanaceví. This
peaceful congregation was attacked by the Tepehuanes, who burned the
church, and killed with arrow, lance, club, axe, and sword, nearly one
hundred people (two Jesuit priests, nineteen Spaniards from Guanaceví,
and more than sixty negro slaves).[9] The image was sullied, cut on the
cheek with an axe, and submerged in the hot spring near the church.
One story has it that during the reconquest a Spanish captain vowed to
renovate the image and its accouterments should the rebellion be suppressed.[10] At any rate, by May of 1618 the revolt was completely sub-
dued, and treaties of peace were ratified with local *caciques* in El Zape
in 1620 and 1621. By 1623, the mission church was rebuilt, this time
being dedicated to the miraculous *Nuestra Señora del Hachazo del
Zape*. Bishop Tamarón visited El Zape, May 31 to June 10, 1763, and
was so overcome by the deterioration of the church and the neglected
condition of the image,[11] that he personally supervised the renovation
(December 2, 1764, to March 4, 1765), and rededicated the church.[12]
Unfortunately, the writer was so preoccupied with the geography and
archaeology of the Zape area, during the summer of 1936 visit, that he
neglected to determine the present location and condition of "Our
Lady of the Axecut of Zape."

No great damage was done to the mining properties of Guanaceví by the Tepehuán rebellion, since a temporary presidio had been established there in 1617. By the next year, Guanaceví was again termed the most important mining camp in the Kingdom of Nueva Vizcaya. From this we may assume that the ranchos and haciendas in the Zape Valley soon returned to normal production. For the next one hundred and fifty years there is little recorded concerning El Zape. Among the resident padres mentioned are: Juan de Sanguesa, ca. 1621; Martín Suarez, ca. 1638; and Francisco Mendoza, 1662 to 1678. In 1662, there was a great pest (probably smallpox, as in 1604 and 1608) that decimated the Indian population. Zapata, in 1678, recorded a Tepehuán population of 52 (seventeen families) in El Zape proper, with a total of 171 in the entire mission *partido*. El Zape was one of the eleven Tepehuán missions in Durango secularized in 1753. Ten years later (1763) Bishop Tamarón counted twenty-seven Tepehuán families, with a total population of 78, in El Zape. Tamarón commented on the poverty of the pueblo, and the indolence of the inhabitants.[13]

During the succeeding years, El Zape became less and less Indian, and more and more Spanish, until, at the present time, there are no families of acknowledged Tepehuán ancestry in the town. The nearest Tepehuán settlements are now a number of miles to the west, in the rugged Sierra Madre. The present linguistic and racial composition is almost entirely Spanish-speaking whites of peninsular origin. Unlike many other portions of Durango, there were never any Mexican (Aztec and Tlaxcaltec) or Tarascan colonies settled in the Zape-Guanaceví-Indé district. When it became difficult to employ native (Tepehuán) labor in the mines, and on the haciendas, negro slaves were brought in by the wealthier Spaniards. However, there is now very little trace of Negro blood in the population. The Spanish Creole (whites of European extraction born in the New World) population claims to derive mainly from Vizcaya, La Mancha, and Estremadura. Credence is lent to this claim by the frequent mention of the "vizcainos y españoles del real de Guanaceví" (as in Alegre, 2. 54). This general area has become so Hispanized that, out of 122 places listed in the 1930 census of the *municipio* of Guanaceví, 108 are Spanish, 10 are Mexican (Nahuatl proper), and only 4 are Tepehuán. This process was accelerated by the colonization, during the *pax Porfiriana*, of unclaimed federal lands by ambitious but landless farmers (mainly Spanish whites). As a result of the Madero Revolution (State Law of October 3, 1913; Federal Law of

January 6, 1915; article 27 of the Constitution of 1917; State "Ley de Fraccionamiento") several of the larger ranchos near El Zape, and a portion of the former Hacienda Santa Ana, have been broken into small agrarian holdings.

At present, El Zape is a pueblo in the *municipio libre* of Guanaceví. This was formerly a part of the onetime *partido* of Santiago Papasquiaro. During the Spanish period, what is now the State of Durango was part of the Kingdom (later Intendencia) of Nueva Vizcaya (1563–1776), subject to the Audiencia of Guadalajara and the Viceroyalty of New Spain; and of the Provincias Internas (1776–1824), independent of Mexico. In 1824, the Mexican Congressional Congress gave Durango its present boundaries. During the existence of the Kingdom of Nueva Vizcaya, a number of "provinces" were set up, which included the province of Santa Bábara. Within this province were the *alcaldías* of Guanaceví, Indé, and Valle de San Bartolomé. During the first years of Spanish occupation, the spiritual affairs were looked after by Franciscan, Jesuit, and Augustinian missionaries. In 1621, the Episcopal See of Durango (Nueva Vizcaya) was established, which was raised to an archdiocese in 1891. Due to the location of various religious, political, military, and other administrative headquarters at Guadalajara, Zacatecas, Durango, Saltillo, and Parral, these cities possess important archives for the history of Durango in general, and of the Zape area in particular. However, these archives are supplementary to those in Mexico City and in Spain.

Archaeology

THE FIRST account of antiquities in the Zape area is incorporated in the "Anuas del Año de 1604 y del Año de 1612," in manuscript, utilized by the Jesuit historians Pérez de Ribas (1644) and Alegre (1767–80). These remains did not arouse interest among antiquarians and archaeologists until Orozco y Berra (1864), Guillemin Tarayre (1869), and Bancroft (1882) published brief accounts. Guillemin Tarayre was the first (since Gerónimo Ramírez in 1604 and Diego Larios in 1612) to describe the ruins from firsthand information (1865, 1866). Orozco y Berra and Bancroft each devoted less than a page to a very generalized summary based on Pérez de Ribas and Alegre. Lumholtz, in 1894, visited El Zape, and later (1902) compressed a few remarks, supplementary to Guillemin Tarayre, into less than half a page. Hewett passed through Zape in 1906, and much later (1936) treated on the archaeology of the area in less than a page. Seemingly no further visits by archaeologists were made to El Zape until 1936, when both Mason (during the first part of the year) and the writer (June and July) investigated the local archaeology.[14] Mexican archaeologists and historians (working from a distance) have mentioned and placed Zape on archaeologic maps (1928), and have summarized some of the published material,[15] but, so far as the writer knows, no Mexican scientist (excepting the geographer Rouaix) has visited Zape.[16] Of course, this statement does not apply to geologists and mining engineers.

The initial account of the ruins at Zape, which Pérez de Ribas (Jesuit missionary in Sinaloa, 1604–16) abstracted from the "Anua del Año de 1604," is as follows (translations by the writer): One of the fathers [G. Ramírez] visited the *ranchería del Çape*

situated on the bank of a river which runs by the foot of a high rock (*peñol*) where, because of the ruins and remains of ho᾽ᵢses larger than those of these Indians [Tepehuanes], and a plentitude of stone idols, and various images (*figuras*), with other reasonable proofs, it was believed that the ancient Mexicans had established a settlement when they left distant lands, taking with them an idol and the devil within it, in the manner in which the Chosen of the Lord carried the Ark of the Covenant, building their fashion of houses and camps, as did the people of Israel in the Land of Promise, and as did the Mexicans at the lake where they settled . . . on the *peñol* of El Çape were found idols, columns, and other remains of ornaments common to the Mexicans.[17]

Thus Pérez de Ribas, or Father Ramírez, gains the dubious distinction of having initiated the identification of El Zape as one of the places of sojourn for the Azteca and related peoples while on their legendary migration from Chicomoztoc and Aztlán to Anáhuac. Alegre and Rouaix, among others, have perpetuated this misinformation.

Alegre made use of the "Anua del Año de 1604" in the following fashion: Father Ramírez selected the site of El Zape. Here

a fountain springs from a rock, and around it the fathers found many idols and pieces of columns like those of the Mexicans. In the valley they observed also some ruins of edifices, which caused them to believe that the Mexicans had settled there, during that famous journey from the northern lands that are always referred to in their histories.[18]

It will be noted that Alegre has confused the spring at the base of the *peñol* (now called Cerro de La Cruz) with the remains that were found on top of the *peñol*. It is probable that Alegre never visited Zape, but relied upon earlier accounts for all of his information.

From the "Anua del Año de 1612" Alegre derives the following material.

We cannot avoid noting here that which we have already insinuated, in another place, concerning the journey of the ancient Mexicans, which seems to have been through this land of the Tepehuanes . . . to which we shall now add the words of Father Diego Larios, missionary in that *partido*, who speaks thusly: "Digging in front of the church which is now being built, there were found frequently many well-covered ollas with ashes and human bones, stones of various colors with which metals and other things are colored (*se embijan*); and that which caused the most wonder were the statues and figures of various animals which were discovered. I wondered especially at one which resembled to the life a religious with his habit and tonsured head (*cerquillo y corona*) very properly depicted. And that which I have been able to learn from very old Indians is that the ancient Mexicans who came out of the North to populate the Kingdom of Mexico stopped here; and they could not have been few in number, since a half league is covered with such items as graves and ruins of buildings and temples."[19]

Guillemin Tarayre's classic description, based upon visits to the Zape area in 1865 and 1866, has only now (1937) been superseded by Mason's account. There is enough material of value in the Frenchman's narration to justify the following free translation.

The rectilinear development of the Sierra Madre has certainly conditioned the route of all the migrations from the North. It is only in the valleys, which are disposed parallel to the mountain chains, that remains of ancient settlements are found. Near Sestín . . . I saw several caves with *ollas* and other objects that denoted an advanced civilization. Farther to the south, in the Valley of Zape . . . I encountered the vestiges of a quite extensive village that occupied all the open part of an enlargement in the valley. The left bank of the river which flows toward Sestín is closed by a series of low hills that slope on one side toward the Sierra de Guanaceví, and on the other side toward the Sierra de Escobar. The summit of each hill is a center of habitations, while along the foot are cultivated lands. It would have taken up too much time to have made a reconnaissance of all of these quite similar places, therefore I limited myself to making an exact plan of the group that is located 700 meters north of the Santa Ana ranch, and six kilometers from Zape.

Plate III [reproduced in Tamarón, *Demonstración del Vastísimo*, opp. p. 100] presents the plan and the cross section of a series of associated courts (*terrepleins*), formed by mounds (*terrasses*) exactly oriented, whose upper sides are delimited by lines of rocks placed in the ground. Four mounds disposed in this manner surround a square court in the middle of which a small edifice is indicated by a number of rocks which also form a square. After this first court, towards the east, other mounds enclose two rectangular spaces, but only on three sides. This disposition recalls that which one finds in the ancient city of Teotihuacán. There, however, a number of mounds, arranged in the same manner, served as pediments for habitations constructed of substantial materials, while those at Zape seemed not to have supported more than houses constructed of flimsy material, like the *jacales* of the mountain Indians. A road with a gentle gradient descends from each side of the principal edifice to the bottom of the hill, into the fields where maize is still cultivated, as it was formerly. These fields extend 600 meters to an arroyo with a permanent stream of some importance that descends from the highlands around the Ciénega de Escobar to joint the Zape River. The other hills of the valley present groups, some of them more extensive, of mounds arranged in the same manner. One might estimate at 50 square kilometers the area over which these structures are spread. There exist some remains, of an entirely different kind, on the large flat-topped rock that dominates the village of Zape; these are the rests of crude irregular structures, built of rocks piled one-upon-another and recalling the cabins that the shepherds of the Old World erect in stony regions. These barbarous works are attributed to the Cocohiomes, a wild tribe now extinct. Less than two years ago [written in April, 1866] an old woman, the last survivor of that people, died in Zape.[20]

Some caves, that served as habitations for the same people, may be seen along the edges of the river to the north of Zape [caves of Zape Chico]; in these caves are found bones, crude pottery wares, and flint arrowheads.[21]

Lumholtz adds very little to this picture. He says:

At Zape . . . there are some ancient remains. As the principal ones have been described by E. Guillemin Tarayre, who explored Mexico under Maximilian, it is not necessary for me to dwell on the subject. Suffice it to say that walls constructed of loose stones are commonly seen on the crests of the low hills and are attributed to the Cocoyomes. Circles and squares made of stones set upright in the ground may also be seen, and nicely polished stone implements are frequently to be found near by. . . . Outside of Zape are a number of ancient burial-caves, which have been disturbed by treasure seekers.[22]

Based upon his horseback journey of 1906 down the eastern margin of the Sierra Madre Occidental, Hewett contributes the following notes.

Their [Tepehuán] archaeological history is yet to be studied. Material for it is abundant. House building was of the "jacal" type (vertical poles for walls, with thatched roof). There are numerous small mounds that have not yet been plowed under. The hills, in addition to being in places terraced for farming, are in many instances furnished with strong fortifications of stone. Among these are structures that suggest religious purposes, but the fortification idea is unmistakable. Here then is evidence of warfare, well supported by Tepahuana tradition. There is no better example than the fortified mountain of Zapé [sic] one hundred and twenty miles northwest of the city of Durango. This is still, as far as I know, the best center for the study of Tepahuana archaeology. In this region, not many miles from the present town of Zapé, one encounters for the first time in southward bound exploration, stone monuments that begin to forecast the monumental remains of the Mexican plateau. These consist of small monoliths of from one to four feet in height, some anthropomorphic, some of phallic motive. As they are set in the valleys, or at least allowed to remain there by the present farmers who regard them with superstitious respect, one suspects a connection with the fructification and growth ceremonials. The Indians neither affirm nor deny this significance.[23]

The above expressed implication that some, if not most or all, of the mounds and other archaeologic remains in the Zape district represent ancient Tepehuán settlements requires some comment. It is historical fact that the Tepehuán were not settled in the Zape Valley when the Jesuit missionaries entered the area (see Pérez de Ribas and Alegre). Judging from conflicting statements concerning Tepehuán culture, we may assume that the Tepehuán-speaking nation was composed of at least two cultural divisions which represented reaction to different environments and contact with differing exterior cultures. The southwestern Tepehuanes lived in an area of greater precipitation and less temperature extremes than prevailed in the land of the northern Tepehuanes. Furthermore, the southern Tepehuanes were in close cultural contact with such definitely agricultural groups as the Huichol, Cora, Totorame, and Xixime. On the other hand, the northern Tepehuanes had easier access to the interior basin nomads (certain Zacatecos, Conchos, and Laguneros bands) who possessed little or no agriculture, than to the Acaxee and Tahue on the west. Granting that Alegre's characterization (see n. 5) held true for the northern Tepehuanes, and that of the "Anua del Año de 1596" for the southern Tepehuanes, then we may assume that the Indian inhabitants of the Indé-Guanaceví-Zape region, at the time of the Spanish Conquest, were no better than seminomads with little or no agriculture. Certainly, the attributing of archaeologic remains to the "Cocoyomes" and to the

"Mexicanos" indicates that these ancient settlement sites were no part of the Tepehuanes's own tradition. Finally, many of the artifacts, and other types of archaeologic evidence, recovered from the Zape sites are not reminiscent of Tepehuán culture (as reported by the Spanish chroniclers, and Lumholtz and Hrdlička).[24] Along this line it will suffice to mention that cremation was not practiced by the Tepehuanes; nor did they build planned villages of large houses and rooms. Until much more is known concerning both Tepehuán culture and Durango archaeology, it will be unsafe to link any of the archaeologic vestiges with any historic people of the area.

The most recent writings on Zape archaeology represent the fruits of an areal reconnaissance of Durango undertaken in 1936 by J. Alden Mason, for the American Philosophical Society.[25] No formal excavations were carried out (except in the caves near Zape Chico), but potsherds were collected and notes were made of the surface indications. To Guillemin Tarayre's description of the Santa Ana site, Mason added plans and descriptions of two other sites near Zape (Zape Chico and Arroyo Quelites), and a brief mention of potsherds and other artifacts. Mason's chief contribution is his identification of the Zape culture as an attenuated form of Central Mexican culture. His principal reasons for this conclusion are: continuity of similar habitation remains from Chalchihuites to Zape; resemblance of ceramics, especially in legged wares; presence of hemispherical spindle whorls.

In the following paragraphs the writer will present his observations and conclusions, amplified by those of the writers cited previously, concerning the archaeology of the Zape area, and its general relationships. The archaeologic remains consist of three types of settlement sites, with associated artifacts revealed through denudation, the burrowing of animals, and the random diggings of treasure seekers. Prehistoric settlements were made in natural caves, on high fortified hills, or *peñoles*, and on low hills, or *lomas*, in the valley.

The best-known cave sites are those near Sestín, and the group just above (south) Zape Chico. Seemingly, only Guillemin Tarayre investigated the Sestín caves, whence he reported ollas and other artifacts belonging to an advanced culture. The Zape Chico caves, three miles by road north of El Zape, are on the right bank of the Rio del Zape, where the river has cut against the foot of a mass of rhyolitic tuff and volcanic agglomerate. At the top of a talus slope, some fifty feet above the present stream, is the main series of caves, which extend for nearly half a mile along the right bank. These caves have been ransacked by treasure hunters for generations. Some of them are now used as storage places for fodder such as maize stalks and leaves. Guillemin Tarayre noted bones, flint arrowpoints, and crude pottery in these caves, which he believed were occupied by the same people that built the structures on the *peñol* of Zape, but different from the occupants of the site near Santa Ana.²⁶ Lumholtz mentioned these caves as much-dug ancient burial-caves.

The caves of the Zape area are natural recesses which were used as habitations and for storage, but seemingly without the erection of house structures within them. There is nothing distinctive about such cave sites as they are found throughout northern Mexico, and have been used since prehistoric times. It is quite probable that peoples of several successive cultures have utilized them. We know, from the missionary chronicles of the sixteenth and seventeenth centuries and from modern accounts such as those of Lumholtz, Hrdlička, Basauri, and others, that many of the Tepehuán and Tarahumar Indians did and do live in natural caves. Remains of the "cliff-house" type, i.e., substantial structures of stone or adobe built within caves or on cliff ledges under overhanging rocks, have not been reported from the Zape area. Such cliff dwellings have a known distribution from northwestern Colorado to southwestern Zacatecas. As far south as the Aros river of Chihuahua-Sonora the associated cultures belong to the Southwestern complex. The cliff-house reported by Hrdlička near Juchipila, Zacatecas, had no associated artifacts. Unfortunately, the several cliff-houses reported by Case (formerly construction engineer of the K.C.M. & O. Railroad) and Holt (a mining engineer who worked in the Sinaloa-Durango-Chihuahua Sierra Madre, 1921–26) in the canyons of the upper Mayo, Fuerte, Sinaloa, Humaya, Tamazula, and San Lorenzo rivers of Chihuahua and Durango, were not investigated for cultural material.²⁷ The nearest of these reported cliff dwellings to El Zape is a group in the mountains east of San Andrés de la Sierra, Durango, some sixty miles air line to the southwest, in the San Lorenzo drainage.

Fortification or defense sites probably exist both to the east and west of El Zape, located at the tops of mountain scarps, and on isolated hills that crown the Sierra Madre spurs. However, only the *peñol* of Zape (Cerro de la Cruz) site has been reported. This *peñol* was undoubtedly used as a defense site, since habitations were constructed on the very top (some three hundred feet above the valley floor) which can only be attained by an arduous climb up steep slopes that are broken in places by nearly vertical rock faces. The nearest water and farm land are at El Zape, on the valley margin. Only the defensive and lookout values could have made the *peñol* site attractive. It is possible that in prehistoric times the inhabitants of the Zape Valley used the Cerro de la Cruz as a site for one of their shrines, but habitation is indicated by the presence of numerous house remanents and of metates, manos, mortar holes, and quartz spalls. Potsherds are scattered all the way from the pueblo to the top of the *peñol*. These shards represent types found in the valley sites. The houses were seemingly of unshaped local rocks piled up to form the walls of roughly rectangular and disconnected rooms. No particular plan or grouping could be determined. No trace of the columns mentioned by Pérez de Ribas was visible.

Similar hilltop sites, belonging to various cultures, are found sporadically over northwestern Mexico, as at Ojitos and Bachimba, Chihuahua; San Darío and Los Remedios, Durango; and La Quemada and Cerro de Sacrificios, Zacatecas. In general, sites occupying defensive positions are somewhat rare in the lowlands, and are not numerous in the Sierra Madre. The *cerros de trincheras*, or terraced hills, of northern Sonora, the cliff dwellings of the mountain gorges, and the above-mentioned random hill sites comprise most of the defensive sites in northwestern Mexico. They seem to be most numerous along the eastern and western margins of the Sierra Madre Occidental.

Most of the archaeologic sites in the Zape area occupy the crests and upper slopes of low hills that extend down to farm land along the Zape River and its principal tributaries. Location of substantial structures, in nondefensive positions, near crop land and water, together with finds of pottery, metates and manos, and charred maize cobs, indicate that these sites were occupied by a sedentary agricultural people.[28] The best known of these sites are El Zape (Pérez de Ribas and Alegre), Santa Ana (Guillemin Tarayre and Mason), Zape Chico and Arroyo Quelites (Mason), and Los Molcajetes (visited by the writer). The main ruin area extends some seven miles within the Zape Valley, from Zape Chico to Hacienda Santa Ana. It is reported that nearly every *loma* has its ruin. The largest of the known sites, that near Santa Ana, is representative of the type.

The Santa Ana or, as it is known locally, Loma Pelona site extends some two hundred yards, WNW-ESE, along the crest of a low, grassy hill or spur situated two-fifths of a mile NNW of the Hacienda Santa

Ana, on the west side of the river. This entire hill has been under cultivation. A *mojonera* on the hilltop, within the ruins, marks the boundary
between the remnant of hacienda lands and the area taken over by
agrarians. No country rock is exposed; the soil is a gray-brown sandy
loam with many rounded and subangular stones, mainly of igneous
origin. The structures were, seemingly, erected on three or four stages,
which may have been terraces as Guillemin Tarayre and Mason state.
All that now remain of these structures are *cimientos*, or rows of stones,
that mark the disposition of the former walls. These walls apparently
were built of puddled adobe reinforced throughout, or in the lower portion, with waterworn stones as large as eighteen inches in length. During the centuries since these habitations were abandoned, the walls have
crumbled into low mounds from which project the stones that once
served as foundation and reinforcement. No walls are now exposed at
the surface, except in several pothunter excavations. As Mason has commented, Guillemin Tarayre's plan of this ruin is greatly idealized.
Although it is hazardous to determine the ground plan of any ruin prior
to excavation, the present surface configuration indicates, to the writer,
the former existence of rooms arranged to form a rectangular compound (☐), a capital gamma (⌐), an inverted u (⊓), and several
minor structures. There is no evidence of any masonry edifice nor, if one
reads carefully, will any suggestion of such be found in Guillemin
Tarayre's account. On the other hand, Guillemin Tarayre's conjecture
that the mounds in this group served as foundations for jacallike structures is erroneous, due to his not being aware that adobe and rubble
walls disintegrate to form just such mounds and *cimientos*. Scattered
over the surface of the site were numerous potsherds, metates and
manos of various materials, several quartz arrowheads, spalls of quartz
and obsidian, one crude, partially grooved axe, two spindle whorls, one
copper and shell earring (?), and one flat stone pendant. Near several
of the pothunters' excavations were human bones, principally molars
and phalanges. Turtles of metal, and idols or figurines of stone and clay
were reported from this site. Mason obtained the stem of a pipe, a
vessel leg or support, and part of a spindle whorl, in addition to potsherds.

No attempt was made by our party to examine El Zape site proper,
since it has been practically masked and obliterated by the Mexican
settlement. However, shards of the same types found at Loma Pelona
and on the Cerro de La Cruz were noted all along the upper (eastern)

portion of the town. One other site worthy of mention is that which was named Los Molcajetes, from the large mortar holes in bedrock. This site occupies the top of a small rhyolitic tuff ridge about three hundred yards east of the upriver end of the Zape Chico caves. Mounds and *cimientos* were somewhat obscured by herbaceous vegetation, therefore no attempt was made to sketch the plan of the structures. At the southwest end of the ridge were a number of circular mortar holes, the largest of which was twenty-seven inches deep and twenty-two inches in surface diameter. A fair number of potsherds were scattered over the site, but no other artifacts were observed. Nowhere in the Zape area did we notice the circular *cimientos* mentioned by Lumholtz. Nor did we locate the graves and temples mentioned by Alegre as being within a half league of El Zape church.

The stone and adobe type of house indicated by the Zape mounds and *cimientos* is widely distributed throughout the higher and cooler portions of northwestern Mexico. Ashlar masonry seemingly was not employed, excepting in very crude form in a few ruins in Chihuahua, in such Zacatecan sites as Chalchihuites and La Quemada, and elsewhere to the south. Houses of puddled adobe, often of many rooms and several stories, were restricted to the extension of the Southwestern culture area into Chihuahua. Walls laid up of unshaped rock, and plastered over, are present sporadically in the northern portion of the Sierra Madre in small one-story ruins, and more commonly in Zacatecas, Nayarit, and Jalisco, where a number of large and multistoried ruins have been reported. The Zape house type is the predominant type in the Sierra Madre and adjacent highlands. As mentioned before, this type of habitation weathered down to a slight mound, with room positions outlined by the upturned stone slabs or pebbles used for reinforcement. These *cimientos* occur in southeastern Arizona and southwestern New Mexico, and are numerous in eastern Sonora, western Chihuahua, western Durango, and southward at least into Nayarit, western Zacatecas, and northern Jalisco. This reinforced adobe wall is the only type known so far from western and northern Durango, as in the sites visited by Tarayre, Lumholtz, Holt, Sauer, Mason, and the writer.[29] There is, apparently, no connection between the *cimiento* sites and any particular pottery ware or type of stone artifact.

Practically nothing is, as yet, known concerning architectural details in the Zape area. When such data are provided they will enable the archaeologist to more definitely place the Zape culture. At present we may assume that the Casas Grandes, or Chihuahuan, and La Quemada, or Zacatecan, cultures were opposed lobes of fairly strong and well differentiated cultures, with an intervening area of nondescript culture.[30] Tau or step doorways, wall niches, and inset fireplaces of Pueblo type have been noted only in the Chihuahuan area. Pyramidal structures, large courts flanked by individual structures, round stone houses, and stairways are known only from Sinaloa, Zacatecas, and southwards. The most northern truncated pyramids recorded are in the Suchil Valley of Zacatecas-Durango, and in the Presidio Valley of Sinaloa.[31] Town courts have been located only in the larger ruins of Zacatecas, and southward. Round stone houses have been reported from the mountain and foothill country of southeastern Sinaloa (near Cacalotán, etc.) and adjacent Durango. Stairways are known archaeologically from Chalchihuites as the most northern site, but the Acaxee and other tribes of western Durango-eastern Sinaloa were reported, by missionaries, to have not only stairways but also three-story communal houses of stone and adobe.

A summary of the archaeologic evidence, other than architectural, from the Zape area may throw more light on cultural affinities. It may be assumed that the prehistoric people of Zape were agricultural, with a primary reliance on maize. Further investigations may reveal that other plants were cultivated, but only rests of maize have been discovered so far. It is virtually impossible to determine if irrigation was practiced prehistorically. When the Spaniards entered northwestern Mexico only the coastal Seri and Guasave, and certain tribes of eastern Chihuahua, Durango, and Zacatecas, lacked crop farming. There is neither archaeologic nor documentary evidence of ditch irrigation being practiced prehistorically or at the time of the conquest in Chihuahua (the case for Casas Grandes is not clear), Durango, Zacatecas, coastal Nayarit, and Sinaloa. Only at the north and south (among the Pima, Opata, and prehistoric Hohokam of Sonora and southern Arizona; and on the plateau lands of Nayarit and Jalisco) do documents and archaeologic investigations indicate irrigation. Bones of various wild mammals and birds are present but not in large numbers. Some of these bones seem to be turkey, but there is no way of differentiating between the wild and tame forms. The comparative picture shows maize, beans, pumpkins, cotton, chile, chia, and guava cultivated, and ducks, chachalacas, turkey, parrots, bees, snakes, and dogs kept, in Jalisco, Nayarit, and Sinaloa. Climatic and edaphic conditions, of course, would have excluded certain of these items from the highlands of Zacatecas, Durango, and Chihuahua.

Spindle whorls (*malacates*) of both semihemispherical and biconical terra cotta types have been found in the Zape area. This would indicate that cotton was known, even if not cultivated. *Malacates* of both types, decorated by punching and incising, were found by us on the Loma Pelona. They were identical in size, shape, and decoration, with many seen by the writer in the lowlands of Sinaloa and Nayarit. Such *malacates* are fairly numerous as far north as the Mocorito and Zape valleys. A few have been collected in Sonora and Chihuahua, and two or three are known from the American Southwest.

Human images or figurines (*monos*) of terra cotta are virtually lacking in Durango. Mason found few, and the writer saw only the fragment mentioned previously, which may not be prehistoric. However, natives of El Zape informed the writer that figurines of both stone and clay had been found in local sites; Pérez de Ribas makes a general statement concerning *figuras*; and Alegre circumstantially details the finding of a human figurine by Father Larios. At all events, the one figurine actually seen is not like any other known from Mexico. We may reasonably conclude that figurines are very rare in the Zape area, and that whatever exist (on the basis of reported descriptions) certainly are not of the specialized large hollow type that seems to be localized in Jalisco-Nayarit, with an extension into the Baluarte Valley of southern Sinaloa. The mere presence of figurines, incidentally, means nothing unless detailed descriptions are obtained, since human figurines of baked clay are found sporadically from Utah to northwestern Argentina. Stone idols (of man and other animals) were not noted by us, but they were reported frequently. Seemingly, these idols range in size from a few inches to more than two feet in height, and vary greatly in nature of execution. Such idols were frequently mentioned, by the Spanish missionaries, as being common among the Tepehuán, Acaxee, and other tribes of the Sierra Madre.

The stone artifacts most frequently noted were mealing stones, projectile points, knives and scrapers, and axes. Not one of these categories, as yet, furnishes a definite diagnostic element concerning prehistoric cultures in northwestern Mexico. The metates of the Zape area were invariably of the legless scoop and bowl types, commonly constructed of local igneous rocks. These two types are found from Utah to Guerrero. Examples can be cited from Arizona, Durango, Nayarit, and Michoacán, that cannot be distinguished apart, excepting perhaps through petrographic analysis. It should be repeated here that, despite Bartlett, Lumholtz, Fewkes, and others, legged metates are not found *in situ* in the prehistoric sites of Arizona, Chihuahua, and elsewhere in northwestern Mexico.

Projectile points seem to be fairly common, since our party picked up more than a dozen whole or nearly entire points, and many fragments and rejects, while reconnoitering the several sites visited. Only based points, nonserrated, varying from one-half inch to somewhat more than two inches in length, were noted. All points were laterally notched, and a few also possessed a basal notch. The points were about evenly divided, as to material, between rather crude points of felsites, basalts, and diorites, and well-made points of chert, jasper, and chalcedony. No points, or any other artifacts, of obsidian were seen; and only a few obsidian spalls were noted. This lack of obsidian artifacts contrasts strongly with both the Chihuahua-Sonora country to the north, and the Sinaloa-Nayarit-Zacatecas country to the south and east. It is possible that now workable obsidian occurs in this portion of Durango. The Zape projectile points are practically identical with points found in many other areas, e.g., in New Mexican sites of Pueblo culture. The principal conclusion that may be derived from the presence of these points is that, unlike many of the lowland peoples of Sonora, Sinaloa, and Nayarit, the inhabitants of Zape made little use of wooden shafts with fire-hardened points.

A few knives and scrapers, of the same materials used in the projectile points, were observed. These did not differ from similar items found in Chihuahua, Sonora, and elsewhere to the north. The long, four-sided, flaked obsidian blade is common north into central Sinaloa and Durango, but is rare or lacking in the northern portions of these states. The writer has seen only one large obsidian item from Chihuahua, a five-inch core about one inch in greatest diameter. Only one axe, a partially grooved crude example of some dense igneous rock, was seen. However, Lumholtz reported various polished stone implements, and local people informed us of several polished, partially grooved axes that had been found in the valley. None seemed to be of the effigy type seen by the writer in Sinaloa (owl head poll, near Verdura), and reported from Nayarit, Zacatecas, and elsewhere to the south. Grooved and three-quarters grooved polished stone axes (Pueblo and Gila types, of the Southwest) have about the same distribution as the scoop and bowl metates. No celts of south Mexican type are known from northwestern Mexico.

Ornaments of stone, metal, shell, and bone were seen or reported in the Zape Valley. From the Loma Pelona site were seen a small, tabular pendant of shale, pierced by two close-set holes on the long side; one-half of a bar, made from some nacreous shell, that apparently had broken in the middle where a perforation had been made; and a ring (one-half inch diameter) of copper wire upon which was strung a perforated disk (one-half inch diameter) of white shell whose edges were rouletted by twenty-four irregularly spaced and sized triangular indentations. In addition, turtles of metal were reported, and Mason was told of gold ornaments. Although the tale of gold ornaments is somewhat incredible, it is quite probable that items of copper and of silver are present. Such items have been found in Sinaloa, and have been reported from the Casas Grandes area.[32] Metals—principally copper, silver, and gold—were placered and worked northward to Culiacán, and possibly in Durango. Beads, pendants, gorgets, and bells (the most common metal artifacts throughout northwestern Mexico), die away in numbers northward until, in Sonora-Chihuahua and the American Southwest, they become so comparatively rare as to be considered trade items. So far, no specific identification has been made of shell artifacts found in Durango. The items noted by the writer seemed to be from the shells of freshwater molluscs. The apparent absence of *Glycymeris* and *Olivella* is in marked contrast with the abundance of these genera in the ruins of Sonora and Chihuahua. Mason reports tubular beads of bone, to complete the picture of known ornaments from northern Durango.

The archaeologic evidence of cremation, as well as inhumation, is very definite. Although not known to have been practiced by the Tepehuanes nor their linguistic close-kinsmen, the Pimas,[33] it was practiced historically by the Chichimecs (certain bands of the interior plateau north of Mexico City), Aztecs, Otomí, and Tarascans, and prehistorically in the Hohokam, Trincheras, Aztatlán, and Toltec culture areas. It has often been explained as an innovation from the north by nomadic or seminomadic Uto-Aztecans, but this theory is not well substantiated as yet. About all that can be concluded is that cremation was neither an Anasazi nor an Archaic Mexican practice, and that the area of distribution contracted southward from prehistoric to historic times.

No ball courts or dancing plazas were noted in the Zape area, but Lumholtz, Mason, and others report them from farther to the south and west. Special areas for ball games and dances were reported by the Jesuit missionaries in the Sierra Madre of Durango and Sinaloa. *Mitotes* are still danced in southwestern Durango, and *hulama* is still played as far north as central Sinaloa. In this connection it should be remarked that many, or all, of the structures labeled "ball courts" that have recently been described from the American Southwest, might just as logically be termed dance plazas. Furthermore, "ball courts" in Mexico were used for such dissimilar games as *tlachtli* and *hulama*.

Potsherds constitute the most valuable diagnostic items available. Such shards are rather plentiful in the Zape area. Although whole vessels (*ollas*) have been reported, from both cave and *loma* sites, only shards were seen by the writer. These shards were usually small, and none was larger than five inches in major dimension. The potsherds observed, from four sites (Loma Pelona, Cerro de La Cruz, Los Molcajetes, Cuevas de Zape Chico), fell into three wares and some seven types. These were as follows:[34]

I. PLAIN MONOCHROME WARE

1. ZAPE BUFF.   Paste—medium hardness; homogeneous to slightly porous; rather friable; light yellow, orange, or buff. Carbon streak—.9 of wall, to none. Temper—fine to medium-fine sand, with occasional large water-worn inclusions of quartz and feldspar. Surface treatment is uniform. A float or a light slip has been worked on or applied. The resultant surface is light buff, occasionally crackled, with larger tempering particles showing through at times. Finished by an even and excellent rubbing and polishing. Walls—.5 to 1.8 cm.; average .7.

This is quantitatively the leading pottery type in the Zape area, constituting 47 percent of the shards. However, it was found only at the Cerro de La Cruz and Loma Pelona sites, where it predominated at the latter. By inference, from rim and body shards, it occurred in bowl and *olla* forms. There is no definite evidence of legs, as the two "legs" found could equally well have served as lateral nubs or ears.

2. ZAPE RED.   Paste—medium to quite hard; compact concrete-like to slightly porous and friable; gray to brick red. Carbon streak—usually large. Temper—fine to medium sand or crushed rock, chiefly quartz and basalt. Surface smoothed, but striations not completely eliminated. A thick, soft, deep-red slip was applied, normally over all, sometimes on exterior and over on to rim (seemingly *olla*) interior, rarely just exterior. Where unslipped, interiors normally buff color. This red slip is very soft and weathers readily. Final treatment, polished to burnished.

Zape Red probably was derived from Zape Buff. It is present at all four sites, predominating at Cerro de La Cruz, and being second at the others. Constitutes 20 percent of the shards. *Olla* and bowl forms.

3. ZAPE BROWN.   Paste—fairly hard; medium fine, but varying from fine dense to coarse friable; dark orange to black. Carbon streak— variable. Temper—fine to medium sand or crushed rock, generally quartz and feldspar. Surface treatment highly variable. Always smoothed to some extent, but scraping marks may be seen on nearly every shard. Unslipped, floated, heavily slipped. Slip was applied all over, exterior only, interior only. The slip usually was polished or burnished, and fired to a dark brown red. This color often shaded into a gray where firing- clouds have blemished the slip. Some surfaces slipped, without polish; other surfaces polished, without slip. Walls—.5 to 1.9 cm.; average 1.0 cm.

Probably derived from Zape Buff. Present at all four sites in third rank, excepting at Los Molcajetes where it is the dominant type. Con- stitutes 17 percent of the shards. Open forms predominate over closed.

4. ZAPE GRAY.   Paste—harder than Zape Buff; sandy, rather fri- able. Carbon streak—commonly present to a slight extent. Temper— medium coarse and somewhat angular to fine rolled sand. Surface slightly smoothed, leaving striations and protuberances. A medium- heavy soft gray slip was applied to both sides of vessels. This slip checked and crackled considerably, and weathered readily. Walls— average .7 cm.

In general, Zape Gray resembles Zape Buff. Found only at Cerro de La Cruz, where it was fourth to Zape Red, Zape Buff, and Zape Brown.

II.   *SMUDGED WARE*

5. ZAPE SMUDGED RED.   This type has the same paste, temper, and exterior treatment as Zape Red. The interiors have been smudged and polished. The smudging varies from a deep carbonizing that ex- tends well through to the outside, and often manifests itself there by firing-clouds or smudge-blurs, to a light blackening of the interior. Represented by a few shards at Loma Pelona and Cerro de La Cruz.

6. ZAPE SMUDGED BUFF.   Identical with Zape Buff, excepting that interior, exterior, or both sides may be smudged and polished. Found at Loma Pelona and Las Cuevas de Zape Chico, where it is dominant at the latter site. Constitutes 13 percent of all shards from the Zape area.

III.   *PAINTED DUOCHROME WARE* (*3 percent of all Zape shards*)

7. ZAPE RED ON BUFF.   Paste, temper, and red pigment are much the same as in the better examples of Zape Red. However, paste seems

to be somewhat sandier, and carbon streak is less developed. The ware is well smoothed, and carries a heavy gray to buff slip. Crude red designs were painted in sloppy fashion, and the whole surface was well polished. Because of the softness of both slip and paint pigment, this polishing caused the streaking out of pigment from the lines or body of the design, and a resultant blurring and lessened effectiveness of the design. Because of this same softness of the slip, many of the shards have lost, through weathering, nearly all of the slip and imposed design. The design elements are circles, wavy lines, enclosing squares, straight lines of varying width, and scrolls. These elements were applied on the exterior of what seemed to be both closed and open forms. There is an indication that all, or nearly all, of the rim pieces were painted red.

Zape Red on Buff was found only at Loma Pelona and Cerro de La Cruz. It is seemingly related to Mason's Chalchihuites Red on Buff,[35] and most certainly is related to Aztatlán Red on Buff from Sinaloa and Nayarit. The writer compared Zape and Aztatlán shards, and discovered that it was virtually impossible to distinguish many of the shards. Any of the Zape shards could have come from the Aztatlán area; but there were a number of the Aztatlán shards (with finer and more skillfully drawn design elements) that were not duplicated among the Zape shards.[36] The implications of this resemblance are discussed later in this paper.

In addition to the above seven pottery types (each based on a study of from 10 to 1,102 shards), there were four other types or subtypes. Four shards were found, at the Cerro de La Cruz, of an orange-slipped ware, painted with red designs that were seemingly outlined in white or with some pigment that burned to a dull, lusterless surface. Also on the Cerro de La Cruz were found three shards slipped with red on one side and with gray on the other. One of these shards was decorated with red on the gray. One shard from the Cerro de La Cruz belonged to a ware otherwise totally unrepresented in northern Durango—incised or carved ware. It seemed to be part of a shoulder from a closed form. Paste— hard, porous, dark gray in color. Exterior is light gray, of a somewhat mottled appearance. Upon this exterior surface had been carved, after the polishing, a design of triangles in a row above a field cut by oblique grooves. The interior had been smudged and burnished. At the Loma Pelona site was found one shard of a very fine, hard, compact paste, terra cotta in color.

Pottery was made or used throughout northwestern Mexico, according to archaeologic and historic evidence. However, definitely prehistoric wares have not been identified as yet from the area between the Sinaloa and Sestín rivers on the south and the Yaqui-Aros and Conchos rivers on the north.[37] In this area most of the wares belong to types still or historically manufactured by the Pima, Tarahumar, Conchos, Yaqui, and Mayo peoples. Unfortunately, it is not known what ceramic types were made by the Tepehuán, Acaxee, and some other of the Sierra Madre tribes.[38]

The distinctive Trincheras, Hohokam, and Chihuahua prehistoric wares have been found southward to the Rio Sonora, Sahuaripa, Rio Aros, and the Conchos. These wares, by their simple forms, lack of tripod supports, and presence of typically Southwestern design elements, belong definitely to the Southwestern culture complex. Chihuahua poly-chrome ware, because of bright colors, frequent effigy forms, and occasional macaw designs, has been suspect as of Mexican origin. But these items, when balanced against the lack of tripod supports, the common use of interlocking scrolls, opposed step designs, and "leaf" designs—in a decorative field set off by framing lines, and divided into panels, with a repetition of elements, and the technique of thumbnail indentations around *olla* necks just below the rim (which is found nowhere else in the region), are not sufficient to indicate a southern origin. Furthermore, corrugated ware (occasionally found in Chihuahua), copper-glazed ware (such as Húerigos Polychrome from northwestern Chihuahua), and hooded effigy pots or *ollas* are not found to the south. Not a single vessel or shard of southern provenience, even from Sinaloa or Durango, has ever been reported from Sonora or Chihuahua; nor has any Chihuahua or Sonora pottery been reported from southern sites. Trade wares from Arizona and New Mexico (such as the Little Colorado, Middle Gila, and El Paso polychromes, and Mimbres and Chupadero black on white) turn up in northern Chihuahua, but not any farther to the south. The ceramic evidence points conclusively towards a cultural unity of northern Sonora and Chihuahua with areas and peoples to the north.[39]

Over most of Nayarit, Jalisco, Zacatecas, western Durango, and Sinaloa to the Sinaloa River, there seems to have been a basic ware (not necessarily the oldest in all localities) which was a red-rimmed pottery, both slipped and unslipped, and commonly decorated with simple designs in a rather fugitive red on a buff background. This ware constitutes the Aztatlán complex which was discovered and traced over northern Nayarit and Sinaloa into the Humaya drainage by Sauer and

Brand in 1930. Many of the shards collected by Sauer in central and southern Durango and around Guadalajara, Jalisco, in 1933, proved to belong to the Aztatlán Red on Buff ware, largo sensu, as is true of Mason's Chalchihuites Red on Buff or Brown on Buff, and Brand's Zape Red on Buff, which were collected in 1936.[40] There are at least five variant types of the Aztatlán Red on Buff ware,[41] which differ somewhat in paste, tempering, and firing, but agree in color and design treatment. Bowl and *olla* forms, more commonly legless than tripod, seem to predominate. This ubiquitous ware is associated with distinctive localized ware in various regions, e.g., Culiacán and Chametla polychromes in Sinaloa, incised, carved, burnished, smudged, and plain monochrome wares throughout the area, and cloisonné ware in Zacatecas.

No stratigraphic excavation has been done in sites containing a ceramic complex (with the exception of Kelly's work in Sinaloa), so that it is impossible to correlate chronologically the ceramic cultures of Durango, Sinaloa, Zacatecas, Nayarit, and Jalisco. From Kelly's work it is known that Aztatlán Red on Buff preceded Culiacán and Mazatlán polychromes, but, at Chametla, was preceded by at least two distinct polychrome styles.[42] Other than the possibility of unrecognized Aztatlán shards, no trade pieces from Durango-Zacatecas have been found, so far, in Sinaloa-Nayarit, and the reverse is likewise true. However, this probably represents merely the lack of stratigraphic work and the small number of sites even casually inspected.

A SURVEY of the totality of archaeologic evidence from the Zape area, in the light of the known archaeology of neighboring regions, leads the writer to agree with Mason that northern Durango represents the most northern extension of a very attenuated form of Central Mexican culture. The writer sees no reason for changing the tentative boundary outlined in 1935 (Brand, "Distribution of Pottery Types in Northwest Mexico," *Amer. Anth.* 37: 294, map 1). No distinctly Southwestern element of material culture is present, while pottery types, pipes, spindle whorls, varied ornaments of metal, cremation, and possibly legged wares and terra cotta figurines, indicate Central Mexican affiliation. One might postulate either: 1] a spread of Toltec-Tarascan culture simultaneously from the Michoacán-Jalisco plateau into the Pacific lowlands, and along the eastern margin of the Sierra Madre Occidental; or   2] an extension of this same generalized culture from the Sinaloa and Nayarit lowlands up the drainage lines of such streams as the San Pedro, San Lorenzo, and Culiacán, into the highlands of Durango. Major problems indicated, in addition to the need for more intensive regional reconnaissance and archaeologic excavations, are: 1] chronology of the various cultures; 2] why did not Central Mexican culture expand farther to the north, into areas seemingly just as attractive as the occupied frontier lands?

3

The Chalchihuites Area, Zacatecas

Manuel Gamio

Gamio's important article, here reproduced for the first time in English, was based on some three months of field work carried out in western Zacatecas in 1908. Noguera (1930) and Marquina (1951) have followed the Gamio article very closely in their own discussions of Chalchihuites archaeology. Gamio's excavations at Alta Vista, reported in this article, until quite recently represented the only excavations in the Chalchihuites area. Even today it is the only published account of the excavation of a major Chalchihuites site, although Kelley and Abbott (1966) have summarized the culture history of the region. Gamio's article also carries the first description of the highly significant fortifications of the Chalchihuites area and the all-important spectacularly developed mining industry of the culture (cf. Weigand, 1968). Understandably, Gamio misinterpreted the "cavernas excavadas" as occupation sites used as places of refuge in time of war.

Our Southern Illinois University field groups have collected extensively at Alta Vista but have not excavated there aside from digging stratigraphic test pits in 1958. However, we have excavated at the nearby sites of La Cofradia and El Calichal, and the position of Alta Vista in the Chalchihuites Culture sequence is quite clear. Alta Vista was a ceremonial center and is the type site for the Alta Vista Phase, dated at circa A.D. 300–500. Potsherds collected from Alta Vista, as well as materials excavated by Gamio, indicate that the site was occupied almost entirely during the Alta Vista Phase.

The materials excavated by Gamio at Alta Vista, and illustrated in his original article include one specimen of paint cloisonné decorated pottery which has a most significant design, that of an eagle clutching a serpent in its beak, essentially the much later Aztec symbol which became the Mexican national emblem. Perhaps this was one of the bits of evidence which led most archaeologists to identify Alta Vista as a Post-Classic site. We now know that its occupation and its affiliations were almost entirely Classic in age.

Some of the material excavated by Gamio at Alta Vista is still available in the Museo Nacional de Antropología in Mexico City, but some has disappeared. In his report reproduced here, Gamio noted that this article was part of a much more detailed manuscript report; to the best of my knowledge this detailed report is not available. The article reproduced here not only has great significance in the history of archaeological research in northern Mexico, but also remains one of the most important basic sources for the student of Chalchihuites Culture archaeology.

J. C. K.

ON ONE occasion, while chatting with Lic. Don Genaro García, Director of the National Museum of Archaeology, History and Ethnology of Mexico, about the paucity of archaeological data from the north of the Republic, particularly in the north and northwest regions of the State of Zacatecas and the south and the southwest of Durango, he indicated a determination to carry out an exploration of such places under the auspices of the institution which he headed.

Having kindly been charged with the responsibility of carrying out that mission, I left the capital of the Republic in the month of August, 1908, headed for the settlement of Chalchihuites, in the State of Zacatecas. I intended to begin my work in the area surrounding that site, owing to its apparently distinct intermediate position between zones of aboriginal culture. Such a position, apparently distinct in nature, was of especial interest.

The expedition lasted three months, part of that time being spent in observing ground-level remains—caves and fortifications—several of which have already been mentioned.[1] Later on, the ruins of Alta Vista were discovered. Their description constitutes the major chapter of this report which, therefore, includes the summary description of remains which had been known previously as well as those discovered during this exploration. There is also brief commentary on this matter, abstracted from a broader study which I did and which cannot be transcribed in its entirety, since it would be to the detriment of more interesting and learned studies, such as this report which will appear in the publication of the Seventeenth Congress of Americanists.

As I said previously, Lic. Don Genaro García approved the exploratory project and subsequently lent his most effective support to it. The authorities and inhabitants of the settlement of Chalchihuites always did everything possible to facilitate my research and other work through whatever means were available to them. Finally, Professor Marshall H. Saville, from New York, United States of America, placed at my disposition his select library, in which books I found valuable data. I hereby express my sincere appreciation to such kind people.

Geographic Location and Historical Antecedents

SINCE THE numerous recognized and discovered remains surround the settlement of Chalchihuites in an area of about 20 kilometers in radius, it would not be possible for me to determine the specific location of all of them. Thus, I shall list here the location of the settlement in question as a central point of reference, and when I describe the remains, I shall indicate their approximate distance from that point.

According to recent scientific data, the settlement of Chalchihuites[2] is located at longitude 104° west; latitude 23°; altitude above sea level, 2,300 meters. It is located 625 kilometers north-northwest of the capital of the Republic.

The climate is temperate with little variation, similar to the Valley of Mexico, since the aridity of the area where it is located is offset by the existence of various springs and arroyos. The vegetation is, generally speaking, cactus and small conifers; but it is more abundant and varied in the lower regions and in the irrigated portions.

The greater part of the population is white, descending from the Spanish colonizers. The *mestizo* population, which is very sparse, is formed by a long-past miscegenation of Spanish with indigenes imported into the area from the south and southwest and, to a lesser degree, with aboriginal peoples. The indigenes have totally disappeared from the region which I explored, so that the visits paid the settlement of Chalchihuites by the Tepehuán Indians who come down from the nearby mountains for the purpose of selling their poor products and buying others, are occasion for great curiosity.

Almost all authors are in accord with affirming that the indigenes found by the Spaniards when they visited this region (approximate date, between 1530 and 1564) were nomads and were uncultured. They had primitive huts for temporary lodging; their warlike nature was extreme to the point that the Conquerors were forced to bring other colonizing indigenes from other areas, particularly the Tlaxcaltecas and the Tonaltecas. Some people refer to those aborigines as Chichimecs, a very widely discussed term owing to its vagueness, since in the final analysis the word means savages and barbarians. Others give them the name Zacatecos, although they do not state if that is their original name, or if it was a name given them by Nahuatl-speaking people who aided in their conquest. There is also a wide divergence of opinion concerning the language which they spoke. Mr. Pimentel says that the Zacateco language existed and he even insists that there was a dictionary written by a priest. Unfortunately, said dictionary has not been seen by any men of science, such as Orozco y Berra, who have made a painstaking search for it. Mr. Elías Amador puts forth the claim of the Jesuit Juan Agustín who says he preached in Zacateco to the inhabitants of Cerro Gordo, Durango. In this case also, there is no more proof than the statement made by the priest. It has been said that Zacateco was a dialect of Nahuatl[3] while, according to other opinions, it was the origin of three dialects: Topia, Acaxee, and Tepehuán. Finally, it has been ventured that Ulmeca, Xicalanca and Zacateco were actually one language.

In summary, if Zacateco either as a language or a dialect ever existed, it is extremely difficult if not impossible today to reconstruct it, since neither in Spanish (which is spoken in the region at this time) nor in the chronicles of the time of the conquest of the area, is there to be found one word which can be attributed to such a language. Neither, insofar as I know, is there any mention of Zacateco as any integral element of any of the indigenous languages[4] of the regions surrounding the area of occupation of the so-called Zacatecos. And this is based on the most outstanding studies that have recently been made of those languages.

In my humble opinion, the language which was spoken in the area at the time of its discovery was Tepehuán (Southern Tepehuán) and the group that spoke it and occupied the region was the Tepehuán Indians who still exist, primarily in the State of Durango.

The reasons which I adduce for such an hypothesis are these: The Tepehuanes live very near the region, toward its northern reaches and, although the number of them who come into the area today is very reduced, in times immediately prior and subsequent to the Conquest, their invasions were quite frequent in the central and south portion of the State of Zacatecas. Therefore, it was logical to assume that they would occupy the intermediate zone (Chalchihuites and its environs), since if another people had lived there, they would not have permitted free passage through their lands. Moreover, when the region was dis- covered, a great number of its inhabitants fled to places not even touched by the Spaniards, and those places could not have been in any other place than to the north-northeast and northwest of Chalchihuites —an area populated today exclusively by the Tepehuanes—since in all other directions the territory was subjugated. Finally, the primitive status unanimously attributed to those peoples hazily called Zacatecos or Chichimecos by the chroniclers, perfectly coincides with the ele- mental culture shown by the Tepehuanes from the time of their con- quest to the present day. This fact can better be observed in their settle- ments in south Durango, which were probably the nuclei whence came those who settled in Chalchihuites and invaded the more southerly areas.

If one takes into account the deficient civilization of the Tepe- huanes (or Zacatecos) of that era, clearly it can be deduced that they were not the builders of the edifices found in the area. Rather, another people of vast culture which were driven out by the Tepehuán or who voluntarily abandoned the locale to be succeeded by the Tepehuanes were the builders of this region.[5]

Caves

Natural caves.   These caverns were formed geologically and consti- tute the most primitive habitations or refuges of all found in the re- gion, and they are very few in number. Existence of man who dwelled in them is proven only by the fragmented rocks and scarce, crude pot- tery remains found in them.

As examples worthy of study, we should mention the Cuevas de la Polvorera, located southwest of Chalchihuites, on the lands of the Hacienda Vergel. The one that I explored consists of a crevice or hole which, at some 4 or 5 meters of depth, is divided into very long, narrow galleries; their floor presents rises and slopes which are very mildly in- clined. Stalactites and stalagmites on the roof and floor of the galleries are noted with frequency. At some distance, at the foot of the hill in which the cave is located, a very meager brook runs; a circumstance that confirms the probable presence of man in such places, which would give him shelter and water. There is also a natural cave in the south face of the Cerro del Chapín; but in this cavern there already appears important adaptations made by man, such as the defensive wall found there and several open pits in the floor and in the walls which, owing to their semispheric and semiovoid shapes, appear to have been for domestic use, such as for the storage of vessels, liquids, etc., etc.

Excavated caves—TYPE NO. 1.   Great is the profusion of these interesting caves, which exist not only in the area explored by me, but are strung out up to some places in the southwest part of the State of Durango. They are generally excavated on the eastern face of hills near streams of water. The excavation work which is required is very easy since the formations are of soft earth, a product of stratification, in which are found alternating conglomerates of calcspar, clays, etc., etc.

As type examples of these caves we have chosen those of San Rafael, which are located southwest of Chalchihuites. Modifying a natural outcrop such as those found on the east faces of the hills, the builders formed a little shelf (*meseta*) on which the outside slope of the rampart or wall rises vertically, and in which they worked out the entrance to the cave. The selection of the faces of the hills for opening up entryways is explained for the reasons that in that way they gained a strategic position, they were safe from floods, and they could easily get rid of the excavated material by shoving it over the edge and down to the foot of the hill. The height of these entryways averages 1 meter 20 centimeters, while the lintel measures 1 meter 60 centimeters; these rather reduced dimensions leads one to suppose that the builders did not want them to be easily visible.

The entrance connects with a large room which always is present in this type of shelter and is one of its main characteristics. Its dimensions vary between 10 and 30 meters in length by 3 or 6 meters in width; the height of the roof or vault is always greater than that of the entryway, sometimes measuring 3 meters. The floor is flat and is covered with the offal from the material knocked loose from the roof and walls.

Currently, some of these rooms have been adapted for habitation or storerooms, for which reason the entry was enlarged and across the entry was built an adobe wall in which a rectangular hole was left and which was provided with a door.

On both sides and at the rear of the room are seen, in no symmetrical plan whatsoever, several openings of lesser dimensions than the

main entry. These doorways lead to secondary galleries whose dimensions are smaller than those of the central room in both height and
width. However, insofar as length is concerned, they are much larger,
some of them reaching a distance of 100 meters. I termed these galleries labyrinths, because they interconnect in a most confusing manner, to the point that I always returned to the same spot after exploring
them. That fact notwithstanding, I believe that they must communicate with other exits. In several of them I found a large quantity of
fragmented limestone, all along one of the walls like a long parapet of
little height, since it never touched the ceiling or vault. Also, from place
to place, one finds little caves excavated in these walls. Finally, some
galleries are sealed by accidental or intentional falls, a circumstance
which also impeded my prolonging the reconnaissance.

Excavated caves—TYPE NO. 2.　　　These caves are generally found on
the upper shelves of hills whose formation is similar to the previous
type, being, like them, near streams of water, but without any determined orientation.

As examples of them, we can mention the ones at El Mezquitalito,
some 3 or 4 kilometers from Chalchihuites, to the northwest.

The entrance to these caves is in the form of a section of an inverted cone whose measurements are, on the average: Diameter, 11
meters 60 centimeters; height, 6 meters, and angle of the generatrix,
50° to 70°.

The lower end of the truncated cone forms the door or portal in
this type of cave, which in the previous type is vertical. In this type, it
is on a horizontal plane or on inclined planes. Through it one goes into
a vertical conduit, while in the first type one goes into the large room.
This vertical or slightly inclined hole has openings in the walls, vertical
doorways which lead to secondary galleries, identical to those described
for the first type.

Perhaps the caves of both type are intercommunicated and are part
of a system, notwithstanding the notable differences in their layout and
the style of entrance.

On the shelves on which this second type of cave is found, one
often finds curious little mounds formed by the same materials from
which the caves are dug. One presumes that they are accumulations of
the diggings from the caves. These mounds do not appear outside the
first type, since they are built on the face of the hills and the tailings

necessarily fall to the foot of the hills. Here, they represent various defined forms: conical, semiovoid, semilenticular, and spherical helmets; some appear to be appendices which makes them take on the appearance of some deformed animal representation.

Fortifications

ONE FREQUENTLY finds rocky hills in this region, and their faces and declivities are not smooth as are those in which the caves are found. Rather, they have large escarpments and pronounced, steep rocks which would make access to the upper shelves impossible if it were not for a few natural places of access plus some others that have been made by man to convert these rocky hills into fortifications. Two of these important promontories are the Hills of Moctezuma and El Chapín.

On the Hill of Moctezuma, the defense works, such as trenches, etc., have virtually disappeared; but on the other hand, there is a small remnant of one of the constructions that was on the upper part of the hill. We do not describe this ruin, because its construction or fabrication, which is the only thing upon which we could comment, is identical to those monuments which we shall describe in detail further on.

Fortress of the Hill of El Chapín.   This hill, which is situated approximately 8 kilometers from the settlement of Chalchihuites, toward the southwest, is a great rhyolitic rock protuberance, rather conveniently adapted to use as a fortification.

The lower portion of the hill is formed by mild slopes which have, with time, been washed and on which ascent is quite easy. In order to obstruct access and to defend the fortification, the builders formed several series of parapets, made with chunks of rock, and these parapets surround the first level like an immense rosary. The second level requires no protection whatsoever, since it is a purely abrupt and inaccessible rock wall.

Generally, on fortresses of this type there are natural chinks and fissures which have been artificially enlarged to give access to the upper tableland. On El Chapín, the layout of the entrance is very interesting. Toward the left-hand portion of the southern face, there is a crevice or chimney which appears to have been artificially enlarged and whose measurements are the following: height, 4 meters; width, 52 centimeters; and length, 5 meters 15 centimeters. On the northern extreme of this gallery, it widens out and becomes a circular area, in whose center is located a rock outcropping and other smaller ones that serve as a ramp to ascend to a shelf. I forgot to say that on the south part of the chimney there are also chunks of rock that obstruct ingress, leaving only a small entryway.

The tableland of El Chapín is a very spacious, irregular parallelogram, from which the adjacent hills and valleys can be dominated.

Over almost the entire surface is found circular and square sites, laid out in symmetrical bands and made of fragments of rock. Perhaps they represent the removal of hut and cabin walls, but I should note that they are not bound with any type of mortar, making them completely different, therefore, from the remains found on the Hill of Moctezuma, since they appear to have been very crude houses—certainly not of any high level of construction.

On the eastern part of the plateau, there is a curious geometric design carved into the rock, constituted of semispherical holes, the radius of which is from 2 to 3 centimeters and which form two concentric circles, a diameter and a secant. There are 260 of these holes in all. I call such a petroglyph a calendar, because Mr. Chavero[6] and Mr. Castañeda (in the article already cited) call it "cycle of the Nahua race" and "religious year of the primitive peoples of the North" (it being, in fact a curious numerical coincidence, nevertheless a thing on which conjecture is pointless).

Also toward the south, and not far from the calendar, there is a hole with water in it, which, according to people from the surrounding area, is an indication of a subterranean spring and not water collected from rain falls. They add that it was there that (thanks to the spring) the aborigines who had fled from the south held off the tenacious sieges of the *conquistadores*.

Isolated Buildings

IF, AS I said previously, the fortifications exist in great number in the area, on the other hand, the isolated habitations or buildings are very sparse in number, probably due to their location in valleys or slightly inclined lands which are plowed year after year, destroying the structures located there, while the others, owing to their inaccessibility, were left alone. (Nevertheless, these layers appear ruined today, destroyed by ignorant people.)

One of the buildings which I could recognize is located near the banks of the Chalchihuites River, some 6 or 7 kilometers west of the village of the same name and on some lands called Las Diezmeras. At first glance a small mound covered with grass is seen; but on ascending to the upper pleateau, some partially buried stones, laid out in quadrangular and rectangular figures, can be seen. These form the cornice of the walls of the building; the sides of the mound are formed by materials carried from other places and placed on the building which was transformed into a mound. This is a most notable and typical feature, which is also observed in the grouped monuments which I describe below.

Grouped Buildings

THE RELATIVE profusion of ceramic potsherds, obsidian points [*dardos*], small engraved stone objects, etc., etc., found on the surface in the locale, as well as the caves and buildings already mentioned, lead us to believe that groups of buildings must have existed there, or perhaps cities where the principal manifestations of culture of the people or peoples that lived there used to flourish. This is because among those vestiges there are some which, owing to their ornamentations and structure, as in the ceramics and carved stone objects, and owing to their construction, such as are seen in some fortifications (ruins such as those on the Hill of Moctezuma) reveal a state of civilization that made all of this necessary.

A happenstance led to my discovery of the grouping of buildings that was hidden on the lands of the Alta Vista or Buena Vista Ranch. The results that I got by uncovering such grouped buildings make up the material for the description below.

Monuments of Alta Vista

IN THE middle of September 1908, taking into account the observations set forth to this point, I was ready to leave for the south of the state, when I happened to find out that on the nearby Alta Vista or Buena Vista Ranch (it is known by both names) there were buried great treasures, according to the people of the area. And they even assured me that some residents by the name of Pérez had dug in some parts where they only turned up human remains and some ceramics.

I went to this ranch and, reconnoitering an area of 2 kilometers, I found a curious grouping of mounds, some of which were circular in shape, having another mound in their center. There was also a rectangle formed by the mounds, and one group took the shape of a right angle.

The mounds are covered with grass, large nopal cacti and mezquite, but on the top, particularly on the one I explored, there were some partially buried stone fragments which, I supposed, and afterward confirmed, are wall cornices. As for the remainder, I saw the excavation that the Pérez family had made previously, and I noted in it several thin flat stones or sandy rocks, that must have been carried there by man and put up in the form of a wall.

On the same day, I began to excavate a rectangular site that was formed by several stones and I discovered the first steps of a stairway that, owing to the mortar on its surface, as well as the ceramic sherds turned up afterward, appeared to reveal that the structure was pre-Hispanic. For two months the excavation work continued with the following results.

Location.   The grouping of structures of Alta Vista is 1,330 meters from the ranch of the same name, toward the southwest. The area which it occupies is difficult to ascertain, since although the principal nucleus consists of only about twenty mounds, there are others at some distance that in other times were linked to the nucleus by roadways or streets paved with flagstones. We shall refer to these below. Further, among these mounds there are some that do not cover buildings, and still others that are made up of accumulations of stone fragments or rubbish. These circumstances make it impossible today to localize the grouping of buildings.

The importance which these grouped monuments must have had for their inhabitants is noted by the great number of fortifications surrounding them and by the prominent place on which they were built and from which a great area of land was taken in. To the north of the monuments, the foothills of the mountains visibly begin their climb and among them the large Jacal Hill stands out like a watchtower. This hill was an invaluable fortification for the aborigines of the area. To the west, elongated buttresses or abutments extend outward, and on top of these was built the fortification of El Chapín, on the one hand, while on the other hand they were cut through by the Chalchihuites River.

At the same time, rising atop the area near the cut or draw on the right hand side were the ruins of another fortification which I call the Rancho Colorado, since it is located near that ranch. And, finally, perceived in the distance are the Pedregoso Fort, the plains of El Suchil and the fortification of Moctezuma. Local humidity conditions give such a clarity to the atmosphere that one can see and appreciate all of the varying aspects and details of the region, as far as the eye can see.

The excavation process. As I said previously, the mounds are covered with vegetation of the locale, and some very old trees (or thickets) and nopal cacti can be seen on some. This growth has never been touched probably because there never has been any planting done on these mounds and, therefore, they have never been touched by the plow.

The work on the mound which I explored began by removing the vegetation and afterward clearing off the dirt and rock fragments which covered the structures. We continually followed the outlines of the walls, floor surfaces, stairs, columns, etc., etc. In order to avoid any destruction whatsoever, the removal of the overburden was effected with small carts which were filled by the workers. These carts rolled over planks laid on the earth to avoid direct contact with the soil which would lead to its destruction.

These buildings had been intentionally covered over, since their doors were closed off with rock and clay walls, or filled in with adobe bricks, and on their outside there had been great accumulation of earth which formed the faces of the mounds.

In my opinion, it is very interesting that the building bears traces of a fire which occurred prior to its burial. Actually, all around there are to be found ashes, burned timbers, partially consumed human remains, and finally, traces of fire on the floor and walls.

Description. The plan of the structures shows a large room, twenty-eight columns, and two entry doors to the large room. To the west of the room, detached from it, are several platforms or terraces and steps, as well as distinct pilasters which at intervals interrupt the last-mentioned stairway.

To the west of the room, hiding its door, is a terrace, a stairway, a rectangular "apartment" or compartment, another compartment and a door which gives access to the rectangular "apartment." Having laid out the general disposition of the ruins which I discovered, I shall now describe them in detail.

Hall of the columns. The boundary of the floor is 3 meters in relation to the upper terrace, which is the plane of reference. Its shape is quadrangular, covering an area of approximately 400 square meters, since each one of its sides measures from 20 meters to 20 meters 5 centimeters; the roof is nonexistent, only pieces of the timbers that once formed it being found; the height of the walls which enclose it varies greatly, since some parts measure a little more than 3 meters, while other parts are 60 centimeters in height. In the middle portion of the north wall there is an entryway that leads to the outside, and in the west wall there is another entrance, whose lintel is higher than the ground-level one and shows, besides, the peculiarity of having, on the part facing the hall, two rectangular dihedral angles, which appear to have been the frame of another door.

The walls of this hall must have been crowned with a series of graceful merlons, one of which was found among the rubbish next to one of the walls. It is "stair-stepped" or staggered and its lateral planes are slightly inclined inward; it is made of clay and has three successive coats of mortar applied on its exterior.

Columns. There are twenty-eight columns in the hall, laid out in four series of seven columns running parallel to the walls. The columns assume four different shapes which, owing to their different dimensions, at first glance, are not in good architectural taste generally shown by the group of monuments I had discovered. Nevertheless, it wasn't always that way, since in one sense all of the columns were of one single type which was in harmony with the size of the hall and of the adjoining compartments. The circumference of these typical columns is approximately 4 meters. For some unknown motive, the builders changed or transformed eight of these columns, adding a large layer of clay and stones to them, over which they added finished cement, the same as for the typical columns. Of the eight which were altered, one represents the form of a prism, another is semicylindrical, and as for the remainder, some are imperfect cylinders, and others are similar to a circular hyperboloid; in the upper cross-section of them can clearly be seen the nuclear column, of the same diameter as the typical ones.

Among the debris of the hall, several objects were found, the most valuable of which were found under the floor of the hall. Their discovery would have been impossible if we had not noticed some small spaces in which there was no mortar or cement, which normally covers the floor, walls and columns. Further on, these objects will be described.

Terraces and eastern stairway.   The great terrace or platform is the highest part of the remains discovered, and it was taken as a point of reference for the boundaries. From it lead two stairs which lead to the lower platforms; one stairway has steps which are larger than its risers and it ends on a platform whereat the excavation work was interrupted. The other stairway, on the other hand, has risers which are larger than the horizontal width of the steps. Four of these steps first lead to a platform, from which two steps continue until they meet the prolongation of the steps of the other stairway, while toward the right-hand part two steps branch off and by which one can descend to another platform. On this latter platform was found a metate [a curved stone, generally in the form of an inclined plane, used for grinding grain], which I shall describe later. I forgot to say that on the first stairway, laid out laterally, rise six prismatic pilasters, and on the right hand side of the other stairway there is a wall that could not be totally uncovered; there are two walls which connect at right angles on the first platform, one of which was as thick as the one mentioned above, while the other was less thick. On the other platform excavation was halted.

"Apartments" (compartments) and western stairway.   Through the hidden doorway previously cited, one enters a quadrangular compartment or room and, climbing the four steps of another stairway, one comes to a small plateau. On the left of this stairway, and running parallel to it, there is a rectangular compartment whose floor is 4 meters lower than the point of reference. Its walls are the same in appearance and makeup as those already mentioned and those which are still to be mentioned. In this compartment there is an entrance or door which, peculiarly, has no wood lintel, but instead is self-supporting since the adobe bricks from which it is built are placed in such a manner that, with some of them vertically placed, some of them inclined, they form a primitive arch. This door gives access to an irregularly shaped room in which there is a wall and a partially destroyed pilaster which separate it from the next room. Its other walls have no other outstanding features. A narrow passage connects this room to another irregular room. On one of its walls, there is a windowlike opening which is closed off with clay and stone. The previously mentioned stairway begins on the floor of

this room, 4 meters deep in relation to the terrace, and the last of its nine steps terminate at the cornice of the walls of the rooms.

Construction materials.   Two types of stone were used in construction: First, fragmented stone of "plutonic" origin, [i.e., lava] was used. These stones were, at times, irregular in shape and, at other times, form more-or-less regular cubes, some of these latter being seen in the semi-ruined building which is located on the top of the Hill of Moctezuma which, as we have said is identical in construction to the Alta Vista buildings. Secondly, flagstones or elongated sedimentary stones torn from the ground by the river's action. In the surrounding area there is, in effect, an excavation or quarry where one can still observe the extraction of these stones.

The adobes found there have the following dimensions: length, 89 centimeters; width, 10 centimeters. The regularity of these measurements in almost all of those I examined leads one to believe that they were made in frames or boxes.

The bricks are of the same size, for which reason I imagine that they are the same adobes mentioned above, appropriately fired, owing to their bright red color and to their relative hardness.

There are two types of mortar: The first is a yellowish gray clay, quite cohesive and adhesive in nature; the second is a mixture of lime carbonates and silicate sands, whose color is very white and whose consistency is hard and more adhesive than that described above.

The cement is of a faded white color and is comprised of a very fine white clay, mixed with a small proportion of carbonate of soda, and whose dehydrating qualities must have been imperfect, owing to the fact that the consistency of the cement is less than that of the second mortar.

Oak, cedar, huizache [Acacia], and mezquite are the trees and brush whose timbers appear in the remains of the excavations.

Disposition of the materials in the structure.   The great solid structures, such as principal walls, columns, pilasters, etc., etc., are made from rubble-work masonry comprised of rounded pebbles and rock fragments, some polished and some rough, laid one over the other and held together by the first mortar alluded to above.

At times, the structures just mentioned appear as lines of stone or brick, more or less perfect in shape, made up of the flagstones mentioned previously.

Dividing walls, stairsteps, merlons and some other parts of the overall construction, whose exact determination is difficult since there was no regular plan adopted, are built of adobes and bricks which have already been described. These adobes and bricks were held together with the first type of mortar mentioned. The adobes and bricks that were used to close off the doors of the hall and its window, on the other hand, had many fragments of the second type of lime mortar. I believe that the discussion of these mortars is of interest, for reasons that I will set forth later.

The entire surface of the structure, be it constructed of rubble-work masonry or in the form of lines of stone or brick, is first covered by a layer of clay to a thickness of 5 or 6 centimeters, in which very fine mixed filaments are perceived, and which were, perhaps, mixed with the clay to give it cohesion. Over this layer of clay, which has corrugations on its surface, another layer of the cement above described was placed, its thickness varying from ½ centimeter to 1 centimeter.

A truly interesting detail in the construction of the walls is in the reinforcement of the walls with stakes [or pickets]. These stakes not only protect the walls, but also the cement, since they reach down to a lower level than the cement. The stakes are set in the layer of clay, between the rubble-masonry and the layer of cement, and they are in a vertical orientation. The ones which I saw in the walls of the room were spaced, on the average, 1 meter 50 centimeters from each other, and their dimensions are from 1 meter 60 centimeters to two meters in height, and 11 centimeters in diameter.

Objects found on carrying out the excavations.   Among the debris which filled the small plateau and the hall, there appeared a great quantity of human remains which were extremely disintegrated, making it impossible not only to describe the position in which they had been, but also the number of them. Basically, the skulls were in such fragile condition that they crumbled on being touched. Nevertheless, we were able to save the following remains: a skull with the mandible missing; fragments of two skulls; several mandibles; femurs and other skeletal remains.

The first-mentioned skull shows a circular perforation 9 millimeters in diameter, in one of its sutures. Dr. Carlos Barajas, M.D., after examining the skull, was of the opinion that the lesion showed signs of healing, which indicates that it probably was made during the life of the individual. A great number of the teeth, especially the molars, are so worn that the chewing surface is entirely smooth; in others, there are rather deep caries. Some of these remains show traces of fire.

An adequate idea of the culture of the inhabitants who built the buildings at Alta Vista is gained through the ceramic objects which were found. The ferrugenous earth that exists in the area constituted the unsurpassable material for the fabrication of all types of vessels. A prolonged pounding of that earth must have made it quite plastic, so as to obtain the compact and firm clay from which the vessels are made. In addition, there must have been various gradations of firing which determined their diverse hardness, fragility, appearance, and coloration. Although the molding of the vessels must have been done by hand, their finishing and ornamentation were probably accomplished with very fine, small sticks, pieces of which can still be seen on their surface.

The ceramic objects which were discovered may be divided into two types: 1] vessels which are varnished or glazed and whose ornamentation was painted on the surface; 2] vessels which are not varnished or glazed and whose ornamentation consisted of inlays or cloisonnés.

The color of the clay in the first type is, generally, yellowish and at times, reddish, while the color of the ornamentation is dark red or black. The surface is smooth and often shiny, owing perhaps to the application of lead salts which abound in the area. I have divided them, by shape, into *comales* [a flat earthenware "pan" for cooking maize cakes], pots and vases. The *comales* take a slightly concave and lenticular shape, although they may also follow a round, bowl shape. Their diameter varies from 10 to 30 centimeters, and their thickness from 4 to 9 millimeters. All of the *comales* are ornamented.

With one exception, all of the pots are broken. The dimensions of the whole pot are 15 centimeters in height; 15 centimeters in diameter in the main body of the vessel; and 8 centimeters in diameter at the neck; its decoration is well delineated.

As in the previous case, only one vase could be found in whole condition. Its dimensions are: height, 6.5 centimeters; upper diameter, 8.5 centimeters; lower diameter, 7 centimeters. Its color is light red and, as the only exception among all of the ceramic objects found, it had no ornamentation whatsoever.

The examples of the second type which particularly show inlay work, are the braziers, which have two perforated handles; a vertical, cylindrical border, where the inlays are generally applied; a lenticular bowl for the bottom, and three supports or feet, whose tips in some cases have ornamental incising. The fabrication of these braziers must have been the same as for the first type, since they show the same consistency, polish and varnish, differing only in the inlays, which are red in color when the brazier is black, and black if it is red. On yellow braziers, the inlays are indiscriminately red or black. It is difficult to determine if the hollows which were made to contain the white clay which was incrusted on were made before or after the firing of the nucleus. I found several whole examples of these braziers, all with ornamentation.

The ceramic pieces with its ornamentation superimposed, i.e., cloisonnés, are made up of a primitive form or nucleus of dark and porous clay, on whose exterior walls is adhered a layer of clay in various colors. To expand on this point, I should say that one first notes a series of spirals of black clay over the nucleus. This spiral, black strip is from 2 to 4 millimeters in width, and the thickness of its relief is from ½ millimeter to 1 millimeter. The free spaces formed by the spirals represent human figures, animals, fruits, flowers and geometric designs, formed by clays inlaid into the spaces, and which, still today, are very bright and varied in color: green, red, blue, and white.

On one of the pieces of this type, which was found broken, there are still found placed, as on a palette, the colors that probably were mixed with the clay; on another whole piece can be seen, inside the lower part which supports it, a goodly quantity of partially burned resin.

The typical form of these ceramic vessels is that of some amphoras or harmoniously designed vases. They are formed by an upper body which is a spherical bowl; the lower being a partial cone, and the neck, which unites the two parts, is paraboidal. As a final observation, I should say that none of these amphoras or vases show any trace of varnish whatsoever, either on the interior or exterior.

When the debris that filled the Hall of Columns was extracted, there was discovered in its southwest corner, in the soil, a circular space devoid of cement; the surface dirt was carefully excavated and at a depth of 20 centimeters was found a hollow where were placed, among other objects, the two mosaics which I shall immediately describe noting the peculiarity that the objects rested on a fire mat [even though] this mat, when it was taken out crumbled into pieces, nevertheless. In the National Museum of Archaeology, History, and Ethnology of Mexico, these pieces are to be found, the analysis of which could constitute an important detail.

The earth and debris which had gathered over the cavity in reference had disintegrated the fragile objects, leaving only some vessels in good condition. Thus, the mosaic, which I call the Breast Jewel, when it was removed, had much of the inlaid work missing from it.

It is formed by a circular clay disc, which is bordered by a wooden ring. The former [disc] is yellowish in color, and had a compact grain, while its dimensions are 7 centimeters in diameter and 9 millimeters in thickness. And, even though the disc does not have any inlaid work remaining, the traces left on the back side of the disc by the inlay permit us to distinguish in great part the design which it formed. This design bears a great similarity to the human representations seen on a vessel found by Mr. Carl Lumholtz at La Estanzuela, Jalisco.[7] Near the outer edge of the reverse side of the disc are two oblique perforations which meet on the interior of the disc. On the periphery of the disc there is also a perforation. The wooden ring which circles the disc is a prismatic band made up of several sections and still covered in several places with inlays. These last mentioned [inlays], although they had dropped out, were all recovered, and are made up of little plates or leaves in diverse forms, as well as little spherical "bowls," both being worked in turquoise, steatite, and beryl. To fasten the mosaic on the disc, use was made of a mixture of clay and resin, the resin alone being used to fasten on the wooden ring band. By its form, and because of the presence of the perforations which I described previously, I supposed that this mosaic was a breast jewel which was suspended from some type of collar. Two circumstances make this mosaic noteworthy, differentiating it from the thirty or thirty-five that exist in the museums of America and Europe. The latter have a simple nucleus formed from one of the following substances: metal (gold nucleus, Museum of Mexico), bone, wood, and stone; while the mosaic from Alta Vista has a compound nucleus, the materials which form it being wood and clay. The latter material [clay] is found used for the first time as a nucleus for a mosaic. At the same time, we believe that until now the use of steatite was never known as a material for inlaying mosaics.

I have given one of these mosaics the name *bezote* [a ring which Indians wear in their under lip], because it is similar in shape to those of other civilizations and not because it may have, in fact, been used for that purpose. To make the description more graphic, I will say that this mosaic appears, at first glance, like a violin bridge. The nucleus, which is made of wood, has two symmetrical figures of alligators carved in it, attached at the belly. Crowning the heads of the alligators are two plumes, each one having two branches. Over the union of the reptiles the nucleus forms an out-jutting square which has a perforation at the point where its diagonals cross. The spirals formed by the carving were filled with platelets and spherical discs of turquoise, beryl and steatite, all of which have been conveniently kept for reconstruction purposes.

Along with the mosaics, there were numerous beryl and turquoise fragments which, owing to their quite curious shape, were probably strung. Some are spherical plaques whose base is not flat, but has two facets which form a dihedral angle; a perforation goes through these two facets in a direction perpendicular to the dihedral. There are also perforated cylindrical samples, which must have required exacting work in their fabrication.

There also appear a great number of mallets and axes. The former are worked in the form of two deformed pockets separated by a throat. The axes are of various types, from the most primitive, which is an elongated smooth stone, to those that have one end [in the shape of] animal heads. On the terrace a metate without any feet or supports was found.

Innumerable small pierced marine shells were found in the hole where the mosaic appeared. In the Hall of Columns a large periwinkle with a perforation in one end was found. Blowing into this perforation, a husky sound can still be produced. I found stones of varying sizes and great hardness which, on some sides, show traces of prolonged scraping; perhaps they served to finish the cement that covers the structures. Many other objects were found, their number reaching approximately one hundred and fifty; but it would be very tiresome to enumerate them, given the nature of this report.

Ornamentation of the objects.   If, in the structures of Alta Vista, there appear no paintings or any drawings, on the other hand, the objects discovered there offer very profuse ornamentation, whose principal representations are human, animal, and geometric.

It is impossible for now to know if this ornamentation is realist or conventionalist or if both characteristics are present, and even the comparative study of the ornamentation, with regard to other regions, would be dangerous, for if I have been able to find some analogies, they would be insufficient to establish a relationship or, for that matter, even to venture an hypothesis.

I BELIEVE it unnecessary to consider, in this account, the natural caves that were described earlier, since the very few traces left by their occupants make their study impossible.

The artificial caves, on the other hand, are of high interest, since they constitute types of truly original shelters. We call them shelters and not habitations because, in my opinion, they were places for hiding and escaping, when necessary. [I draw this conclusion] from the numerous secondary galleries which form a confusing labyrinth. Actually, the position of the entryway, on the sides of hills, makes them difficult to see; the average height of the ceiling in the main room is low, and the [ceilings of] secondary rooms even lower, circumstances which would make permanent residency there very difficult. The presence of palisades of fragmented rock appears to offer a supply of projectiles and, finally, I must note that in none of them did I find evidence of any protracted living, e.g., carbon and hearth ashes, bones of animals which were eaten as food, potsherds, etc., etc. For the remainder, the existence of fortifications on every summit and every outcropping indicates that the dwellers of that day lived on constant alert and that they had a vast defensive system, formed by the fortifications in reference, on the heights and by the subterranean shelters in the caves. This vast defensive system must have had as its main objective the protection of the peoples that inhabited the valleys and the people of whom, probably, the group of buildings at Alta Vista is a genuine representation.

With the object of making some general comments concerning the nature of the structures in the region I explored, I have selected the monuments of Alta Vista which, since they had been buried, are found in a good state of preservation.

These monuments appear to be the manifestation of a most interesting, transitive state, since in them we find, in conjunction, characteristics of quite distinct pre-Hispanic civilizations, aside from some totally original details. Thus, the manufacture, form and makeup of the adobes used in construction; the metate found on the terrace without any feet or supports and which was hollowed out of a flagstone; several stone axes and some amulets, such as the frog made from steatite—all constitute peculiarities [found] inherent in the ruins of Casas Grandes, which form a part of the civilization of the "Pueblos."

The pilasters or columns are identical in structure and form to those of La Quemada, since almost all of them are formed by flagstones superimposed the one over the other in a straight line.

Although the stair-step outline of the merlons is common in the original ornamentation of the "Pueblos," merlons were not used, appearing in profusion, on the other hand, in the architecture of the Nahuatl civilization.

The stairways offer particular interest, since in the same building, and even within one set of stairs, there appear three distinct types: step lower than the riser; step larger than the riser; and step virtually the same as the riser. The first type and, rarely, the third, (stairways of the old temple, or *teocalli*, in Mexico in the subsoil of the patio of the Ministry of Public Education and Fine Arts), exist in various structures made by the Nahuatlacan families. The type of the second group can be seen in the buildings recently uncovered at Teotihuacan. Also, in these last monuments, there has been noted, as at Alta Vista, that a great fire occurred in them, and that later several of these buildings were filled with clay, earth, and debris and the doorways sealed or closed off with rubble-masonry of adobe.[8]

The finding of the mosaics and the more valuable pieces of ceramic in the subsoil of the Hall of Columns brings to mind the custom which some peoples had of burying, as a good omen, precious objects in the cement of the buildings they were constructing—a ceremony which took on great importance, according to the chroniclers, when the erection of the main temple was begun at Tenoxtitlan [Tenochtitlán].

One noteworthy peculiarity which the buildings present is the absence of inclined planes, which were of such common use in almost all of the architectural works of other civilizations. Among all of the numerous ruins not one, single pyramidal structure was found.

The dimensions of the walls, stairways, columns (the thick columns as well as the prismatic and semicylindrical ones constitute later innovations), etc., etc., are judiciously chosen for, while at the same time they represent solidity, their aspect is harmonious and beautiful, with straight lines predominating in the general style.

There is no room for doubt about the close relationship between the monuments of Alta Vista and others that are found in the states of Zacatecas and Jalisco, as are those of La Quemada, Totoate, Monax,

Teul, Tlaltenango, Mezquitic, etc., etc., since, in addition to all of this being testified to by the similarity in structure of their buildings and the system of fortified areas for the defense of major settlements, there exists an undoubtable testimony witnessed by the presence of ceramics with superimposed ornamentation or another of cloisonnés, which is characteristic of that great group of pre-Hispanic constructions. Probably the first ones to find such ceramics in those places were Professors Aleš Hrdlička and Carl Lumholtz, which they illustrate in their interesting writings "The Chichimecs" (in the *American Anthropologist*, vol. 5, pl. 39) and "El México Desconocido" [*Amer. Anth.*, 2: 448–49, pl. 13], respectively. Moreover, it must be said that truly inlaid ceramic, i.e., that in which colored clay which served as ornamentation is put into spaces or holes made aforethought in the nucleus of the vessel, does not appear in other sites that have the cloisonné style of ceramic, while at Alta Vista, both types are found.

In conclusion, the monuments of Alta Vista comprise the northern limit of structures that count as distinctive architectural elements: stairways, pilasters (or columns), and merlons, whose elements tie them to the structures of the center, the south, and the southeast of Mexico. On the other hand, as has been said, other elements deny the influence of the "Pueblo" civilization. They constitute, therefore, a true transition between the northern regions and the southern regions.

When all of these monuments will have been discovered, one will have ample and sufficient data with which to begin a limited comparative study which may filter and confirm what has been said to this point on material which is so little known.

I bring these lines to an end with the hope that the numerous errors will be corrected and rectified by people of good will, which will smooth the road for the better success of future studies on this matter.

4

Navacoyan: A Preliminary Survey

Agnes M. Howard

The late Agnes McClean Howard was an amateur archaeologist who lived with her family on their ranches near the city of Durango, Durango and near Mezquital in the mountains to the south. Mrs. Howard worked actively in the Durango region throughout the 1950 decade. In addition to her own studies, she served generously as hostess, advisor, and friend to archaeologists and other scientists who visited there. She made her collections freely available for study to all interested persons, and joined with Robert H. Lister in writing the first definitive account of the Chalchihuites Culture, an article based primarily on analysis of her collection (Lister and Howard, 1955). Her collection also supplied the basic data for Johnson's article on similarities between Hohokam and Chalchihuites artifacts (Johnson, 1958) and we have used it freely in our Southern Illinois University series of studies.

Much of Agnes Howard's collection came from the site of Navacoyan which she describes in this article. As presently known, Navacoyan is the second most important site of the Chalchihuites Culture in the Guadiana Valley region, surpassed only by the Schroeder Site located a few miles to the west. Navacoyan appears to have been primarily a burial site, although some masonry structures are found there. During 1957–58, major vandalism took place at this site, virtually destroying it as far as archaeological research is concerned. Most of the pottery and other artifacts recovered by the vandals eventually came into the hands of the late Federico Schroeder of Durango, another outstanding local amateur archaeologist who aided professional archaeological research in the region in many ways. Schroeder allowed us access to his fantastic collection from Navacoyan in the summer of 1958; his collection has now been brought to the United States and at last report was being offered for sale in El Paso, Texas.

From our analysis of the Schroeder and Howard collections, and using the data presented by Mrs. Howard in this article, it is clear that Navacoyan was occupied, or used as a burial ground, throughout the entire span of the Chalchihuites Culture occupation of the region, or through the Ayala, Las Joyas, Rio Tunal, and Calera phases of that culture, from circa A.D. 550 to 1350. The abundance of vessels of such pottery types as Nayar White-on-Red, Otinapa Red-on-White, Madero Fluted, and Canatlán Red-Banded in the collection, together with the large numbers of smoking pipes, copper artifacts, etc. found suggests that the principal occupation or use of the site took place late, during the Rio Tunal and Calera phases.

Mrs. Howard's paper is the only available published account of Navacoyan and accordingly is a basic source for the archaeology of the Guadiana Valley and the Chalchihuites Culture.

J. C. K.

THE NAVACOYAN site is on a hill situated about eight kilometers (five miles) east of the city of Durango, Mexico. It is covered with nopal cacti and small vegetation—in fact, "Navacoyan" means nopal. The hill stands alone and commands a view of the entire Valley of Durango which is some miles in extent. The Rio Tunal runs along the eastern slope and there are permanent springs on the northern slope, one of which is hot. There are two villages at the base of the hill, Conteras and Navacoyan. The latter was the site of a huge hacienda in former times and so the name has been chosen for the archeological site as well. This hacienda was so large that the Howard ranch, sixty miles away, was once a part of it. Foundations of structures are to be found on all sides of the hill and archeological materials may be found in the stone fences which surround the present-day houses of the villagers.

An idea of the richness of the site may be formed by considering the fact that the writer has more than six hundred and fifty axeheads—whole or broken—from the site. Spindle whorls of all sorts from the crudest, poorly fired, undecorated sort to highly polished, elaborately decorated ones may be found. Predominant are those of the polished black engraved type.

Beads and pendants are probably of the greatest interest and are very numerous. The pendants range from anthropomorphic and zoomorphic examples to abstract triangular, circular, square, and irregular forms. Many are skillfully carved from stone, shell, bone, jasper, quartz, chert, turquoise, obsidian, and even coral. Whether by intention or coincidence, most of the turtle effigies are carved from greenstone.

One pendant depicts a long-nosed hunchback. This is of special interest in view of a recent report (Lambert, 1957) of a hunchback figure from the Schroeder site in Durango which is only about five miles from Navacoyan. In this connection the statement by Parsons (1939, p. 1008) that "of all extant Uto-Aztecan peoples, the Cora-Huichol tribes of the Nayarit sierra in Jalisco are closest in culture to the Pueblo" is of interest as Navacoyan is well within the area of Cora-Huichol culture. We will discuss some other possible relationships to the United States Southwest later.

A tiny human figurine is perfect in every anatomical detail, though it is only about three-quarters of an inch, or two centimeters, in length. It is apparently not intended as a bead or pendant, as there is no hole for stringing or suspension.

It is probably unnecessary to point out the similarities in style, and even in the basic materials used, between these objects from Navacoyan and many from the Hohokam area. If we add to the objects already mentioned such items as the copper bells, projectile point types, and ceramic styles and motifs found at Navacoyan and compare them with Hohokam and other Southwestern United States materials, the conclusion is forced upon us that there must have been some rather important relationships between the areas. Copper bells found at Navacoyan appear identical with one illustrated by McGregor (1941, Fig. 59) which he notes as being "almost identical with bells found in Mexico." However, there are still other evidences of extensive trade between Navacoyan and other areas in Mexico and perhaps in the United States which be noted later.

There are many figurines in stone, shell, bone, and pottery. Many of these are beads or pendants as already mentioned. These show marked differences in appearance. Some have resemblances to United States Southwestern figurines and to Pima figurines (DiPeso, 1956, Fig. 11); others are not unlike West Coast (Sinaloa) materials; and still others are quite similar to some from the so-called "Tarascan" area. In this latter connection, Carl B. Compton reports (personal communication) that . . . [one of the Navacoyan figurines], is almost identical in appearance with one which he collected at Cerro del Chivo, a site near the city of Acambaro, Guanajuato, Mexico. This site, incidentally, has a material culture quite aberrant from the "Chupícuaro" culture of the surrounding area.

Spindle whorls, already mentioned, are also of uncertain affiliations. Some are definitely of Chalchihuites type; others show West Coast influence. Some are quite likely of spontaneous local manufacture or, in other words, strictly utilitarian objects made with little thought for design aside from the purely functional design imposed by the dynamics of threadmaking. It might be remarked that the *malacate*, or spindle whorl, was a very important object in Pre-Columbian Mexico and many of them are objects of considerable beauty. They must have required great artistic ability to make as well as painstaking craftsmanship.

Pipes are found in considerable abundance and vary widely in form. The two shown are not unlike some from the Tarascan Tsintsuntsan [*sic*] area, but others appear to be from the West Coast area and are of highly polished red, black, and white engraved ware. One example has a squash form which is virtually identical with the squash-form vessels of Veracruz. Even the paste seems to be similar, though thus far no tests have been made to determine this. Still other pipes are bird-effigy in form. Some of the pipes appear to be incipient "platform" pipes, but this may very well have been unintentional; no actual pipes of "platform" type have been found at Navacoyan.

Stamps made of baked clay as well as many carved from soft stone are found in both cylinder and "block" or flat form. One cylinder stamp has a female figurine motif. This identical motif was also found at Navacoyan as a design on a pottery sherd, but this design was painted on and was definitely not made by means of a stamp. It is probably impossible to print a design on pottery with a clay stamp excepting in the case of the "stamp impressed" type of pottery where the design is pressed into the clay with a ceramic stamp. Others of the stamps have animal motifs and some are so stylized as to be nonrepresentational in appearance. In general, the cylinder and flat stamps have about the same motifs. These Navacoyan stamps are practically the same, if not entirely the same, in motif and appearance as those which are common all over the Mesoamerican area, though of course specific motifs are not duplicated.

Pottery at Navacoyan is chiefly white-on-red but Chalchihuites types are found as well as the Coastal black, white, and red incised or engraved. The Chalchihuites pottery is highly polished black or brown. There is some red-on-cream pottery and an occasional polished-red sherd suggestive of the polished-red of the "Tarascan" Chupícuaro region. Some of the spindle whorls are apparently of "paint-cloisonné" but this pottery is relatively rare at Navacoyan, though found in sites not far distant. Some pottery which appears to be similar to certain Nayarit styles is found.

A considerable number of stone balls have been found at Navacoyan. Most prehistoric peoples collect such naturally formed spheres when they are found. People of our own culture often prize them highly as curiosities. The Museum of Michoacán in Morelia has many of them in the patio and General Cardenas used them as "newel posts" at his home in Patzcuaro. They have been found in huge size in the Maya area and as small objects in Eastern United States Archaic, Hopewell, Californian, and many other sites. For the most part, they are either volcanic in origin or were formed in potholes in swiftly running streams, though some may have been man-made. There is nothing to indicate that these examples from Navacoyan are man-made. They may have been used in some sort of game, as Wedel (1941, p. 68) thought they might have been in California, or merely prized as curious objects because of their near-perfect spherical shape.

Among the other objects of material culture are many trough metates, two-hand manos, one-hand manos, full and three-quarter grooved axes, paint mullers, and palettes (Howard, 1955). Polishers of onyx, basalt, jasper, and other stones are numerous and are of all sizes from one to six inches in length. A fine obsidian cruciform also came from Navacoyan. Others have been found in this region (Howard, 1954). Polished ceramic beads made on a straw which burned out in the firing process are common, as are bone heads of various sorts as mentioned above.

The projectile points present some interesting problems. By far the most numerous are small, even tiny, arrow points. A very few large points are to be found—a representative large one is three inches in length—but some points are less than one centimeter in length.

All, or nearly all, of these points are side-notched but otherwise present rather wide variation. Many of the points are quite similar to Hohokam Colonial and Sedentary points (McGregor, 1941, Figs. 48, 58) as well as to Upper Pima (DiPeso, 1956, pl. 130, c). As an assemblage these points resemble to a remarkable degree those called Harrell Points in Texas (Suhm et al., 1954, p. 500, pl. 129), which also are found generally from Canada through the Southwest and eastward to the Mississippi River. It was apparently a highly satisfactory form. The very small serrated and rather crude points are quite frequent among the Hohokam and among the points of West Central and Trans-Pecos Texas where they are known as Toyah Points (Suhm et al., 1954, p. 508, pl. 133, D, E). Similar points are found in North Texas and in Oklahoma and elsewhere. The Navacoyan examples are made of almost any available material such as quartz, jasper, obsidian, and chert.

THE NAVACOYAN site is one of the richest in the entire Chalchihuites area of Mexico if we may judge from surface materials. It seems to have been an important "crossroads" in Pre-Columbian times. As one well-known archeologist remarked after seeing the site and the collected material: "This must have been a summer resort for all Mexico."

Without stratigraphy, dating is, of course, only speculation. However, in the light of certain pottery type-periods recently established, at least tentatively, for the nearby Schroeder site (Kelley, 1957) we may make certain cross-references and assumptions. From the materials collected thus far we would assume that at least the most intensive development at the site about A.D. 1000 and later. However, and again with cross-reference to the Schroeder site, we may reasonably assume that there were earlier occupations of the site, possibly from earliest Formative times.

Navacoyan is admirably situated from every point of view. As mentioned, it even had hot and cold running water in the form of springs. The locality commands a view of the entire valley of Durango and would have been easily defended. The valley is rich and ordinarily well watered—an excellent agricultural area. The springs and the Rio Tunal would provide ample water for irrigation if that were desired. All in all, Navacoyan may well have been a Pre-Columbian land of plenty and ease.

5

The Region of the Ancient Chichimecs,
with Notes on the Tepecanos
and the Ruin of La Quemada, Mexico

Aleš Hrdlička

Hrdlička's turn-of-the-century reconnaissance in southern Zacatecas and the northern extension of the State of Jalisco produced valuable data regarding the archaeology of the Rio Malpaso-Rio Juchipila drainage, including especially the great site of La Quemada, and that of the Rio Bolaños barranca to the west. Today a paved road leads directly to La Quemada and a major Mexican highway follows the course of the Rio Malpaso and the Rio Juchipila. The Rio Bolaños barranca, however, remains almost as inaccessible as it was in Hrdlička's day, although road construction is now moving steadily towards it on two fronts. La Quemada is now comparatively well known to archaeologists but it is a remarkable commentary on the contemporary status of archaeological research in northern Mexico that this article, published sixty-seven years ago, still represents the only published account of the archaeology of the Bolaños barranca. Even the site of Las Ventanas on the lower Juchipila is known primarily from Hrdlička's description of it in this article.

Hrdlička's excavations at Totoate on the Rio Bolaños are of especial interest because of the large quantity of paint cloisonné decorated pottery vessels which he reports finding there, reputedly in association with cremations in many small rooms of a "buried" building. In 1963, our Southern Illinois University field party dug at Totoate for two weeks. Included in our work was the reopening of Hrdlička's trenches. We found that the structure excavated by Hrdlička was not at all as he described and illustrated it. The structure was actually one unit; a large circular masonry walled court with groups of platforms and rooms attached on the cardinal points. In the center of this court was a circular stone tower, actually a series of concentric circular stone walls possibly representing multiple rebuilding of the central tower (four stages), which appears to have been filled inside with rubble to form a circular platform. Hrdlička's trenches—very nearly as shown in his illustration—were clearly visible, cutting into the circular platform from all sides, running straight through the concentric heavy masonry walls. Apparently, Hrdlička's many small rooms, in which he reputedly found cremations with associated paint cloisonné vessels, were the spaces between these walls. The building is much smaller than described by Hrdlička and his small rooms were very small spaces indeed. We found no traces of cremated bones and no paint cloisonné sherds in his back-fill or in the unexcavated parts of the tower. Indeed, we found only three sherds of paint cloisonné pottery in all of our excavations at the site. The discrepancies between what we found at Totoate and Hrdlička's descriptions are very great. It is difficult for us to believe that the cremations and the large number of paint cloisonné vessels (which are now in the American Museum of Natural History in New York City) actually came from the structures to which he attributes them.

Nevertheless, Hrdlička's article is required reading for anyone who plans to do archaeological work in the Bolaños area. His field reconnaissance represented a remarkable journey for the time and place. Incidentally, on the Bolaños, Hrdlička crossed the trail of another great scientist-explorer, Carl Lumholtz, but the two men did not actually meet in the field.

In addition to the archaeological work, Hrdlička made a field trip in 1898 and two additional ones in 1902 to the Tepecano town of Askeltán (Azqueltán) in the Bolaños Canyon south of Totoate. From the comments of Mason (see elsewhere, this volume) who visited the same settlement in 1912 it would seem that Hrdlička was the last person to see the Tepecano as a functioning aboriginal group. It is quite valuable to compare Hrdlička's Tepecano as of around 1900 to the Southern Tepehuán of fifty years later.

J. C. K.
C. L. R.

THE GREAT mountainous region of northern Mexico that bore originally, with the Spanish, the name of Nueva Galicia and of which, somewhat subsequently, a large part was included in the Provincia de San Francisco de Zacatecas, is to this day an almost unknown country to anthropology. This region extends from the Valley of Nochistlan in the east to the sierra of the Guachichiles or Huicholes in the west, and from the Rio Grande or Santiago in the south to the Tepehuane country in the north; that is, from a line about half a degree east of longitude 103° to a little west of longitude 104°, and approximately between 21° and 23° of latitude. The territory comprises the northern part of the present Mexican state of Jalisco, southern Zacatecas, and the western point of Aguas Calientes.

To the early Spaniards this was preëminently the country of *bárbaros, caribes, mekkos*, and *chichimecos*, among whom were distinguished mainly the "Cazcanes," "Teules-Chichimecos," "Tepecanos," and "Zacatecos."[1] The term "Chichimec," whatever may have been its meaning originally, or in the valley of Mexico, was here applied as a term of derision, or rather as a communal surname, expressing very much the same sentiment as *bárbaros*, to all the tribes indiscriminately and without any expressed intention of connecting them ethnically with the Chichimecs of Anahuac or even with each other.

Judging from the number of warriors met by the Spaniards in this section, it is evident, even if an allowance be made for possible exaggeration, that it must have been well peopled; but there is only limited knowledge of the actual settlements. The best known of these were apparently Nochistlan and Teul; other larger towns occasionally referred to[2] are Juchipila and Colotlan. La Quemada is mentioned, but already as a ruin. All that is recorded of other settlements is that they were situated generally on steep and barely accessible elevations.

As to any possible remains of these settlements, or of the natives who built them, nothing is known. The great La Quemada alone has been visited and described by several archeologists.[3] Lumholtz, on his journey to the Huichols, touched the northwestern corner of this territory, but did not make any explorations or collections. Miss Britton, an American lady interested in an amateur way in Mexican archeology, visited, a few years ago, Totatiche, Teul, Juchipila, and Nochistlan, but thus far has published nothing on her observations.

The work on which I shall here report was largely unplanned and incidental. My presence in Mexico was in the interest of physical anthropology, and even in all the exploration and excavation that I finally undertook, the principal motive of my search was the physical remains of the prehistoric people. If I gathered anything more, it was for its intimate association with the skeletons and to save it from destruction, or, what is but little better, dispersion. In the more remote parts of Mexico, such as I speak of, nothing is saved. This is the home of the periodical treasure hunter, who, as soon as the dry season sets in and affords him leisure, goes to dig for money, buried during revolutions, wherever there is a cave or a ruin. That is usually the last of the human remains of whatever nature that the cave or ruin contained, most of them being broken on the spot and the rest sold to the first comer or given to some friend or to children. Under these conditions Mexico itself should be grateful to those who at no small risk at times save here and there the relics of its past cultures.

The notes here published are a part of the results of three expeditions, from the last of which I returned at the close of 1902. The expense of the first of these journeys was borne by the American Museum of Natural History; the second by Dr. Frederic E. Hyde, Jr., and the last by Mr. B. Talbot B. Hyde, of New York, the whole work being under the general supervision of Prof. F. W. Putnam.

It was on a journey from Mezquitic to the remnant of the Tepecano Indians, in the valley of the Rio de Bolaños, northern Jalisco, after having visited the Huichols early in May 1898, that I learned of certain ruins in the neighborhood and made the first explorations. In the early half of 1902 I extended these researches southward through the valley mentioned, and in the latter part of that year pursued them farther southward and eastward to Zacatecas. My journeys are indicated on the accompanying map. [Not included here.]

The present notes are given not so much as a record of results as an incentive to further investigation in the region; and they are made to follow, without regard to chronology, the route of travel. The descriptions of the archeological objects recovered and of the skeletons, as well as the detailed observations in physical anthropology, are reserved for future publication.

The Valley of the Rio de Bolaños

THE VALLEY of the Bolaños is a deep barranca, in places several miles broad, situated between two parts of the sierra. It begins practically at Fresnillo, but more definitely a little above Mezquitic,[4] and extends in a south-southwesterly to a nearly southerly direction to and beyond

Askeltan [Azqueltán], the seat of the Tepecanos. The whole valley is traversed by the stream from which it takes its name and which was largely influential in its formation. Above Mezquitic, and again some distance below Nostic,[5] the valley is more or less "filled up" with secondary elevations and mesas, among which the river of Bolaños and its tributaries run in often narrow gorges with here and there high, steep to nearly perpendicular walls. The greatest width of the valley at its base may exceed eight miles (a little south of Mezquitic); in other places, as at the hot springs, it is but a narrow cañon. Geologically the whole region is granitic and volcanic. The river is mostly shallow and offers no obstacles to travel during the dry period, but becomes quite impassable at the height of the rainy season. The population south of Nostic to Askeltan is insignificant, and with the one exception to be mentioned later, is wholly mixed or Mexican. No Indians except the Tepecanos are now settled in the valley; but occasionally one here meets traveling Huichols and even Coras. The valley is the westernmost of four (Nochistlan, Juchipila, Tlaltenango, and Bolaños) extensive and nearly equally deep, parallel depressions, that run, separated by high mountain ridges or narrow plateaus, from north to south through the region under consideration.

Indian Occupants North of Askeltan [Azqueltán]

In the Mezquitic part of the valley there are some rather vague traditions among the whites in regard to Indians who occupied the district "a long time ago." There are other and more definite traditions of occupancy of parts of the valley more recently by the Huichols. I was shown caves near Mezquitic with remnants of rude stone habitations, where it is said these Indians have dwelt, and I have found figures of deer on stones looking very much like those made by the Huichols of today. As the mountain range of this tribe forms one of the western boundaries of the valley, the fact that there were at some time some Huichol settlements in the valley itself is quite possible.

In Nostic there still lives a single pureblood Indian (Macias) who is a remnant of those who occupied the pueblo during the first half of the nineteenth century. This man, who is about seventy years of age, informed me that during his childhood the natives in Nostic were still numerous, but were annihilated by epidemics and during a revolution. They spoke the "lengua Mexicana," which is the Nahua (a fact con-

firmed to me independently by the Tepecanos); this makes it probable
that they were the progeny not of the original people of the pueblo,
but of the introduced fronterizos of Tlaxcaltecos.

Ancient Ruins in the Valley of the Rio de Bolaños

Remains of Indian occupancy, such as stone implements, shell
ornaments, pottery, etc., are found throughout the valley of the
Bolaños; but there are also a number of more or less large and well-
defined settlements which will repay further study.

Mesitas.   The first ruins of any extent occur southeast of the town
of Mezquitic, and are situated about halfway between this and Nostic,
on a part of a smaller irregular plain or terrace at about the middle of
the eastern slope of the sierra of Monte Escobedo. The terrace is over
a mile in width, and where the ruins are situated it is riven by a number
of deep, narrow gorges. These gorges converge from all directions into
a common cañon, which, in the form of an ellipse, completely surrounds
an oblong, central elevation, the top of which is diamond shaped. The
result of the formation is a number of converging points of land with
the isolated part in the middle. During the rainy season this central
part is completely surrounded with water, and is then actually an island.

The surfaces of all the points, as well as that of the central part,
are level, and show in most places only the bare bedrock; but in a few
spots there is a thin layer of black soil. The sides of the points, as well
as those of the central part, are steep, and most of them can be scaled
only with difficulty. From a yard to several yards from the top the rock
on some of the points is perpendicular, and this feature is very pronounced about the entire central portion.[6]

The central mesa measures two hundred paces in length and forty
in maximum width; and it, as well as the various points, is covered with
ruins. The place bears no name, but from its character it will be referred to as the Mesitas.[7]

The more important ruins are found on the middle portion. There
were apparently habitations as well as other large structures on this portion, and there was also a conical mound of moderate size. The remains
invariably consist of low, square or oblong foundations, built of quadrangular stones, of moderately large dwellings. Most of the dwellings
were somewhat larger than are the average huts of the Huichols today.

The foundations are quite regular in form. They consist of one, two, or exceptionally of three superimposed layers of flat, quadrangular stones, varying from a foot and a half to more than three feet in length, from a foot to two feet in width, and from two to four inches in thickness.[8] The stones were apparently carefully selected, so as to form a fairly compact and regular wall. Some of the stones seen were nicely hewn or rubbed into the desired shape. No cement or mud mortar now remains in the joints of the masonry.

The main body of the house must have been of wood or reeds, as there are but very few loose stones about to account for the superstructure; however, I have never found a trace of wood on or in the ground about the foundations, which absence probably speaks for the age of the ruins. According to all indications the wooden parts of the dwellings were placed but superficially, and in time were completely washed away or destroyed by other agencies. No fireplaces are visible, these also probably having been washed away. The foundations of the houses are in some places almost entirely exposed, resting on the bedrock; in others they are nearly covered with accumulated earth. The entire group of ruins bears indication of having been abandoned in the far past, and of having been disturbed but very little since, except by the elements. There are no traces today of ancient cultivation of the soil in the neighborhood.

Potsherds and pieces of obsidian were found scattered in all the ruins, but were not very numerous. The potsherds collected[9] are mostly thick, crude, and unpolished, but some are decorated with incisions or painted red on one surface. Besides these, however, there were found fragments of thinner and finer pottery, nicely colored on one or both sides, generally in red or brownish, and in most instances polished.

The central mesita is exceedingly difficult to scale, and it has probably been visited but very few times since it was originally abandoned. The place was apparently fortified, for there still exist accumulations of stones, well adapted to defensive purposes, along the edges and particularly about the single possible approach, toward the northeast. A number of the structures here were much larger than the ordinary dwellings, and two or three of them were situated on a slight artificial elevation. The foundations of all these larger houses are like those previously mentioned, quadrangular and very regular, but there are more hewn stones found in them than in the foundations of the dwellings proper. All the large buildings and the mound are situated on the northeastern three-fifths of the mesita.

Examination of the surface and slight excavation in the ruins and mound resulted in finding two large, well-made stone mortars; two slabs of stone with markings; a small, nicely made stone fetish (animal figure); a well-chipped white stone arrowpoint; and many potsherds and chips of obsidian. The larger mortar, made of the hard trachyte of the region, crumbled to pieces from the effects of long exposure, as if made from very soft sandstone. The mound was almost wholly made up of stones and proved to be a burial mound, containing the remnants of a number of cremated human bodies. It was here that the animal figure was discovered. A cave was found in the southeastern wall of the central mesita, but it contained only a few potsherds.

Information from all sources was gathered concerning other ruins in the valley, and gradually a considerable number of localities where some one knew of ruined *fincas* were recorded. But the information was generally meager and not always reliable. Many of the localities mentioned were distant as well as difficult of approach, but the results of my visits generally proved to be more interesting than was expected.

Nostic, La Escondida.   On the mesas to the east of the little town of Nostic are some remnants of old habitations. From one of these I have seen a very well made, even somewhat artistic, large, circular stone that probably served as a pedestal to a statue. In the fields about Nostic ancient objects are found quite frequently. To the west of Nostic rises a hill called Potrero de Chimulco, or Cerro de Chimulco, upon which ruins are found; and farther in the same direction, at the foot of the Sierra Huichol, near the rancho La Estancia, is a large, important ruin called La Escondida. In this ruin, which was explored only superficially, there are many remnants of dwellings similar to those at Mesitas and also larger structures and mounds. From this ruin I obtained several objects, among which is a fine ceremonial axe; and from an apparently ancient burial in a nearby cave was excavated a complete skeleton.

Totoate.   The third ruin, and one that proved to be of much archeological interest, lies a little less than three miles south of Nostic, on the point of a long, isolated, generally steep-walled but not lofty mesa, which for two-thirds of its extent is river-bound. The point which projects northward like a ∧ into the expanding part of the valley is covered with the ruins of an ancient settlement. This is known as Totoate, a name apparently of Nahua origin and pertaining to water. This is the only ruin that was explored at all thoroughly, and the results were very surprising.

As at the Mesitas, the southern portion of the point is covered with ruins of smaller structures, probably dwellings, while on the extremity itself, to the northeast of the body of the ruins, I found a group of mounds, a rough sketch of which is given in the accompanying illustration.

The ruins consist only of foundations, or bases, and are of the same general character as those at Mesitas or La Escondida; indeed this is true of all those yet to be mentioned in this region. Hewn or rubbed, oblong building stones are more numerous at Totoate than in the other ruins. The smaller structures, mostly of quadrilateral but a few of circular form, are rather close together. The surface soil is rich in fragments of thick and crude as well as of finer, painted pottery, and in chips of obsidian, chalcedony, and other stones.

The first noteworthy find in this ruin consisted of a considerable number of stone slabs and several portions of the bedrock (one of which measured over six yards square), with peculiar, unusually well made and deeply graven petroglyphs. These carvings are all executed in a similar manner, and are very different from those generally seen farther north. They consist of broad, deep grooves, principally curves, and of cup-shaped hollows in the course of the lines. Many of the forms represent a coil or a part of one, others a humanlike figure with a head-dress or striae radiating from the head, and there are still other designs. These carvings, although deeply made in hard trachyte, are so greatly weather-worn as in some instances to be barely traceable.

Owing to limitations of space I shall omit details and restrict myself to the statement that in search for burials I excavated mounds A, B, C, and a part of D. Mound A was nearly two hundred feet in circumference and over eleven feet in maximum height. It consisted of a thick outer layer of stones (including some broken slabs with petroglyphs), beneath which was a large quantity of stones and earth, and of a central stone house of seven or eight rooms, a part of which was filled with stones and earth and a part with stone-covered cremation burials.

The walls of the house were over seven feet high, well built of selected but unhewn flat stones laid in and plastered with adobe mortar.

This adobe coating (a piece of which is preserved in the American Museum) was mostly destroyed; but the remnants found show many small parallel tubes, such as could be produced by extended stalks of *zacate*.[10] There were small doorways and little square niches in the walls, recalling similar structures in the ancient pueblos of New Mexico.

The remnants of cremated bodies were closely packed in three of the central rooms, and with them were buried many fine specimens of pottery, some of which are unique in character, as well as other objects. There were also charred remnants of well-woven cloth, large shell trumpets, shell nose-ornaments, ornaments of pyrites, amazon-stone pendants, obsidian knives, a fine ceremonial axe with a well-carved human face, etc.[11]

Mound B, less than half as large as mound A, was composed of stones with some earth. Near its floor was an ordinary burial. No objects other than the bones were found here and these soon fell to pieces.

Mound C, which was large and flat, was composed of stones and earth, and yielded a number of burials of the ordinary type, some crude and some fine pottery, a quantity of amazon-stone beads, etc.

Mound D (uncompleted excavation) was found to be composed of probably four originally separate structures, the ruins of which have coalesced. Remnants of stone walls and two burials were found.

The cremated bones from mound A, all of which, though in small fragments, were preserved, belonged mostly to men, but there were also the bones of some women and children. Judging from these remnants, over fifty bodies must have been deposited in the three rooms. Many of the skulls are remarkable by reason of the thickness (nonpathological) of the cranial walls. Enough was reconstructed of two or three skulls to show their identity with those of the ordinary burials, as well as with the skull obtained near La Escondida, and with another later found south of Totoate. They all belonged to a subbrachy- to brachycephalic people of not very large stature (as shown by the remnants of the skeleton) or other proportions.

Cerro de Chivo; Cerro Prieto.   To the west of Totoate, on the opposite side of the river, rises a more readily accessible mesa of similar height to the last. It is known as Cerro de Chivo (Goat Hill) and its point shows numerous remnants of habitations similar to those of Totoate and Mesitas. A little farther to the west rises a higher, isolated ridge called Cerro Prieto (Dark Hill), on which are also many remnants of ancient dwellings.

To the east of the mesa of Totoate lies a shallow valley, and here, as well as farther south, in the valley of an arroyo that opens from the east, are many low remains of stone habitations and also stone ridges that had been employed most probably for some agricultural purpose.

Banco de las Casas.   Seven miles south of Totoate, and at the base of the southern extremity of the same mesa, is a small, now Mexican settlement called Temoaya. A little west of this, on the southernmost point of the mesa, is a quite extensive ruin. The locality is known in the neighborhood as the "Banco de las Casas."

The ruin extends over two terraces of the mesa. It consists of many low stone foundations such as those at Totoate; but on the lower and more southerly bank there are remnants of larger structures, a number of *mogotes* (mounds), a ruin that probably was a temple, several very low, small, regularly square mounds, and a number of walls and patios. A brief survey and a little digging resulted in the finding of a remnant of a large metate carried on the back of an animal figure, probably a turtle; several larger stones with petroglyphs, somewhat similar to those of Totoate; a number of oblong, conical stones without marking, some of which stood upright in the ground, apparently as originally planted; fifteen or sixteen oblong, nicely worked stone slabs with a large angular notch in the middle of one of the longer sides;[12] two slabs with central circular perforations, and a number of other larger worked stones; a ceremonial, animal-form axe, and a few smaller articles. Slight digging was done in one of the conical mounds, but nothing was discovered.

The "temple" was a nearly square structure fifty to sixty feet in diameter. The stone walls are still six to ten feet high above the ground and on the top nearly six feet thick, built of selected but unworked flat stones. No trace of mortar is now visible. The inside of the structure had been intentionally filled with stones. Apparently the structure was originally a large, low pyramid or base, with possibly a wooden super-structure. In the filled area I found a large central depression, and near the sides a number of filled, crude stone cysts or holes leading down-ward; a few fragments of human bones were recovered from the only one of these which we explored somewhat. Later on I came across an almost identical cyst in the stone-filled court of the temple of La Quemada.

Torreón; Ocota.   Looking directly west from the Banco de las Casas ruins, one sees rising a few miles distant from among the flatter elevations an isolated, steep, moderately high cone, locally known as the Torreón. The hill can be approached only by a circuitous road and with considerable difficulty; but at its base, on the Banco de Zapote, as well as on the top, are found ruins of a large pueblo. Not very far from here, to the south, is a ranch called Ocota. The character of these ruins is the same as that of those already described.

La Peña.   A little south of Temoaya, and on the east side of the river, is a steep eminence, called La Peña, which is accessible only with difficulty. The somewhat saddle-shaped top of this hill was apparently a fortification, and there are also well-preserved ruins of structures that probably served for religious purposes.

Mesa del Encanto.   Proceeding southward from La Peña one soon reaches a place where the river flows through a narrow cañon, between high and steep granitic walls that reach a particularly great height toward the east. Not far below this point, at the base of the eastern wall, is a large spring of hot water containing considerable sulphureted hydrogen. In the rocks of the neighborhood, and farther southward, are a number of caves, in some of which I came across chips of obsidian and other traces of Indian occupancy; none of the caves, however, contains structural remains.

Below the "ojo caliente" the country on both sides of the river down to Askeltan contains many more or less isolated mesas, and on several of these are found remnants of ancient habitations. In at least three of these localities the ruins are of sufficient importance to deserve separate mention. One of these locations, known as the Mesa del Encanto, is an oblong, entirely isolated piece of tableland, generally similar to although larger than the central portion at the Mesitas. This tableland, which is known also as the Cerro de Vonash, is a part of a larger elevation, called the Mesa de las Moras, and is situated a little more than three hours' horseback journey northwest of Askeltan.

The entire surface of the Mesa del Encanto is covered with the well-preserved foundations of stone structures, of the same general character—low, square or oblong, or more rarely rounded—as those of the ruins previously described. All these are constructed of stones more or less worked. There are three larger ruins, two mounds, and a sort of broad, long avenue bounded by very large slabs standing on edge. A part of the mesita (where at all accessible) was apparently fortified with stones.

Borego.   In nearly the same latitude, but on a mesa east of the river and best reached from the town of Monte Escobedo, lies the ruin of a large settlement called Borego (a sheep). I did not visit these remains, but according to information from a number of persons they are essentially identical with all the ruins previously described, and, like the others, give promise of rich reward for prolonged and careful investigation.

Cerro de Colotlán.   The ruin known as the Cerro de Colotlán lies only about four miles by circuitous roads north-northeast of Askeltan. Although not very large, this seems to be one of the most promising ruins of the Totoate group for archeologic exploration.

The main part of the ruin is situated on a small but steep mesa, accessible from but one direction, on the right bank of the Rio de Bolaños, which at this point makes a sweeping curve. Several stone mounds, one of them particularly large, arranged much like those at Totoate, are found at the northwestern base of the mesa.

The ruins on the flat top of the cerro must have served some important religious purpose. On the northwest extremity of the hill is a large, square patio or court nearly fifty feet in diameter, surrounded by a stone wall (three to eleven feet high), or rather ruin, for in some parts of it there very probably were rooms which are now filled or covered with building stones. Next to this large court, on the southern side, is a smaller one, formed on a low stone terrace about two feet in height, ascent to which is facilitated by three stone steps. A short distance eastward from this is a large, low, flat, quadrilateral mound. One or two other separate parts of the ruin are seen a little to the eastward of this mound. Throughout are found stone structures and foundations similar to those in the Banco de las Casas and in other ruins of the Totoate group.

In the large court a number of interesting antiquities were found. Near the middle of the place, in the ground, lies a large, ancient, worked and slightly decorated slab of stone. As its surface is still fully exposed and on a level with the surrounding surface of the court, there is no doubt that the slab has been used or cared for by the Tepecanos in recent times. On approaching the stone I was warned by my Tepecano companion not to touch it, and especially not to remove it, for "anybody who should move it," he said, "would die," i.e., would be punished by the gods.

Near this slab lay a smaller hewn slab, two others with petroglyphs, two damaged stone idols, and several pieces of similar figures. None of these objects seemed to have been used recently, and, judging by the weathering, all indicate ancient origin. Some parts of the petroglyphs are now quite indistinct, but enough is left to show workmanship generally similar although slightly inferior to that at Totoate. On each slab is a distinct coil figure, such as, with more or less variation, is common at Totoate. The two idols, each almost a foot and a half in height, are each made of a single piece of hard stone and consists of a hewn pedestal, a neat, deep groove around above this, and a somewhat crude recumbent figure of a mountain lion on the top. The details of the figurines are better than their general form. The mouth is large, while somewhat conventionalized teeth are exposed all around. Unfortunately the head and the mouth of the figures are the parts most damaged. The fragments referred to are those of one or two other stone lions. It is of interest to note that on the Cerro de la Liona, situated a little south of Askeltan and affording an imposing view from the Cerro de Colotlán, the Tepecanos (judging from the descriptions given us) up to this day keep and venerate two apparently similar lion images of stone. We made a laborious excursion to obtain or at least to see these figures, but as my inquiries about them had alarmed the Tepecanos, we found, on reaching the summit of the Cerro de la Liona, only an empty court with traces where the idols had stood.

On the highest part of the eastern wall of the large court, in a circular depression of moderate size, is a small, crude Tepecano shrine in which these Indians still place their *chimáles*, or prayer sticks. On the extensive, low, flat mound lay a number of nicely hewn stone slabs, varying in length up to three feet and of slightly less width. Their use is not apparent.

The Cerro de Colotlán ruin is the most southerly one of the Totoate group in the valley of the Rio de Bolaños. A little to the south is Askeltan, where there are some recent but apparently no ancient ruins. South of Askeltan, to Bolaños, the country is very rough, and I could obtain no information of any important ancient settlements within it; however, this region, as well as the valley south of Bolaños, seems well worthy of exploration. I have heard of ruins and even a graded pyramid near Tule, south and a little west of Askeltan; and the ruin known as Orcón, to the southeast of Askeltan, is less than a day's travel from the latter pueblo.

The usual lack of means and time, my unfitness for this class of work, and the existing Mexican laws—under which there is no restraint to destruction, but a stern prohibition against taking anything away, even though purely for the benefit of science—all obliged me to make but flying visits where days and weeks of arduous labor should profitably be spent. Consequently, I am able to give only brief notes instead of such an exhaustive account as would, owing to the richness of the field, be of considerable value to Mexican archeology.

Yet even from the little I was able to do it is plain that the region through which flows the Rio de Bolaños, between the towns of Mezquitic and Bolaños and very probably farther southward, was in some forgotten, though probably not very ancient time, the center of a considerable population; and the remnants of the works of this people, and especially the objects recovered, speak in many ways of a high degree of culture peculiarly its own. If there were any subsequent *bárbaros* here, such as the Spaniards described, they left no visible traces. I hope to be able to throw more light on the people when my physical studies are completed, as well as by the detailed description of the specimens to be published later; but it may be stated here that my further researches tend to identify the Totoate group of people with that great population which occupied, up to the Spanish conquest, the whole of northern Jalisco and southern Zacatecas, of which the great fortress of La Quemada was once the northernmost bulwark, facing the country from which descended the waves of Tepehuanes and possibly other invasions.

I wish here to acknowledge the valuable services rendered me, in connection with all my work in this region, by Don Cruz Vázquez del Mercado and by Señores Vicente Medrano and Genaro Santibáñez, of Mesquitic, Jalisco.

The Tepecanos

Previous knowledge of the tribe.　　The Tepecano Indians, the remnant of whom lives in northern Jalisco, is one of the least known native tribes of Mexico, whether considered historically or in the light of present knowledge.[13] The present causes of this lack of knowledge are the smallness of the tribe, the distance of the region occupied by it from any considerable white settlement, and the very rough character of the country and its approaches. In addition to this the Tepecanos are feared by their superstitious white neighbors, partly on account of a supposed ferocity and partly for their "witchcraft," which hinders free intercourse and prevents the acquisition of much information concerning them. Even from their nearest neighbors one learns more imaginary tales and reports about the tribe than actual information.

Historical references to the Tepecanos are very meager. The entire region from the river Tololotlan (Rio Grande) in the south to the town of Jerez in the north, a territory which in all probability embraced the early home of the Tepecanos, was included in what is known as the "conquest of New Galicia." The initial reduction of this province to Spanish power was accomplished in 1530 by Oñate and Chirinos, two of the captains of Nuño de Guzmán. The indefinite records of this conquest, which are particularly poor in allusions to distinct peoples, contain no direct reference to the Tepecanos or to their country.

When the tribe of Tepecanos is mentioned by the earlier writers[14] it is considered as a branch of the "Chichimecan" family. Thus the only reference by Bancroft to this people is found among his notes on the "Chichimecos." A direct reference to the tribe is found in Orozco y Berra.[15] According to this author (p. 279), "The Franciscan friars assure us in their narrations that the monasteries which they founded at Colotlan, Nostic, and Chimaltitlan were situated in the regions belonging to the family of Teules-Chichimecos, who used a special language called *Tepecano*." And again (pp. 284–85): "But the same Teules-Chichimecos were subdivided into fractions, with particular idioms. The first family were the *Cazcanes*, who occupied the region above (or from) the Rio Grande, and their neighbors were the Tecuexes and the Tepecanos."[16]

Orozco y Berra, usually so well informed, considered the Tepecano language to be extinct; but on his map he allots to the tribe an extensive territory, much larger than it occupies today or has occupied within the memory of its oldest men. In 1826 Capt. G. T. Lyon crossed from Zacatecas to Bolaños and gave an account of his journey[17] without referring to the Tepecanos.

Of modern students of Mexican ethnology or archeology only Lumholtz has approached the Tepecanos; he came within a day's journey of Askeltan, met a few of the Indians, and collected a few words of their language. Dr. Nicolas León, of the City of Mexico, published in 1902, through my incentive, a brief vocabulary of the Tepecano language, obtained through a padre from one of the nearby Mexican settlements. But the tribe, as well as the whole valley of the Rio de Bolaños, is, with the exception of the work here referred to, a virgin field for anthropology.

Present location.   Today the Tepecanos are confined to the pueblo of Askeltan[18] and to not exceeding one hundred and fifty square miles of the valley of the Rio de Bolaños and the adjacent mountains. The nearest white or other Indian settlements, of any moment, to the Tepecano country are Nostic on the north, Santa Catarina and San Sebastian (Huichol) on the west, Huilacaltitlan (few Tepecanos) and especially Bolaños on the south, Temastian (descendants of introduced Tlaxcaltecs), and, farther on, Totatiche on the southeast to east.

Dwellings.   The pueblo of Askeltan consists of about forty dwellings, some of which are clustered on a low, rather unattractive hill or point, two-thirds of which are surrounded by the river, while others are scattered along the river itself. The village contains a small, old, Spanish-built church, and in general has a sort of semicivilized appearance; this was further enhanced during the latter part of 1902 by the Tepecanos permitting a Mexican trader to settle in their pueblo for the first time in its history.

The dwellings of the Indians, where not modified by Spanish usages, consist of one or two rather small, low structures, built from irregular, unworked stones, with or without mortar. Occasionally there is in addition a more or less open shed built from boughs. The roofs of the houses are gabled or ∧-shaped, as are those of all the more primitive Indian dwellings in Jalisco, Tepic, and Zacatecas. The houses consist of a framework of native bamboo covered with *zacate*, or grass. A small separate group of such structures is usually surrounded by a rude stone enclosure. These dwellings are generally quadrangular, and the ruins of some of them are quite indistinguishable from the ancient ruins in that region. In the vicinity of the church are a few houses of more modern construction.

Dress.   All the male Tepecanos dress in a loose, collarless blouse shirt made of the cheap, unbleached but durable Mexican muslin; and in loose pantaloons of the same material, reaching below the calves, but

often worn rolled up much higher. The head is protected by a home-
made straw hat, somewhat of the shape of the ordinary Mexican som-
brero, but smaller; on the feet the men wear simple rawhide sandals. A
few of the men have in addition nice homespun belts or pouches. The
women wear a rather short muslin shirt, and a muslin or calico skirt,
but seldom (except when visiting or traveling) any head-covering and
apparently never any sandals. The little children run about nude or in a
long shirt; older children dress like the parents.

The hair of the men is worn trimmed from three to six inches in
length, while the women wear their hair in braids down the back. There
is no tattooing, and ordinarily, at least, no painting. Ornaments are now
almost wholly restricted to women and girls, and consist of cheap rings,
earrings, and beads.

Population.   The Tepecanos in the Bolaños Valley estimate their entire number to exceed three hundred. Askeltan, which is their headquarters, could hardly accommodate more than about one hundred and
fifty inhabitants. A small Tepecano community some years ago emi-
grated from this neighborhood and now live near the Rio Santiago
(Rio Grande).

Occupation; food.   The tribe subsists almost entirely by agriculture
and on the native fruits, such as the pitaya, tuna, vamuchile, and others.
They cultivate maize (which is consumed mainly in the form of tortillas, but is also cooked whole), some beans, calabashes, and watermelons. For the watermelon they show a fondness equal to that of most
Indians, and, it may be added, an equal disregard for its ripeness before
eating. Some of the cactus fruits are dried in the sun on stones and
preserved in cornhusks.

The Tepecanos raise some sheep, goats, and cattle, and keep
chickens; they also hunt and fish a little. A few of the men occasionally
conduct a little trade or engage in work for others. There are no
artisans.

Ancient money.   In 1898 I accidentally came across and finally obtained a small string of ancient shell beads, or wampum, which the
owner declared had still a definite exchange value, although they were
used very rarely on account of their scarcity.

Organization.   The Tepecanos are practically independent. They
elect from their midst a *gobernador* and an *alcalde*, who are nominally

subject to the Mexican authorities, but they virtually do as they please. There are some indications of a more primitive, probably clanship, organization. There is no established school, no education; but several of the Tepecanos have learned in the neighboring pueblos more or less of reading and writing.

Religion.   Occasionally a Catholic priest comes to hold a brief service in the village church and to baptize or to marry those who so desire. The Indians have apparently assimilated some of these usages into their own religion, somewhat in the manner that they have adopted some Spanish terms into their language; and so long as the visitor keeps within certain bounds he has no difficulty. After the padre has departed the Tepecanos resort very largely again to their primitive deities and fetishes, which are represented by objects of stone or of other material and which are kept carefully hidden in their homes or in caves and sacred spots in the mountains. I have thoroughly reliable information of two quite large, crouching lions of stone, with wide mouths showing teeth;[19] a stone cat or leopardlike figure; and a stone snake, decorated with *chaquira* (beads). All these figures and two *chaquira*-decorated skulls are kept somewhere on or near the Cerro de la Liona (Lion Mountain), a little south of Askeltan, and several times each year are brought to an artificial patio (court) on the summit of the high mountain and there used in certain dances or ceremonies. It is probable that these figures are ancient. I myself have obtained from the Tepecanos two probably ancient and one modern, small, lithomage figures, one representing the sun, one a chicken fetish, and the third a god of war; also a small stone disk with a hole in the center and radiating lines on the surface, probably representing the sun. The esteem with which the Indians regard all the old objects found in the ruins, and even the ruins themselves, is remarkable.

Twice every year, in the latter half of May and in September, the Tepecanos give *quentas* to the "great god" and other deities, the sun probably being foremost among them. These offerings consist of several kinds of sticks, to which are attached loose cotton, cotton-yarn "badges," feathers or beads, etc., or most often several of these objects together. The finished sticks are known as *chi-má-les*, or *ki-vá-res*. The latter term, I was told, is the proper Tepecano one, but the former is heard much more often.

There are two principal varieties of *chimáles*, namely, those with and those without the "badges." The differences in the two classes, as

well as the many individual modifications, are, so far as my informant
could tell, more of an esthetic than of a symbolic nature. Two kinds of
sticks are used—one thin, looking like a split bamboo, from four to ten
inches long; the other of light, white, native wood, much more common, is cylindrical, about three-quarters of an inch thick and from nine
to fourteen inches in length, pointed at one end and blunt at the other.

The cotton used is a native variety and is cultivated by the Tepecanos for ceremonial uses only. It is used loose and made up into a
moderately thin yarn. The loose cotton is wrapped about the *chimále*
stick, or about the ends of the ribs of the badges, or hung on the stick
in tufts or in the form of pendants. It represents clouds and is used
particularly on the May *chimáles* as a prayer offering for "good" clouds
and water.

The badges vary in size, some being over five inches in diameter.
They are generally plain white, but sometimes they are colored in two
tints, pale blue and red being mostly employed. The colored and white
yarn, where the two are employed, alternate in bands, when there are
no other figures. In shape most of the badges are hexagonal; others are
diamond-shaped, and in one instance I found a cylindrical one.
Although I questioned the Tepecanos on this point a number of times
(and I had the same experience among the Huichols), I was unable to
learn that these badges had any significance other than that they are
"nice" and "agreeable" to the deities.

The feathers are mostly, although not exclusively, those of a species
of hawk; they may be used singly or in bunches, fastened to the top of a
stick and pointing upward, or hanging as pendants. The beads fastened
to the *chimáles* represent money and form a figurative tribute to the
deity. The most valued beads are those of shell, found in the old ruins,
but glass beads also are used. Occasionally a diminutive bow and arrows
are attached to the *chimále* as pendants.[20]

The Tepecanos have several definite spots where, from season to
season, they deposit their *chimáles* by sticking the sharp edges into the
ground. One of these shrines, to which an Indian led me and whence
came the *chimáles* here illustrated as well as a number of others in the
American Museum, is a small, artificial structure of stone, partly covered but open eastward, constructed on the top of the main portion of
the wall of the large patio in the ruin of the Cerro de Colotlan, a few
miles north of Askeltan. It seems that each such depository belongs to
a certain group of individuals. Here the men come after the middle of

each May and deposit their *chimáles,* each man his own and separately, with prayers for abundant water (on which their crops depend), but only "pure" water, and for freedom from tempests, disease, and other malevolent things. The cotton and badges and pendants are conceived as representatives or messengers of this prayer; the feathers symbolize the desired swift flight of the prayer, while the beads are an expression of a consciousness of indebtedness and a figurative tribute. This much could I gather from the discourses of my informant. During September (any part of the month, the end of the rainy season) and before the harvest fiesta, new *chimáles* are made, and each individual, again the men only, passes the prepared sticks in a certain way around the head and body for "purification," then gives thanks to the deities and deposits his *chimále.* At times the *chimále* is used for supplications other than those here mentioned, and even in sorcery. Gourds, to which beads and cotton are pasted, are also deposited as offerings at the same places as the *chimáles.*

Sorcery.   The Mexican neighbors of the Tepecanos greatly fear the latter on account of their supposed powers in sorcery. On one occasion I met two individuals each of whom knew of some "idols" of the tribe, but both refused all offers to lead me to the locality for fear the Tepecanos would revenge themselves by causing the right arm of the informant to wither. Eventually, on my last expedition, Don Nicolas, an exceptionally honest and intelligent ranchman who knows the Tepecanos better than any of their other neighbors (a part of his ranch being situated very near Askeltan), brought to me a wooden figure found in a cave where it had been deposited by one of the Indian sorcerers. This figure, I was assured, was a faithful representation of a certain Mexican who, some time before, did some injustice to the Tepecanos. One of the sorcerers of the tribe made the figure, affixed it to a plumed stick or *chimále,* and deposited it in the cave from which it was later taken. The Mexican was soon afterward taken sick; but another Tepecano told of the figure, and as soon as this had been torn from the stick and removed from the cave the man rapidly recovered.

     The harm-belief need not of course be considered; but what is of particular interest is the fact (of which, after all I heard on the subject and with the wooden image in my hand, there can not be much doubt) that the Tepecanos actually practice some "witchcraft" ceremony. This is probably a form of prayer which, like every other more important prayer, is represented by a prayer stick and other object and deposited in one of the sacred shrines.

Traditions.   Among the Tepecanos there is one old man, highly regarded by all, for whom, on account of his wisdom and general behavior, I could think of no more fitting term than "Nestor"; and, curiously enough, he has been known to others, ever since my first visit, as Nestor Aguilar. According to this stage—and he talked in the assembly and with the expressed approval of a number of the other men—the Tepecanos came a long time ago "from the north, from a *Rio Colorado,*[21] and were of the same people as the *bárbaros* there. Those of Nostic were originally Tepecanos, but later became mixed with other people and talked their 'lengua Mexicana.'[22] The Tepecanos extended to the Borego and Mesitas [both now apparently ancient ruins]. The Borego settlement was very old. Askeltan, Temastian, Acapulco, Huila (Huilacatlan), Santa Catarina, and Nostic were once occupied by branches of the same nation, who were originally a part of the *mecos.*[23] The *bárbaros* made war on the Tepecanos, but were repulsed. Then those of the Borego warred with those of Askeltan. It is long since this war took place, but it was after the white men came. The cause of it was a miraculous image of San Lorenzo which both villages claimed. Askeltan was then for a time called San Lorenzo. The pueblo received the name of *Askeltan,* from *askelas,* 'ants,' on account of the many people who lived there—as many as ants. The Tepecanos were themselves once *bárbaros* after coming from the north."

A good deal more is known by the old man and by other Tepecanos, but it is rather dangerous ground to tread upon and should be left to students better qualified for such a line of investigation.

Social customs.   No marriage is allowed until after puberty. The husband not infrequently takes two wives, but a woman has never two husbands. There is a little marital infelicity and some irregular prostitution.

The Tepecanos denied the occurrence of suicide in their tribe. They hurt or even kill each other occasionally, but only when made drunk by sotol [*xoto*] or tequila. Transgressions are usually of a minor character and the punishment is either incarceration or lashing. A murderer, if caught, is delivered to the Mexican authorities.

In the last century, during periods of disturbance, several of the men became highwaymen and were killed by the Mexicans. The dead were formerly buried in caves, but now many remains are interred in an old as well as in a new cemetery at Askeltan.

Intellectual qualities.   After one has gained the confidence of the Tepecanos and they recognize in him a friend, and particularly one who does not deceive them, they become pleasant, display keen intelligence, and even become close companions; under these conditions they are in every way preferable to the ordinary Mexicans. But to reach such a stage of acquaintance and then retain the confidence of the Tepecano (owing, no doubt, to the usual experience of the Indians with whites) is quite a difficult matter, as may be seen from the following.

I made, in all, three brief visits to the Tepecanos, one in 1898 and two in 1902; and as every one warned me of the suspicious nature of the people, I chose but a single guide and companion, Sr. Cruz Velásquez. On reaching Askeltan, in the first week of May 1898, we found the town almost deserted, most of the inhabitants having gone to the sierra to pick the ripening pitayas. We saw a few women from afar, but, on perceiving us, these immediately sought seclusion, so that aside from a female patient to whom I was brought later, I did not see on this first visit, which occupied two days, a single woman make her appearance. The few male inhabitants, whom we found after some search, received us with much reserve and apparent distrust of our intentions, which we did not succeed in overcoming for many hours. We were conducted to the *gobernador*, or head of the village, who, after receiving some gifts, gave us one of his huts for shelter.

As an illustration of the distrust which the Indian felt toward us, I may mention that for more than half a day we were unable to buy, in the entire village, even with the aid of our host, a single goat, sheep, chicken, or egg, although there was no scarcity of such things in the settlement, and indeed we were thus restricted in our purchases of the necessaries of life even after promising to make a general feast with the things bought. Gradually, however, the distrust gave way to kinder feelings. The people learned that I was a physician, and some called me to see the wife of one of the men who was very ill with malaria. Later the husband of the patient brought us as a gift a gourd full of fine tunas (cactus fruit), and all became more friendly. Finally, when evening came, the house and the yard were filled with visitors, and the latter part of the evening and the following day were spent in complete confidence with all those who were in the village—the women, however, still remained in hiding. The Indians, some of whom were brought from the nearer mountains by their friends, surrounded us at all hours, and I was able to measure them and to make inquiries at pleasure. They even promised me two skulls which they kept in the village for certain of their ceremonies, but during the night these were spirited away to the mountains.

My second visit, in the spring of 1902, was very pleasant and profitable. I was enabled to record more physical data and also to make photographs; but the women, although they did not run away nor hide, still remained sufficiently distrustful to prevent me from measuring or photographing them. On my third visit (toward the close of 1902) the mere repetition of my visits and some photographs of individuals of the tribe which I brought with me, aroused new suspicions; all of which shows the care necessary in dealing with such people and indirectly reflects anything but credit on their past relations with the whites.

Medical and physiological.   Information on these subjects, except where they bore on certain ceremonies, was given by the Tepecanos without hesitation.

The tribe, according to the information obtained, increases but little, if any, on account of the high death rate. The most frequent causes of death among the adults are "fever" (in all probability typhoid), calentura, dysentery, and "a chest disease of short duration accompanied with pain and fever" (probably pneumonia). Calentura is quite prevalent.[24] The mortality of children is large, and is due chiefly to intestinal disorders, often caused by eating unripe melons and other fruits. Calentura is also frequently fatal among children. Smallpox has appeared occasionally and its ravages caused numerous deaths. A certain percentage of women die as a result of accident or from disease while pregnant, or at or shortly after childbirth.

The most common minor affections among the Tepecanos are pains in the joints (rheumatism?), headaches, some vertigo (the latter two mainly the effect of drinking to excess, which is not frequent, or of calentura), and conjunctivitis. Tumors occur occasionally. Insanity is very rare and is believed by the natives to be incurable.

The materia medica of the Tepecanos consists of many herbs, and, when these fail, of certain ceremonies. The herbs most commonly used are *palo amargo* (native cinchona), *herba de San Antonio*, and oak-leaves, for calentura; *palo mulato*, mainly for pains; *hi-ku-li* (obtained from the Huichols), *vervena, rosa de castilla*, the root of *ko-ho-te*, the seed of *ci-ci-va*, etc. There is no higher degree of surgery, but the Tepecanos can well take care of broken limbs.

If a patient does not improve, the medicine man is called. When he comes the patient lies down; the medicine man prays and talks to the winds and spirits; then he lights a cigarette, draws in the smoke, and applies his mouth to the painful part of the body, which he bites a little or sucks, then puffs the smoke away from the patient, and spits into his own hands. With the saliva comes usually some small object—a cactus spine, a little stone, or the like—which the medicine man either breaks up in his palm or throws into the fire. He then throws away the saliva. Occasionally the medicine man gives also some remedy internally; but his prayers and touches, especially with the fingers moistened with saliva, and the exercises of his magic power are the essentials.

Conception generally follows very soon after marriage. Most women have four to six children, but there are some who have given birth to ten or even twelve. Only a few women are naturally sterile; others, I was assured, induce artificial sterility by means of herbs. Artificial abortion, also by means of herbs, I was told is not very rare.

The period of gestation lasts, according to the Tepecanos, nine months with a boy, but only seven or eight months with a girl. The mother has no means of guessing the sex of the child before parturition. The period of gestation is reckoned from the last menstruation. There are women who give birth to a child every year, and there are many who become pregnant before the last child is weaned.

Infants are suckled generally up to two years of age, though in not a few instances considerably later; but in addition they partake also of all the kinds of food which the mother eats as soon as they can masticate a little. As among all Indians, the health of the child is often sacrificed through the desire of fully satisfying its appetite, and whatever the degree of medical skill in the tribe, there is, inexplicably, no knowledge or practice of prevention.

Children walk when about one year of age; they do not begin to talk before eighteen months or two years. The Indian mother does not stimulate the talking of her child as the white mother does. Before walking the Tepecano children crawl like white children, or even run a little on all fours.[25] The first dentition occurs most frequently in the latter part of the first year, in a minority of cases at about six months. The occasional mother who "has no milk" nourishes her infant on the milk of goats or cows.

Parturition is generally accomplished with the aid of one or more related or friendly older women. There are no professional midwives, and the woman in childbirth is not secluded from her family or friends. The average labor occupies about twelve hours. The woman is usually delivered squatting on her knees and toes, or on knees and toes and hands, with the lower limbs separated. In difficult labor the husband or brother will encircle her abdomen from behind with his arms and try to expel the child by pressure, which is continued without intermission as long as the man or the woman can stand it. If this heroic treatment does not accomplish the purpose, the medicine man is called, and he proceeds with the woman much as with any other patient, but gives her at the same time a decoction of *herba buena* or *rosa de castilla*.

The newborn begins to suckle usually within two hours after birth. The infant is washed at once with lukewarm water, but the mother is not thoroughly cleansed until after four days. Women often have "fever" after confinement, which sometimes results in death. The abdomen of the mother is bandaged with the ordinary man's *faja*.[26] After confinement the woman is urged to remain abed as long as possible, and she generally stays indoors eight to fifteen or even thirty days.

Mealtimes and food are not so regular as among the whites; this, however, is the rule among all Indians. Intoxicating drinks, as with other Indians, have a rapid and, in the beginning, generally exhilarating effect. Tobacco is used very moderately. As all Indians, the Tepecanos are good travelers. In pacing, two steps (from one mark of one foot to the next mark of the same) are counted as one. Both the men and the women are good although not steady workers.

Physical characteristics.   However interesting the Tepecanos may be ethnologically, they are even more so from the point of view of physical anthropology. They are the shortest in stature and the most brachycephalic of all the Mexican tribes north of latitude 21°. They show quite close physical relation with the Tepehuanes, Huichols, Coras, southern Jalisco (Tuxpan) Nahuas, and Opatas, but this relation does not amount to tribal identity. My investigations afford reason for the belief that all of these people, as well as those now wholly or nearly extinct throughout Jalisco, a large part of southern Zacatecas, much of

Durango, at least parts of Sinaloa and Sonora, and many now scattered over even a much wider radius, descended from one physical *souche*, or type; but this subject will be more appropriately treated in another place.

The physical appearance of the Tepecanos, aided by but not wholly due to their costume, is such that many of them can be quite easily distinguished from the Huichols; yet there are among the Huichols, as well as among the other tribes above mentioned, not a few individuals who, if met near Askeltan, would be taken for typical Tepecanos.

Almost all the Askeltan natives appear short and rather thickset. The color of the skin is generally a medium brown, not far from the ordinary mulatto tint, but with a slightly greater tinge of red than of yellow. The women are not lighter than the men, and some of them, as shown by their bare arms and the upper part of the chest, have the identical, fine, slightly reddish brown common among pureblood Indians of the United States. The hair, as in other Indians, is of the same color as the black mane of a horse. The eyes are dark brown, hazy, conjunctivae yellowish.

The heads of the Tepecanos are generally rather large, rounded, regular, and free from artificial or other deformity. The face is usually quite broad and seldom handsome, but it increases in interest or pleasantness with animation. The forehead is generally of good height and breadth, occasionally sloping backward in its upper half. The malar bones are large, but not excessive. In men the nose is quite short and broad, but not low or thick as in the Negro; it is of moderate dimensions and of a nicer form in the women. The lower part of the face is generally strong. There is little, if any, facial but more of alveolar prognathism. The supraorbital ridges are well marked and in some individuals are large. The eyeslits are nearly as straight as in the whites to slightly oblique. The bridge of the nose is usually moderately convex; the point is generally blunt and thick, and frequently, especially in the older ones, overhangs somewhat the nasal septum and the borders of the nasal openings (pendant point); or the whole septum shows a descending inclination. The mouth is large. In the majority of cases the lips are slightly thicker than those of whites, but never like those of Negroes. The chin is rather broad and of medium prominence, never receding. Both the upper lip and the chin in men are covered with straight, rare, rather coarse, black hair, from two to five centimeters in length. As among Indians generally, no beard grows on the sides of the cheeks. The teeth are well developed and regular. The ears are of medium size and well formed, but the lobules are in some cases attached. The body is generally regular and strong, the chest well developed and rather deep at the base. The hands and feet of the Tepecano men are well formed, somewhat short, not large. The toes gradually recede in size from the first. The legs are of almost the medium dimensions of those of whites, not so small as among other Indian tribes.

Without entering into further detail in this place, I append . . . brief tables which illustrate certain of the physical characters of the Tepecanos compared with those of several other tribes of northern Mexico. The relation of all these is obviously very close. The Tepehuanes as well as the Opatas show a larger proportion of mesocephaly, which is probably due to admixture with their neighbors, the meso- to dolicho-cephalic Tarahumares. It is quite possible that the Tepecanos were originally but a part of the once great Tepehuane tribe and that their name is but a slight perversion of the term "Tepehuano."

The Nasal Index average was, for Tepecanos (27 persons) 83.6; Southern Tepehuanes (no number given) 83.3; Huicholes (no number given) 82.2; Coras (no number given) 83.3; Southern Jalisco Nahuas (no number given) 81.8; Opatas, Sonora (no number given) 81.1.

There remains the question whether the immediate ancestors of the Tepecanos dwelt at Totoate, Torreón, etc. This question physical anthropology can answer only so far as to assert that they are of the same type of people; but whether they are of the same tribe can be determined, if at all, only by archeologic and ethnologic research.

The Language of the Tepecanos

The majority of the people, particularly the women, know but little Spanish; among themselves they employ the Tepecano dialect. The language sounds more pleasant than do some other Indian languages. It is quite easy to follow and reproduce the sounds and to distinguish many of the words. There are no harsh constructions and no unpleasant or unusual inflections of the voice; the pronunciation, however, differs slightly with different persons. I append to these notes a brief vocabulary and some phrases and sentences collected by me during intervals in my somatological work; and I give also for comparison a few words

1. Physical Characters of the Tepecanos Compared with Those of Other Tribes of Northern Mexico; Comparisons of Persons Are In Percentages

	STATURE					
Height in Centi-meters	Tepecanos (25)	Southern Tepehuanes (40)	Huicholes (30)	Coras (53)	So. Jalisco Nahuas (50)	Opatas, Sonora (31)
153–155	12.0	...	3.3	1.9	...	...
155–160	36.0	17.5	16.7	13.2	12.0	22.6
160–165	40.0	30.0	36.7	35.8	46.0	19.4
165–170	12.0	42.5	36.7	37.7	32.0	29.0
170–175	...	5.0	6.7	11.3	6.0	16.1
175–180	...	2.5	...	1.9	2.0	16.1
180–185	...	2.5	...	...	...	...

	UNDEFORMED HEADS					
Cephalic Index						
Below 75	...	2.5	3.3	2.0	10.0	6.4
75–76	...	...	6.7	2.0	...	3.2
76–77	...	22.5	3.3	8.0	8.0	6.4
77–78	8.0	5.0	3.3	6.0	8.0	19.3
78–79	...	20.0	6.7	8.0	6.0	10.0
79–80	8.0	7.5	6.7	14.0	14.0	13.0
80–81	12.0	7.5	13.3	14.0	14.0	13.0
81–82	4.0	2.5	13.3	16.0	10.0	10.0
82–83	4.0	12.5	6.7	8.0	6.0	13.0
83–84	28.0	10.0	10.0	6.0	14.0	...
84–85	16.0	10.0	13.3	...	4.0	6.4
85–86	...	...	3.3	2.0	4.0	...
86–87	4.0	...	10.0	2.0	2.0	...
87–88	...	...	...	4.0	...	...
88–89	4.0	...	...	...	...	...
89–90	4.0	...	...	...	...	...

These percentages do not always add up to 100. We here simply reproduce the figures as they appeared in the original article. For simplicity's sake, the Nasal Index given originally in table form is here placed in the text.

obtained later among the Southern Tepehuanes of the district of Santa Maria de Ocotan, Durango. The terms were obtained in both cases from a group of men, which is safer than similar information from any single individual; they were also repeated by me to the men and only when easily understood were allowed to stand. There is no doubt that a good linguist, in a reasonable time and without much expense, could conduct among this people, as among several other remnants of north Mexican tribes, a work of much value.

Tepecano Vocabulary and Examples of Speech,
with Some Equivalents in the Southern Tepehuane Dialect[27]

NOTE.   In recording the Indian language, not being an expert linguist I found great difficulty in using the English alphabet, so finally employed that of my native language, the Czech, in which I found very nearly all the sounds used by the Tepecanos, as well as by other Mexican tribes. Most of the sounds of the letters in this alphabet, as well as in those of the various Slavonic languages, are identical with the Spanish and Latin (Continental) sounds, but there are a number of additional letters with sounds that represent exactly what is most difficult to represent with the English alphabet. In order to avoid all confusion I present herewith the exact and unvarying sound of every letter employed. [Spanish terms given as printed in the original article. We have also modified a few of the linguistic symbols for purposes of clarity.]

THE ALPHABET

a, as *a* in *marrow*.

ā, as *a* in *mar, garden*.

b, as in *ball*.

c, has the sound the nearest approach to which in English can be expressed by *ts* or *tz*; it is found pure in such Latin words as *terćius*; it is a clear elementary sound, not a combination.

c, has a softer, moister sound than c, and stands intermediate between this and č;

it, as well as š, is common in other Indian languages, as the Hopi.

č, as *ch* in *cherry*.

d, as in *dull, dollar*.

d, or soft d, has a sound the nearest approach to which in English is probably the combined sound of the d and i in some words with the combination of *diê*.

e, as in *bet, tempest*.

e, as *ê* in *fête*.

f,   as in F*aust*, f*ish*.
g,   as in g*all*, g*et*.
h,   as in *home*, *hot*.
ch, as in the German b*rauchen*,
     lachen.
i,   as in *lily*, b*oil*.
ī,   as *i* in *machine*.
j,   as in the German language,
     as *Jesu*; it is used where in
     English *y* would be em-
     ployed.
k,   as in *kine*, *peak*.
l,   as in *lion*, *tool*.
m,   as in *mother*, *boom*.
n,   as in *near*, *bean*.
η,   has a nasal sound somewhat
     similar to *ng*, as in many
     Chinese words.
ñ,   as *gn* in the French *mig-
     non*, that of *ni* in *pinion*.
o,   as in *mother*, or as *u* in *sun*.
ō,   as in *strong*, or as *a* in *ball*.
p,   as in *peak*, *heap*.
r,   as in *rain*, *tear*.

ř,   is a difficult, soft, vibrating
     sound, the nearest approach
     to which in English can be
     made by the combination
     rz; yet in the true ř, which
     is common to many Indian
     languages, no trace of *z* or *s*
     is audible.
s,   as in *salt*, *last*.
š,   as *sh* in *she*, *hush*.
t,   as in *tear*, *meat*.
t,   is soft *t* corresponding to
     the soft *d*.
u,   as *ou* in *Louis*.
ū,   as *oo* in *tooth*.
v,   as in *very*, *weave*.
w,   as in English (from which
     it is adopted).
y,   is closely related to *i*, but
     has a broader sound, as that
     of *y* in *Styria*.
y,   is a prolonged y.
z,   as in *zenith*, *Zulu*.
z,   as in *azure*.

NOUNS

F*ather*, ta-ta (hin-čāt).
mother, na-na (hin-ñān).
brother, en-ha-dōn, ha-dūn (hin-
   čiš).
sister, en-ha-dōn, en-mow-da
   (hin-zi-kō).
brother of my father ⎫ hād-ni-den
sister of my father ⎭ tā-ta-pe.

Old man, ko-li-gi-ja.
old woman, o-ki-gi-ja.
priest [*padre*], om-ōg ["head"].
god [*one of the gods*], sī-do-kam.

son, a-li.
daughter, a-li.
children, mā-ma-li.
grandfather, bā-ba-li.
grandmother, kā-ha-li.
man, ti-ōt, ti-ōn.
woman, wo-ūf.
brother of my mother ⎫ hād-ni-den
sister of my mother ⎭ nā-na-pe.

a dead person, iš-mūg.
child, ār.
pretty girl, zap-māš.
another one [*person*], gu-maj.

Head, um-ōgh [initial *u* and terminal *gh* in all feeble].
neck, um-baik-tow.
chest, um-bās.
hand, um-nōb.
foot, um-tōn.
finger, um-dē-do [from Spanish].
fingernail, um-hōst.
hair, um-kūp.

beard, mustache, um-tum-wo.
eye, um-wuj.
ear, um-nā-nak.
nose, um-dāk.
lip, um-tun.
tooth, um-ta-tam.
tongue, um-nūn.
chin, um-kas.

Deer, el-suj-mar, ko-kōn.
   (so-ī-mā-k.)
dog, go-gōs.
bird, ču-īt. (u-ē.)
sheep, to-tōk.

pig, ek-vi-mar.
quail, to-so-ru-i.
chicken, ta-vu-a.
goose, ha-a.
cat, mi-sō

Day, ta-tāb, te-ši-mā-ši. (ta-nōk.)
night, to-ka, t'-ka', tē-wa-tok.
   (to-kāk.)

week, humat-si-mān [probably from Spanish *semana*].
month, hu-mat mas-za. (ma-sān.)
year, hu-mat oj-da. (mā-km.)

Sun, to-nōr. (hin-*te*-hōg.)
moon, mas-za. (ma-sān.)
star, hōp-pa. (hu-wag.)
earth, bī-t-d, oj-da-kam. (den-wēr.)
water, sūr-di, tsū-di, s ū-di. hā-va [from Sp. *agua?*]. (sur-de-i.)
village, kī-da-or, kī-dagh-ra.
Askeltan, Kī-dagh-ra.[28]
hat, mō-bar.
muslin pantaloons, hi-na-twāř-kar.
health, šav-hu-van.
sky, g-t-wan-gi.
Inferno, ne-ziš-ko-ōk.
stone, ho-daj. (hor-da-ji.)
tree, ūš. (u-ūc.)
fire, taj.
road, voi [from Spanish *voy,* I go?].

arrow, u-u.
bow, gāt.
wood, ko-āg.
house, kī-ta-mi.
great house, gu-wa-āk.
roof, wa-āk, wa-āh.
room, bīd-wa-āk.
cold, iš-tu-čū-pi.
lightning, hp-tg-wa.
thunder, ne-ō-ki-him.
darkness, sa-sa-va-či.
sickness, kōg-da-ra.
malaria (calentura), iš-to-kōk-da.
the mountains, hok-km-dam.
maize, hūn.
tostilla, sā-mit.
a laborer, dād-ge.
a word, ni-jōk.

PRONOUNS

I, a-ne, āl-ne, an-te, a-ni.
thou, ā-pe.
he, she,it, ap-te.

we, ā-tip, te-ti.
they, [male or female], hu-ga.

ADJECTIVES AND NUMERALS

Good, e-ši-ōb, a-me-ři-ōn.
better, e-me-řap-toj.
bad, e-a-nu-ōb, ja-map-toj
  [worse?]
small, liš-puk.
great, large, gū-eh.
stout, fat, sāv-lak.
thin, šī-gak, kam.

high, tōb.
sweet, eš-maj-ka-kam.
bitter, šī-wu-kam.
warm, niš-ho-ōk.
much, vi-ja.
many, muj [probably from the
  Spanish].

White, iš-tā-kam. (š-čo-a.)
black, eš-tō-kam. (štuk.)
yellow, e-šām-kam. (i-šū-vam.)

green, tyr-do-kam.
blue, eš-tyr-do-kam. (ču-ū-da.)
red, ež-wuk-kam. (ši-wuk.)

One, u-ma, hu-maj, hū-mat.[29]
  (ma^n [the terminal *n* but
  slightly audible].)
two, gōk. (gōk.)
three, vajk. (vajk.)
four, mā-ko, mā-ko-ba. (mā-ko.)
five, eš-to-mān. (ča-mam,
  šta-mam.)

six, šev-uma, šiv-hupnaj. (ši-
  huma^n.)
seven, šil-gōk. (šiv-gōk.)
eight, ši-vajk. (šiv-bejk, šiv-vajk.)
nine, ši-māko. (šim-māko.)
ten, mā-huř. (mam-buš.)[30]

MISCELLANEOUS PARTS OF SPEECH

Today, u-wī-mo. (now-šīf.)
tomorrow, wu-ī-mo, as-ta-wī-mo
  [Spanish *hasta?*]. (wuj-mok.)
day after tomorrow, asta-ma-ši-
  je-va, dog-ma-ši-jeva.
yesterday, ta-kāb, ta-kāv. (ta-kāv.)
last year, hm-āk.

until }
up to } hau-a, maj-kā-va.
far, ko-ra. (mk.)
yes, a-ā-a. (hn-dō.)
no, ja-ni. (ča-m, čam-mō.)
what, a-ša-psu-po-haj-da.

VERBS[31]

I go, an-ty-ki-hi, an-te-va-hi.
(an-va-hi.)
I am, āl-ne.
thou [you] art, āpe.
it is, u-iš, ñiš.
I say, au-te po-toj.
thou [you] sayest, a-ni po-toj.
he says, ap-te po-toj.
we [nos todos] say, wu-e-šir te-ti
po-toj.
I have, a-ni vi-ja, a-ni, ni-vi, ja.
he has [or holds], šiš-tōn.
I know, an-te-šmāt, a-ni-šmāt, a-
niš-to-māt-ys.[32]

thou [you] knowest, a-ne-am-to-
māt-ys, a-pe-miš-to-māt.
he [the other one] knows, g-ma-
jiš-to-māt-ys.
we [all] know, wu-e-šir, to-mat-ys.
I want, a-ni, so-ši-mym, a-niš ho-
chi, a-ni-zāk.
I shall say [I shall tell to all],
wūš au-te po-toj mū-hā-der.
I said yesterday, ta-kāv au-te po-
toj.
I cut, a-ni-hik-ta.
I eat, au-te-va-to-hōk.
I hold, šiš-to-nōm.
I return, an-ti-ba-nōr.

COMPOSITION[33]

One man, hu-maj ti-ōt.
two men, gōk te-ti-ōt.
many men, muy ga-te-ti-ōt.
many sons, muy a-la-li.

many women, muy wu-wo-ūf.
many children, muy a-ār.
two years, gōk oj-da.

Greeting on meeting, šav-hū-van
[health]; en-gan-do šav-hū-van.
response to same, a-hwa-nā-pe,
who-pa-nā-pe.
How far is it to Askeltan? Hō-
šiš-mō-kor ki-dagh-ra?
It is not far, Ja-m-ko-ra.
It is very far, U-iz muy ko-ra.
When are you going? Huyř-kat
a-pso-hy-mi-ja?
When will you return? Huyš-kat
a-ps-ha-gu-šija?

greeting on parting, ki-nē-ki an-
te-va-nor.
greeting for "good night," a-te-
ř-hū-ro.
Where are you going? Pā-pe-c-ki-
hi?
I go to Askeltan, An-ty-ki-hi ki-
dagh-ra.
I went yesterday, Ta-kāv-an-te-ki-
hi.
Where are you going, Pā-pes-te-
wa-hi?
Where did you go? Pā-mo pe-c-
oj-ma?

I shall come tomorrow, Wu-y-mo ne-ha-g-ši-ja.

I shall go tomorrow, An-te-wa-hi as-ta wy-mo.

You travel very fast [*Andas muy apriesa*] }
You are a good traveler [*Es muy andador*] } Pta-ki-ja m-šim-da.

You returned promptly [*Pronto dios la vuelta*], P-je mš-mā-tat oj-ma.

I shall go to Mezquitic tomorrow, Wu-y-mo ni-chy-mi-ja wī-hok-tam.

I go to the mountains, A-ni-wa-hi hok-kom, dām.

I return from the mountains, An-ti-ba-nōr hok-kom-dām-de.

Tomorrow I go to the sierra, Wu-ȳ-mo hok-kom-dām ho-ni-hin-da.

I went to the mountains yesterday, Ta-kāv-an-ti-hi-mok hok-kom-dām.

Two men go to the mountains, Gōk tōt am-hī-mi-ja hok-kom-dām.

Many men go to the sierra, Muy am-hī-mi-ja hok-kom-dām.

What news is there? Hās-to šiš-to mo-yn.

There is no news, Nada [Sp.] ni haš-to.

I shall tell tomorrow, after I have thought of it [given spontaneously: *Yo le diré mañana, voy apensarme*], Wu-y-mo eu-pou-vān em-tur-de ne-kau-te-me-mo.

All of you know except myself [given spontaneously: *Ustedes todos saben menor yo no se*], A-pe miš-to-māt a-nem-to-mā-tys.

I do not want any one [given spontaneously], Jam-ki-ja mem-ki-hō-hi.

What is your name? [*Como te llames*], He-sap so-po-tōz?

Come to eat, Baj-to-hōk.

I am eating, An-te-wa to-hōk.

Give me, O-maj.

He has malaria, Šiš-tōn iš-to-hōk-da.

Juan has much money, Juan muy vi-ja vaj-no.

That man has much money, Muy vi-ja baj-num ti-ōn.

Go take a bath, Maj-kvo-to-a-tē-po.

Give me a stone, O-maj ho-daj.

Bring a stone, Baj-ši-bu ho-daj.

Make fire, Ši-to-nād-taj.

It is cold, Niš-iš-chi-jōb.

He drinks water, Neš-iš-to-nōm tsū-di.

I live here, A-ne-kid or-ki-jo.

I want to marry, Niš-ta-hōn-tam.

Somebody is dying [*Se muere otro*], Te-a-po-mo gu-maj.

I want to sleep, Niš-iš-hō-šim kō-šam.

I want you much, A-ne-ni-šim hō-chi.

I am a laborer, A-neš-to dād-gi.

Shoot there, A-ni-to-mo-ja.

114 THE NORTH MEXICAN FRONTIER

Songs of the Tepecanos

A sacred song, of which the Tepecanos would not give a translation, follows:

> Hauk ty-tā-vi ka-mi.
> Či-hajn-dū-du ka-mi.
> Hā-va gū-gr te-tu-wa-vo-ta i-po-oj-da-kam.

The following incantation is sung "al sol y nube" (to the sun and cloud) at the commencement of the rainy season. It is usually much longer than given here (with variations and repetitions it may last, I was told, upward of two hours), but the construction is similar throughout, the first verse being repeated with each successive stanza. Owing to their imperfect Spanish, the Tepecanos were not able to give me a literal translation of the song, but apparently it is mainly a rejoicing at the coming of the rains on which depends the whole sustenance of the people.

> Hā-va-ū[34] tu-tā-vi ka-ma ši-hajn-dū
> Ū te-a-ta wē-ve u-tu-tā-ve
> Hā-va g-t-wan-gi [the heavens] oj-da-kam [the earth].
>
> Hā-va-ū tu-tā-vi ka-ma ši-hajn-dū
> Hā-va um-ā-ran-ghim
> Hā-va te-vāg um-tū-tun-ghim.
>
> Hā-va-ū tu-tā-vi ka-ma ši-hajn-dū
> Hā-va t-wāg hp-tg-wa [the lightning].
>
> Hā-va-ū tu-tā-vi ka-ma ši-hajn-dū
> Hā-va vp-gū-ve.
>
> Hā-va-ū tu-tā-vi ka-ma ši-hajn-dū
> Hā-va ne-ō-ki-him [the thunder].
>
> Hā-va-ū tu-tā-vi ka-ma ši-hajn-dū
> Hā-va bi-wah wa-ū-ta.[35]

Another incantation of the Tepecanos, also sung before or at the beginning of the rainy season, and given to me by another man, is as follows:

> Hā-va tā-ta hā-li ō-li
> ka-ma ši-hajn-dū, dū-ka-ma.

Hā-va g-tu-wan-gi
u-tañ-a-vi, ojn-da-ka-ma.
Hā-va tu-va-gi u-tā
hā-vi o-in-da-ka-ma.

The idiom, as will easily be seen on comparison, although related particularly to the Tepehuane, and also to the Pima and the Nahua, presents numerous differences from each of the latter tongues. This fact would seem to indicate either an admixture of distinct languages or a long separation of people originally speaking the same dialect.

Explorations in Other Parts of Northern Jalisco and in Zacatecas

Tlaxcaltecos.　East of the Tepecanos are the rough mesas and barrancas of the district of Colotlan, and here in many spots are found traces of an ancient population. After almost a whole day of difficult journeying toward the east and slightly south from Askeltan one reaches a group of Indian pueblos known as Temastian, Azcapotzalco (about three miles east-southeast of Temastian), and Santa Rita (about seven miles nearly south of Azcapotzalco). One or two of these settlements are probably ancient, but as I learned from carefully preserved records, they were all peopled, in the early part of the eighteenth century, by Tlaxcaltecs, who were introduced by the Spaniards for defense against the "Chichimecos." Thus, in the three villages there are examples, persisting with their introduced population to this day, of the pueblos fronterizos, which played such an important part in the pacification of the country. Judging from their physical characteristics, the present inhabitants of the three villages are no longer pure Tlaxcaltecs, but the result of a union of these and some of the "Chichimecs." Nor do any of them now speak the old "Mexicano." There exist considerable friendship and even physical likeness between the natives of Temastian and the Tepecanos.

Ruin Orcón.　About six leagues southwest from Azcapotzalco, in a barranca, there is, according to the natives, a large ruined pueblo named Orcón, or Cerro de Orcón, similar in character to the ruins north of Askeltan, with petroglyphs, *piedras labradas*, etc. The inhabitants of Azcapotzalco, which is an old settlement, believe that Orcón was the original seat of those who founded their own pueblo.

Ruin Momax.   Seven miles east-southeast of Santa Rita is a comparatively large and now Mexicanized town called Atolinga; and four and a half leagues from here, in the broad valley that bears its name, lies the large old Mexican town of Tlaltenango. About five leagues north of the latter and nearly midway between it and Colotlan is an ancient ruin called Momax. The licenciate Románez in Tlaltenango informed me that the ranchman on whose property the otherwise not pretentious ruin is situated, needing some stone, destroyed a mound and found in it many burned and also some unburned human bones, together with various art objects, among which was some good pottery. Sr. Románez preserved one of the skulls, which I was able to measure, and he also kept a few damaged pieces of the pottery, one of which I obtained for the American Museum. The pottery exhibits different forms, but has the same artistic paint-inlaid decoration as the best pottery from Totoate, and even somewhat similar figures.

Natives of the Valley of Tlaltenango.   At Tlaltenango, and especially throughout the valley south of it, the proportion of Indian blood increases, and there are ranches and even pueblos where not a few apparently purebloods can still be found. These natives are probably largely the descendants of introduced Tlaxcaltecs, for their facial and body type approach closely that common in Tlaxcala and in the valley of Mexico. A large and almost wholly native pueblo, of known origin, called San Pedro, lies in one of the tributary valleys to the east of that of Tlaltenango, about half a day's journey from Tlaltenango itself. I shall later recur to this village.

Teul.[36]   A little less than a day's horseback journey south-southwest from Tlaltenango lies the famous ancient settlement, religious center, and fortress of Teul, once the most important seat of the "Teul-Chichimecs." Just north of Teul itself are several old native villages, the inhabitants of which show not a little mixture. What is known as Teul today is a fair-sized Mexican town at the foot of the ancient settlement, which was situated on a high, isolated hill, scalable only with difficulty, just south of the present Teul. The hill consists of a base of steep and in places vertical walls; a broad, inclining, circular bank of land, trending eastward, on which is found a spring and a cave-reservoir of water; and a large, conical elevation somewhat west of the middle. On the northern, eastern, and southern quarters of the belt-land are the remains of ancient Teul. These consist of mounds and large ruins with patios, as well as smaller ruins, all built of stone and in practically the same manner as the ruined structures of the Totoate group. The surface is everywhere overgrown and partly hidden by rank vegetation. The total area or mass of the ruin is not so great as one might expect from the notoriety of the place—it is smaller, for instance, than the ruins at the Banco de las Casas, south of Totoate—but there is no knowledge as to how much of Teul lay at the base of the hill, nor of how much has been obliterated by time and through the Mexicans. Enough remains, however, to deserve thorough exploration, for the largest mounds and structures have hardly yet been disturbed and appear to give promise of fruitful results to the archeologist.

The soil about the ruins is rich in fragments of mostly crude, but also some rather nicely painted or incised pottery, and in chips of obsidian and other stones. A quite extensive part of the belt is cultivated. Human bones are found occasionally, but thus far none has reached any museum. I saw dug from the bank a mesocephalic cranium, rather small, and in general of strong texture.

Among the few specimens which I obtained at Teul are the head of a small stone idol with a flat face and a small axe with an animal head carved in profile on the butt. The latter corresponds exactly with the axes from the Totoate group, as well as with the two from La Quemada, recently made known by Batres,[37] that have human or animal designs on the blunt end.

Living remnants of the "Teul-Chichimecs."   While at Teul I learned that two old villages of fullblood Indians were situated about six leagues west of Teul, and between the latter and the barranca of the Rio de Bolaños. These are San Lucas, or, as it is known to its inhabitants, Tepetitlan, and Tepisoac or Tepisoake. San Lucas, which lies about two leagues south of Tepetitlan, is probably the pueblo that Mota Padilla (p. 58) speaks of as having been founded in 1530 by Oñate, and in all probability was peopled by some of the inhabitants of Teul after the reduction of the latter place. At all events there is a tradition among the natives of Tepetitlan that their ancestors inhabited the Teul district before the whites came, and I found nothing to controvert this belief. The introduced Tlaxcaltecs and their pueblos fronterizos were situated a day's journey to the north.

On reaching Tepetitlan, which lies in a pleasant and fertile depression in the highlands, I found it entirely deserted. It is a village of moderate size, with the houses mostly scattered. The dwellings, which are of stone, or of stone and adobe combined, are all quadrilateral, with gable-shaped *zacate* roofs—a type of structure common throughout the entire region. The absence of the inhabitants was partly due to the corn harvest, but mainly, as we found later, to the suspicion that I might be a government agent coming as the result of a recent revolutionary plot. Fortunately I had with me a man (the owner of the Teul hill) in

2. Measurements of Men at San Lucas (Tepetitlan)

Approximate age.	30	55	35	65	42
Height (cm.)	156.0	158.5	161.9	165.5	165.9
Head, diameter ant.-post. max. (cm.)	17.0	18.3	18.7	18.35	19.5
Head, diameter lat. max. (cm.)	14.6	14.6	15.1	15.2	15.2
Cephalic index	85.9	79.8	80.75	82.83	78.0
Height of head from biauricular line (cm.)	13.1	12.8	13.5	12.8	13.55
Face, chin-nasion (cm.)	10.6	10.9	11.8	12.2	11.8
Face, chin-crinion (cm.)	17.3	17.5	18.8	17.1	17.0
Diam. bizygom-max. (cm.)	14.0	14.25	13.4	13.6	14.5
Diam. frontal min. (cm.)	9.9	10.2	10.1	10.1	10.7
Diam. bigonial (cm.)	9.8	10.4	10.1	10.1	11.0
Nose, height to nasion (cm.)	4.55	4.75	5.2	5.2	4.9
Nose, breadth max. (cm.)	3.75	4.25	3.9	4.25	4.25
Nasal index[38]	82.4	89.47	75.0	81.7	86.7
Mouth, breadth (cm.)	6.0	5.8	5.7	5.9	6.0
Hand, length (cm.)	16.8	18.2	17.3	18.1	17.8
Hand, breadth (cm.)	8.1	8.2	7.8	8.0	8.2
Foot, length max. (cm.)	22.8	25.6	23.6	25.4	25.2
Foot, breadth max. (cm.)	9.9	9.5	9.0	9.3	10.0

whom the Indians had more confidence than they usually have in white men, so that eventually a few were induced to return, while others were sought and measured in the cornfields. I include in full the measurements of five full-grown men, from which it will be seen that these Indians are of small stature, often with relatively broad head and face, and a quite broad and short nose, in all of which, as well as in general physical appearance, they closely approach the Tepecanos.

Tepisoake, having been reported to be also deserted, was not visited; but from what I could learn the two pueblos differ in nothing material. The only occupation of the natives of both is agriculture. All now speak Spanish, and even the old men could or would not inform me of any one who remembered any of the original language. The Indian name Tepetitlan is Nahua, as are practically all the native names in northern Jalisco and southern Zacatecas. Of Tepisoake I have not found the derivation.

Other probable remnants of the "Chichimecos."   In a shallow valley about five leagues northeast of Teul and a little more than that distance southeast of Tlaltenango, near the foot of the Cerro Chino, lie two larger and still almost wholly native pueblos, known as San Miguel and San Pedro. Both were among the settlements founded by Oñate in 1530.[39] San Pedro is the larger village, numbering over a hundred men.[40] The principal occupation of the inhabitants of both settlements is agriculture. The dwellings are similar to those at Tepetitlan; the mode of life of the people is the same throughout the region among both whites and Indians, and is as above described. The only language current today is the Spanish. Some admixture with the whites is apparent and very probably some with the Indians of Tlaltenango valley.

On account of the general disturbance caused by the suppressed revolution previously alluded to, and of the fear arising therefrom, my stay in the San Pedro district was brief. I was able to measure only four full-blood men. It would seem that the San Pedro natives in general are somewhat less brachycephalic than those of Tepetitlan; and both the San Pedro men and women, although the nose is also short and broad, appear generally to be of a somewhat more refined physical type. But there are some physiognomies that are very much like those of the natives of Tepetitlan or those of the Tepecanos. The measurements of the four men are as follows:

3.   Measurements of Men at San Pedro

Approximate age.	45	35	40	22
Height (cm.)	163.7	161.7	161.3	159.8
Head, diam. ant.-post. max. (cm.)	19.0	17.9	18.2	18.3
Head, diam. lateral max. (cm.)	15.1	14.0	14.6	14.8
Cephalic index	79.5	78.2	80.22	80.87
Height of head from biauricular line (cm.)	13.3	12.9	13.15	13.05
Face, height to nasion (cm.)	11.5	10.5	11.6	11.0
Face, height to crinion (cm.)	17.5	16.3	17.2	17.2
Face, diam. bizygom. max. (cm.)	14.4	13.2	13.8	14.1
Face, diam. frontal minim. (cm.)	10.4	9.4	10.2	9.6
Face, diam. bigonial (cm.)	10.4	10.0	9.8	10.4
Nose, height to nasion (cm.)	5.1	4.5	4.85	4.6
Nose, breadth (cm.)	4.35	4.25	4.15	3.85
Nasal index	85.3	94.4	85.6	83.7
Mouth, breadth	6.5	6.2	5.8	5.9

Cerro Chino and neighborhood. The high mountain known as Cerro Chino, which is on the road from Teul to Mixton, is a prominent landmark, being visible, except from the east, from almost every elevation from a little south of Jerez to below Teul. With Mixton it forms a part of the long and rather narrow ridge that separates the Tlaltenango from the Juchipila valley. About its base are often found stone implements, particularly arrow and spear points, as well as decorated clay whorls, potsherds, etc. The mountain itself and the level parts of the ridge seem to be devoid of extensive ruins, but I learned of the remnants of many stone *fincas* in a fold of the ridge, some distance to the eastward of Cerro Chino, probably in the slope of the Juchipila valley.

Mixton. My next visit was to the famous Cerro de Mixton, half a day's journey to the northeast of Cerro Chino, the last stand of the united natives against the invading Spaniards in 1541. The mountain is easily accessible from the land side and is not imposing. It covers a part of the flat surface of the ridge, with a moderate conical elevation near the border, bounded on the west and south by a deep barranca, while on the east its usually steep, high walls face the Juchipila valley.

So far as I was able to see or learn, there are no suggestions of the re-ported great conflict that took place here, but the area of the moun-tain is extensive and I was not able to stop long enough to explore it thoroughly. I returned from Mixton to the Cerro Chino, and, traversing a considerable part of the ridge southward, descended to the Juchipila Valley.

Ancient remains in the Juchipila Valley.   The practically unexplored district south of Juchipila, or Xuchipila, abounds with evidences of an ancient population. About three miles south of Juchipila is an elevation that projects like a wedge northward into the valley. The extremity of this elevation consists of two hills, the more northerly of which bears the peculiar name of Cerro de Chihuahua, while the other is designated Cerro de las Ventanas. Both of these hills, and especially the saddlelike concavity between them, contain many remnants of ancient habitations. On the northeastern face of the Cerro de las Ventanas, for about one-third its height from the top, is an almost perpendicular wall, in a large niche at the base of which is found the most interesting part of the ruins, namely, a regular and well-preserved cliff-house. In all probability this is the most southerly cliff-house on the continent. It resembles con-siderably some of the cliff-houses I have seen in the cañons of Utah, New Mexico, and Arizona, but it has the peculiarity of being painted on the outside. The structure measures a little more than forty feet in length and is about ten feet high. The walls are thick and are well built of selected but unhewn stones, the mortar used having apparently been of mud containing considerable lime and mixed with much broken grass. The ruin consists of but one wall, with no subdivision of the quite small cave behind it. Both faces of this wall are plastered with cement of the same kind as that used in the joints. The outer surface shows six broad vertical stripes that were once white. These stripes, which alternate with others of earth-color, equally broad, are clearly visible from the valley and for some distance toward Juchipila, and it is from their resemblance to windows that the cliff-house bears the desig-nation "Las Ventanas." The four actual openings in the wall are all small, not unlike similar openings in many of the cliff-houses and pueblos in southwestern United States. The lowest of these (door?) openings is nearly two and a half feet by slightly less than two feet in width. The three higher openings (windows?) are each about a foot and a half by a foot in height and width. The cave itself is empty and barren.

Another cave may be seen in the wall of the hill above the cliff-house, but it is not accessible by ordinary means. There are several other caves in the two hills.

The ruins between and on the hills consist mostly of low stone foundations. There are several small elevations, possibly mounds. The whole settlement was comparatively large. It is possible that these ruins are those of the original "Xuchipila," reduced by Oñate in the six-teenth century.[41]

The broad valley south of the Cerro de Chihuahua and that of Las Ventanas are covered with small elevations, and on many of these, for miles southward, are found remains of ancient occupancy. There are ruins on the Mesa de Guaje, near the Rancho de la Cantera, at several points near Pueblo Viejo, Rancho Tempiske, etc. At various places in the valley I heard of painted earthenware idols, painted bowls, stone axes, shell objects, etc., as having been found accidentally or by treas-ureseekers, but most of these objects were, as usual, broken and the rest dispersed. All that I was able to recover from the people of the valley are a single small bowl, much like some of the painted bowls from Totoate, and two interesting clay figures which remind one of similar objects from southern Jalisco and Tepic. One of these figures shows a series of nose rings in place.

During my inquiries I was repeatedly informed of bone caves and bone discoveries near the Pueblo Viejo, above mentioned, which is a moderate-sized village of mixed-blood Mexicans, a little more than ten miles south of Juchipila. On visiting this locality I found some ruins and caves, but all had been despoiled. Engaging some of the natives, I excavated at several places, and during the few days at my disposal found several old burials which yielded seven valuable skulls, as well as a few choice art objects including an onyx ceremonial axe, several cop-per nose rings, and some decorated shell ornaments. The most interest-ing object recovered, however, is a piece of a human skull with two, apparently postmortem, artificial perforations. It was in this village that I purchased the little bowl, dug out in a field some months before, that so much resembles the painted pottery from Totoate, although the two places are separated by a distance of about one hundred miles. In gen-eral character the ruins themselves are much alike in the two localities.

North of Juchipila ruins seem to be more rare, but I had only limited opportunities for personal exploration, and the ignorant natives cannot be trusted. Between the ranches of Cofradia and the large artificial lake south of it, near the road from Juchipila to Jalpa, I found a large, apparently ancient, regular, quadrilateral mound about two and a half feet high. This promising *mogote* has not yet been disturbed.

From Jalpa to Tabasco[42] the country is more sparsely populated, and I obtained no information or actual knowledge of value as to its archeology. The Juchipila Valley up to Tabasco is mostly inhabited by a mixed population, which in some localities approaches more the white, in others the Indian type. Among the more Indian physiognomies there is a general resemblance to those of Tepetitlan and San Pedro, and the skulls from near Pueblo Viejo show apparently the same type of people.

From Tabasco, continuing northward, the road leads toward Villa Nueva and the valley of La Quemada. This valley is separated from that of Juchipila by a low mountain ridge, on the southern slope of which are the ruins of another quite large ancient pueblo. There are many low stone foundations, many mounds, or *mogotes*, of stone or earth, and some walls or remnants of walls that probably once served for retaining the water and the soil. The whole ruin has thus far been left untouched by despoilers. The site of the ruin is known among the *arrieros* [mule skinners] as Guayavo. Other ruins probably exist in the mountains to the northeast and west of this place.

La Quemada

THIS GREAT ruin, favored by its situation near Zacatecas, as well as through reference to it by early historical writers, such as Torquemada, Tello, and later Frejes, has received a fair amount of scientific attention, yet thorough exploration is still desirable. The best description and plans of the ruin are those of M. Guillemin Tarayre, published in 1869.[43] The included plan by C. de Berghes is particularly valuable on account of its detail, which shows the ancient roads and many of the smaller habitations now difficult of location. During the present year L. Batres published a monograph on La Quemada[44] with some good photographic illustrations but very little new descriptive matter. Other accounts of the ruin have been published by Gutiérrez, Lyon, Esparza (Rivera's account), Burkart, and Nebel.[45] In the light of these studies, my own observations can convey but little that is new or of special value except that they may in a general way give indication of the character of the ruin as it exists today and point to certain important resemblances between it and the Totoate group as well as other ruins herein mentioned.

The Spanish name La Quemada signifies "the burnt (one)," but there is nothing now visible which justifies the name. If signs of fire in the structure existed when the Spaniards first saw it, they have disappeared, at least from the surface. Apparently Bancroft[46] is entirely correct in his opinion that "the name Quemada, 'burnt,' is that of a neighboring hacienda" and that "there is no evidence that it has any connection with the ruins," the local name of which is "Los Edificios." Yet the ruin is so generally known by the name La Quemada that the term has been retained in this paper.

The ruin is situated on a low, isolated mountain with three summits, a little south of the middle of the narrow valley which extends from the base of the mountains of the city of Zacatecas to some leagues below Villa Nueva. The mountain or hill of La Quemada is nearly thirty miles by road from Zacatecas, twelve miles north of Villa Neuva, and nearly four miles north of the Hacienda de la Quemada. From the highest point of the Cerro de los Edificios it is possible to view almost the entire valley as well as the slopes of the sierras that bound it laterally.

The ruin itself is unquestionably a remnant of the most remarkable ancient structure north of the Rio Santiago. In compactness and plan, in structural quality, and especially in differentiation of purpose, it exceeds not only the more northern Casas Grandes of Chihuahua or Zape in Durango, but also the celebrated Tula in the south. It represents a vast amount of labor and must have occupied, even with swarms of workmen, many decades in its constructon; yet the entire structure seems to show unity of plan and continuity of execution. The ruin exhibits evidence of considerable age, but notwithstanding this and some recent spoliation, such as the removal of building stones for fences, it is still remarkably well preserved and is well worthy of further archeological study.

La Quemada is not the ruin of an ordinary town, although it contained some inhabitants. It was plainly a defensive structure, and unquestionably is the most elaborate ancient fortification in northern Mexico; at the same time it probably served as a theocratic center.

The ruin consists of: 1] Some outlying structures and terraces on the south.   2] A great temple and courtyard on an artificial (or at least partly artificial) high stone terrace that runs from the main ruin hill

eastward. 3] A main pyramid, built on an artificial stone terrace on the
east of the main ruin hill, a little northward from the temple. 4] The
main ruin hill structures, built on several more or less artificial stone
terraces. 5] Two structures between the main ruin and the more south-
westerly hill. 6] A structure on the summit of the southwestern hill.
7] A structure in the depression between the northwestern and the
northern hill. 8] Fortifications. 9] Connecting avenues and diverging
roads.

1]   The outlying part of the ruin consists of a pyramidal stone
structure, now crumbling; a large, low flat terrace; a single straight row
of ruined houses extending toward the base of the main ruin hill; and
a broad, elevated avenue, paved with slabs laid flat, extending from the
low terrace to that on which stands the temple. On the lower part of
the southewestern slope of the main ruin hill are several regular, terraced rows of ruined dwellings which connect with the other outlying
structures by the single row of houses above referred to.

2]   The temple is nearly square. The walls, which are built of
selected flat stones of medium size, still reach a maximum height of ten
feet and are five to eight feet in thickness. Within the temple are
eleven, mostly well preserved, perfectly cylindrical pillars, about five feet
in diameter, built of selected smaller flat stones, laid in adobelike mortar (now largely washed out) and reaching approximately the same
height as the walls. The temple opens into a large, stone-filled court.
The walls of the latter structure are lower than those of the temple;
they are also not so thick and are not so well preserved. The row of
columns that M. Tarayre mentions as having existed here have disappeared. One particular feature which I encountered in the court is some
stone cysts, exactly like those found nearly seventy miles distant in the
"temple" at the Banco de las Casas ruin in Jalisco. Near where apparently the entrance to the temple courtyard was situated, and just at the
proximal end of the paved avenue leading from the outlying structures
to the temple, is a small, conical mound of stone. On and about this
mound, and between the stones composing it, I found a number of
fragments of pottery, among which were several with the paint-inlaid
variety of decoration such as I recovered from Totoate and as was found
at Momax, north of Tlaltenango.[47]

3]   The great pyramid stands quite isolated in a large, quadrilateral, courtlike space which opens eastward. The structure was apparently connnected with the temple by an avenue or plaza. The stones from which it is built and the manner of building are similar to those of the walls throughout the ruin. It still stands about thirty-five feet in height on a wider stone terrace from six to twelve feet high. The pyramid is quadrilateral, each side measuring sixteen meters at the base,[48] with diameter gradually diminishing toward the summit, which is blunt and partly destroyed. The sides of the structure are oriented, although not perfectly. The walls are cracked and otherwise damaged, and only a mild earthquake, fortunately rare in this region, would perhaps suffice to demolish it. At the base of the main ruin hill and nearly in line with the pyramid is a cave of moderate size, the floor of which is paved with flat stones while the walls are blackened by smoke.

At some distance from the pyramid and cave there are some small scattered ruins, and the earth is sparsely mixed with small sherds of crude as well as of a better quality of painted earthenware. A stone flake may be found now and then. The whole place is thickly overgrown with tuna, making a full view of the lower structures very difficult.

4]   The main ruin hill presents three large, more or less artificial, stone-built terraces which are barely accessible. Each of these terraces contains ruins of dwellings as well as of structures that probably served for ceremonial purposes and for assembly. Throughout the terraces the quadrilateral form of construction prevails. In one spot only, on the middle terrace, may an exception be noted in a circular, kivalike outline in the middle of one part of the ruin. The walls are always thick and are built throughout, in the same manner, of not very large, selected, more or less flat stones, the exposed face of many of which has undoubtedly been roughly fashioned, but in no case nicely hewn or rubbed down. It is probable that the stones were laid in some sort of adobe mortar, as mentioned by Tarayre and others, but if so it has weathered away. The terraces, which must have cost an immense amount of labor, are in regular but steep slopes, and are built in nearly the same manner as the walls of the various other structures.

The character of the terraces and walls is much like that of the ruins of the Totoate group and of those in southern Zacatecas, but the proportion of masonry in La Quemada is incomparably greater than that of any other ruin group. The construction in La Quemada reminds one also of that of the ruined stone-built pueblos in New Mexico and Arizona, although there are some pronounced differences between the former and the pueblo ruins of the north.

On the eastern portion of the first terrace is a ruin of a structure that consisted of a number of rooms of medium size. Farther westward are other ruins in poor condition. The middle terrace, apparently the most important one, shows high, fairly well preserved walls of large buildings which originally must have been at least two stories high. There is also a quadrilateral court, near the northern side of which is a small, flat-topped, stone-built, terraced pyramid, about ten feet high. The third terrace contains smaller ruins. On the southern slope of this part of the three-peaked mountain are, as mentioned before, five or six rows of ruined dwellings on low terraces. The very top of the main ruin hill is barren.

5]   In the shallow saddle between the mountain last mentioned and the southwestern part is the ruin of a massive quadrilateral structure, and near this is the remnant of a stone terrace.[49]

6]   The summit of the southwestern hill contains the ruin of a large stone house that must have been of more than one story and which contained several rooms. There is also near this house a pyramidal stone mound.

7]   From the ruin just mentioned an avenue, not indicated on Tarayre's plan, slightly terraced and paved, leads downward toward the northern part of the mountain. Just at the base of this part is found, on a high terrace, the well-preserved ruin of another building of moderate size. Slightly behind this building is a regular space and some low ruins.

8]   The entire northwestern hill and the whole of the northern hill are surrounded by a well-built defensive stone wall, ten feet broad (and even broader at the northwest), and in places from ten to twelve feet high. Formerly, according to Tarayre's plan, a similar wall extended also along the northern side of the southwestern hill, but today only traces of this remain. Some rude breastworks are intact on the western slope of the main ruin hill, commanding the saddle between this and that on the west; and there are various other structures which probably served as fortifications. Wherever the walls of fortifications end, the mountain presents either steep or totally inaccessible sides, or the bulwarks of the stone-built terraces. Altogether there rises before the visitor an imposing, massive, walled fortress of stone, not unlike some of the feudal strongholds of medieval Europe.

9]   Besides the avenue leading from the outlying works to the temple, that from the temple to the great pyramid (now traceable only with difficulty), and that leading from the ruin on the top of the southwestern hill to the one at the base of the northern part of the mountain, there can be made out, especially after the first rains of the wet season, owing to the difference in the color of the earth and other signs, several roads radiating from La Quemada in various directions. On occasions, I was informed, these roads can be traced for considerable distances.[50]

Nowhere in or about La Quemada have I found petroglyphs[51] or worked slabs of stone, such as are common at Totoate. Potsherds and stone flakes may be found almost everywhere about the ruin, but they are in no place abundant and at many points are scarce. Aside from the fragments of pottery above mentioned a day's search resulted in no important find.

With La Quemada the stone ruins of southern Zacatecas and the neighboring region practically end. It appears as if this structure was built through the combined efforts of a great people living farther southward and possibly including the entire population of the valley of Juchipila, Tlaltenango, and Rio de Bolaños, as a protection against northern invaders. The great ruined fort and *teocalli* can not be separated culturally from those to the south and southwest of it. The inlaid and painted pottery, the ceremonial axes, some of the idols, the ordinary axes (pictured by Batres), the peculiar stone cysts near the temple, the form of the stone structures, all connect it more immediately with Totoate, Momax, Teul, and other ruins referred to in this paper, than with those of any other region. There is some resemblance in type between the ruins of La Quemada and those at Zape and its vicinity (there are small stone ruins as far as Santa Catarina de los Tepehuanes), but from Zape to La Quemada, without any known connecting link in the way of ruins, there lies a stretch of nearly three hundred miles. There is also typical relation with more southerly ruins, but the first attention is claimed by those in the vicinity.

I TRUST that this account, superficial and imperfect as it necessarily is, will stimulate further and more extended research in the country of the "Chichimecs," a country hitherto supposed to be barren. As to the physical anthropology of this part of northern Mexico I shall have something more definite to present when the elaboration of my somatological material is completed.

In conclusion I feel obliged to refer, in a few words more, to the treasure hunters in Mexico. There is no law to restrain such people, yet they destroy each year more ancient remains of every description than do the elements and all other sources combined. Wherever I searched for osteological or other remains of the ancient people, I encountered traces of this vandalism. As spoliation is here very largely due to ignorance, the Mexican civil authorities, men of science, clericals, and newspapers could do much good to local archeology by inspring a proper regard for these interesting monuments and for the objects connected with them.

6

Late Archaeological Sites in Durango, Mexico, from Chalchihuites to Zape

J. Alden Mason

This article is another illustration of the vast range of interest and ability that characterized the work of J. Alden Mason. The archaeological reconnaissance, which provided the data for the article by Mason, was carried out in the Mexican states of Durango and Zacatecas in 1935, incidental to a largely unsuccessful search for Paleo-Indian sites. The article itself brought to the attention of American archaeologists the existence of peripheral Mesoamerican cultural remains in north central Mexico. Mason conceptualized the existence of a more or less coherent Mesoamerican culture in the area ranging from Chalchihuites, in western Zacatecas, northward to Zape in northwestern Durango, and named it the "Chalchihuites Culture." More recent archaeological work in this region has confirmed the existence of the Chalchihuites Culture and has shown that it developed first in western Zacatecas, beginning at about A.D. 200, and then expanded northward into Durango and along the eastern foothills of the Sierra Madre Occidental almost to the southern boundary of the state of Chihuahua. Mason pointed out that the culture had disappeared before the Spanish conquest of the area. Recent work confirms this conclusion and suggests that the Chalchihuites Culture disappeared about A. D. 1350.

The Mason article stimulated much later research in the area and is used by most contemporary archaeologists working in northern Mexico as the primary and basic source for the archaeology of Durango and western Zacatecas. However, Mason did not realize that there were two ceramic cultures—Chalchihuites and the somewhat simpler "peasant" Loma San Gabriel Culture—represented in the area. Actually, what Mason described and illustrated as a possible ball court is now known to represent one of the residential compounds of a Loma San Gabriel site. Mason also

erred in including the great site of La Quemada in the Chalchihuites Culture—but archaeologists currently working in the Zacatecas area did not themselves discover that La Quemada belonged
with a separate (Malpaso-Juchipila) peripheral Mesoamerican
culture until recently! Actually, the Mason article not only is of
historic interest because of its relation to later archaeological work
in the Zacatecas-Durango area but also has value even today as a
general introduction to the archaeology of the region.

J. C. K.

THE FIRST four months of 1936 I spent in archaeological researches
in northern Mexico, mainly in the State of Durango and a little in adjacent parts of Coahuila. The expedition was one of three financed by
a grant from the American Philosophical Society, the main purpose of
all three being a search for traces of most ancient man in America with
an emphasis on the Folsom Horizon. The official concession from the
Mexican Government granted permission only for excavations in caves,
old lake terraces, and such presumably ancient sites, and excavations in
more recent sites were not allowed. However, since the more recent
archaeology of the region visited is practically unknown, superficial
observations were made on all sites heard of, and surface collections of
potsherds and other objects and notes and plans of the principal sites
were made. The results of the cave investigations, which, although this
work occupied the greater part of the time, were unfortunately not great
or important; of the linguistic researches and of the notes upon petroglyphs, are reserved for future publications, but the data upon the late
Pre-Columbian sites are here presented, by and with the kind permission of the American Philosophical Society.

The type site of this region, and the southernmost site visited by
the expedition, is that of Chalchihuites in the northwest of the State of
Zacatecas, just over the border from the State of Durango. This is the
northernmost archaeological site in the Mexican highlands that is scientifically known until one reaches the region of Casas Grandes, of
Puebloan affiliations, in the State of Chihuahua. Here Dr. Manuel
Gamio[1] made excavations in 1908, and Sr. Eduardo Noguera[2] at a later
period. The site is, however, far from completely excavated, and the culture only superficially known. Nearby are other unexcavated sites, such
as those of the Cerro de Moctezuma or Montedehuma.[3]

The excavated ruins at Alta Vista, Chalchihuites, are impressive though not large. There are mounds, courts, plazas, plastered stairways and other features that definitely connect the builders with the cultures of southern Mexico. Especially is there a large hall with many round columns of plastered masonry that evidently supported a roof. This and many other features demonstrate an especially close connection with the larger and better-known site of La Quemada[4] in Zacatecas not far to the southeast. Both ruins are built of rude stone slabs originally covered with plaster, the plaster at La Quemada having practically disappeared. The latter is a very large ruin, apparently primarily a fortress, covering a high hill, the walls standing far above ground level. Chalchihuites is a smaller site, and most of the features, including the columns, were not evident until after excavation.

As one travels northward in Mexico the cultural level of the archaeology gradually diminishes; investigations establish this expected fact. At one site after another certain features found further to the south have disappeared. La Quemada is culturally poorer than the Valley of Mexico, Chalchihuites poorer than La Quemada. All these sites have yet to be tied up with their proper tribes and cultures; they are still too little investigated for any stratigraphical researches to have been made, and whatever deductions are made as to tribal and cultural affinities and relative age must be done on purely comparative grounds. On the whole, La Quemada and Chalchihuites certainly pertain to the same culture, but certain features present at La Quemada, such as stone pyramids, seem to be missing at Chalchihuites. Noguera, with good reason and probably correctly, believes this culture to be a peripheral and slightly degraded phase of the Tarascan culture, which is centered in Michoacán and southern Jalisco.

We may here anticipate a little and state that our expedition found, north of Chalchihuites, no stone masonry that we could identify as Pre-Columbian.

Except for pottery, there is such slight differentiation in small artifacts that these can in few cases be used as criteria for the identification of culture phases. For instance, from the Tarascan region northward the stone axes are grooved or semigrooved, in contradistinction to the ungrooved axes characteristic of south-central Mexico. Pottery, with its infinite number of possible variations, is the best criterion for culture distinctions, and most of the present article will be concerned with pottery.

Unfortunately the pottery types of La Quemada are but slightly known; the only collection of pottery made there, by Batres, has unfortunately disappeared. That of Chalchihuites is well known, from the excavations of Gamio and Noguera. Pottery from small neighboring sites is known from the excavations of Hrdlička and Lumholtz.[5]

At Chalchihuites, three main types of pottery are found, painted, carved or incised, and inlaid or cloisonné. The latter is very peculiar ware, unique and of limited distribution. An ornate design is carved out on the surface of the vessel to an appreciable depth, and then filled in with mastic in many colors; the latter are in soft pastel shades and the result quite agreeable. While the technique is undoubtedly related to the lacquered gourd work done by the Tarascan Indians today, the designs and general effect are much more reminiscent of Teotihuacan frescoes, and I believe the ware to be intimately related to Toltec. The shapes of the vessels are also different from those employed with the other wares. At Chalchihuites they are mainly annular-based cups and bowls, the designs mainly geometric, while at Estanzuela, near Guadalajara, they are mainly round-bottom ollas, the designs of naturalistic panels with human figures. Noguera says that this ware is not found at La Quemada, but both Hrdlička and I have picked up sherds of it there. The present expedition found no fragment of this ware anywhere, and Chalchihutes may be accepted as its approximate northern boundary. It probably has a cultural horizon and geographical distribution different from the other wares, but unassignable at the present.

Incised or carved decoration is generally, if not always, found in a band around the rims of tripod bowls; the design was apparently carved after the vessel had been baked, the bowls generally have a black surface, and the incised designs are often painted with another color. This type of ware is not recorded at La Quemada, but probably should be found there. Examples of it are common at Chalchihuites, and a few examples were found or seen by the expedition at several places further north.

The most characteristic ware of Chalchihuites is one with red or brown designs painted on a buff or cream base. The designs are generally small and dainty with rather fine lines and dots, generally geometric and most frequently curvilinear, but conventionalized animal figures are also found. The ware is usually thin, highly polished, and on the whole an excellent ceramic type. It is found mainly on shallow bowls, tripod bowls, and small-necked round-bottom jars or *ollas*. This ware may be found at La Quemada but seems to be not typical of that site, as it is of Chalchihuites.

As regards peculiarities of shape, the rims of the Chalchihuites tripod bowls are often raised and perforated at two opposite points, apparently for suspension. The feet are rather short but not mammiform, and apparently solid. The tripod bowls from La Quemada seem to be a little different in shape.

Potsherds of the typical Chalchihuites brown-on-buff ware were collected on the surface at three sites in Durango State, which therefore pertained, at least at one period of their occupation, to the Chalchihuites Culture. None is large enough to afford much of an idea of the shape of the vessel, but most of them seem to be parts of bowls, the decoration either on the exterior or interior; in one case it is on both. The average thickness is from .5 to 1 cm. and the extremes 2 mm. to either side of this. Several of the sherds, apparently from bowls, indicate two surfaces meeting at an angle with rather sharp edge; the interior is rounded, producing unusual thickness at the junction angle. [One] is a fragment of a leg or handle, of oval cross-section. Five sherds . . . are from Antonio Amaro; the first . . . is from Cueva Susana, the other four from Pueblito; four [others] . . . were secured at Los Remedios.

Los Remedios and Pueblito are suburbs of the city of Durango which lies, in a straight line, about 100 kilometers or 62 miles northwest of Chalchihuites. The sites, however, differ considerably in nature. The Cerro de Los Remedios is a high, rocky, and rather precipitous hill about 100 m. high, just on the outskirts of the city. Except at the base, the earth is shallow and in pockets between the rocks. Possibly all the objects found on the slopes had washed down from the summit. Unfortunately here is a church, the hill was fortified during the French occupation and whatever aboriginal structures there may have been were destroyed. Nearby residents reported that there formerly were lines of stones outlining aboriginal structures, and that skeletons, complete pottery vessels, stone axes and other similar objects had been found there. A permanent stream flows by the base of the hill, and most of the finds were apparently made near the foot, though we picked up a number of typical sherds on the summit. Among these there seem to be a larger number than usual of vessel legs, handles, and types other than fragments of simple vessels.

Pueblito is a village about 5 km. south of Durango City. Near here is a large surface site close to the Rio de Tunal, a permanent stream. The ground is relatively flat on a natural terrace above the stream. The soil has been ploughed for years and all traces of structures of any kind obliterated. A road has been cut through the deposit to a depth of some 2 m., and in the cut potsherds, stones, and flint and obsidian chips may be found to a depth of at least 1.85 m. They are very infrequent, however, especially towards the base, and in the opinion of Mr. Merrill the earth is 90 percent wind-blown loess. It contains, however, many large stones that must have been brought in. The few sherds recovered from the lowest layers show no obvious differentiation from those on the surface. Most of the specimens were picked up on the surface of the ploughed fields. In addition to the potsherds, fragments of metates and metate manos, other stones, and flint and obsidian chips were found. Undecorated pottery predominates, but there is a good amount of typical Chalchihuites brown-on-buff ware, and lesser amounts of other types of decorated ware. Some of the sherds are thick, up to 2 cm. in thickness. A number of tripod legs and some long handles were secured.

Villa Antonio Amaro is a new town about 70 km. northeast of Durango City and 80 north of Chalchihuites. At Las Peñitas, about two miles from the town, is a large horseshoe-shaped valley with a large spring at the bottom. In many places on the crest and upper gentle slopes are seen traces of aboriginal sites. These are, as throughout this entire region from here north to Zape, straight lines of stones interred so as to form rectangular sites of various proportions and sizes. I think I remember sites of the same type as far south as Azqueltan in Jalisco. The stones are laminated slabs, interred vertically so that only their tops show above the surface, and interred to a depth of about 40 cm. Few of the rectangular sites are entirely complete, one or two sides being often missing or unidentifiable, and the interior is most often on the same level as the ground outside. The dimensions of some of these sites were measured as 4.5 x 3.5 m., 5 x 5 m., and 5 x 10 m.

The sites are on terraces on the sloping hillside. The lines of the sites are approximately parallel, with the longest sides approximately on a magnetic north-south line. Many sherds were picked up on the surface, especially where earlier excavations had been made, and excavations were made in several sites which had already been dug into. Sherds were found to a depth of 1 m., as well as fragments of metates and metate manos, and scattered human and animal bones. Some shallow mortar holes, about 15 cm. wide and 4 cm. deep, were seen in rocks. The metates are shallow and not well made, relatively rectangular, troughed and without legs. The manos, of heavy lava, are relatively symmetrical and thin, two measuring 18 x 11 x 5 cm., and 20 x 10 x 4 cm. The used surfaces are slightly convex, the upper surfaces more so.

Two types of objects are clearly shown in the sherds from these three sites, tripod bowls and long handles to some object. The tripod legs are characteristic. They are solid and relatively short. Several, from Antonio Amaro and Remedios, are relatively small and taper to wedge-shaped bases. These seem to be from plain black or buff vessels, and approach the form that seems to be typical of Chalchihuites. Most of them are massive and quasi-conical, and all seem to possess a characteristic knob or enlargement near their tops on the outer side. One of these, from Remedios, is from a typical red-on-buff Chalchihuites ware vessel; the others are more rudely painted in red and buff. Another, from Antonio Amaro, is of carved gray ware. Two fragments of handles from Remedios would seem to be from "basket" handles, as they have relief knobs and brown-on-buff painted designs on the convex side; they may be ladle handles, however. The stem of a tobacco pipe was found at Pueblito. This is short and broad with a flat base and narrow shaft; the bowl was apparently low and circular.

Other types of ware were found at these sites. At Antonio Amaro were found three examples of carved gray ware, in one of which the triangles had been filled in with red paint. In another the raised section of the rim with the perforated hole that is characteristic of Chalchihuites is seen. At Pueblito several unusual wares were found, a fragment of finely incised black pottery and one of buff ware with decorative knobs. The most unique ware, however, is represented by a series of sherds with a dark red surface and designs painted in white lines, generally fine and parallel. Also, in addition to unpainted or plain red sherds, some were found of red-on-buff ware, but the lines are thicker and the designs simpler and more rectilinear than in the typical Chalchihuites ware.

To summarize, at all three sites typical Chalchihuites red-on-buff pottery was found. At all sites pottery of other types of ware was found, but at Antonio Amaro none seems to be of a type not already known at Chalchihuites, while at Remedios and especially at Pueblito wares and shapes are found that are apparently foreign to Chalchihuites. The origin of these is at present unknown.

The next site observed, going northward, was at Guatimapé, on the west side of Lake Santiaguillo about 90 km. north of Durango City. Here, in the valley of the Canyon Molino, are many house sites by a permanent stream. These are mainly rectangular and outlined by buried stones as at Antonio Amaro, often in terraces one above and behind another. Some of these terraced sites are up to 9 x 15 m. in size. There are also some smaller round sites 2.5 to 3 m. in diameter made of larger boulders. There are the ruins of a rude rectangular masonry structure about 7.2 x 4.2 m. in size with walls built of massive stones 60 cm. thick to a present height of about 1.5 m., but we could not certify it as being aboriginal. Parts of the site were retained by stone walls. Many manos and metates were found, some small rude animal figures of lava, and a few potsherds, including one ladle handle of red-on-buff ware. The metate fragments found indicated that they were trough-shaped, without legs. The manos are of lava or granite, quasi-rectangular, and rather thin with one or both faces convex.

At Hervideros, some 150 km. in a straight line northwest of Durango, is a large site that has been considerably dug. It occupies much of the top and slopes of a large high hill that overlooks the Nazas River; at its base is a spring of boiling water. Here are many rectangular sites outlined by lines of stones interred to almost their full length. Most of these lines are parallel, with their long axes up and down the slope, and often with a low retaining wall at the lower end. There are also some smaller round enclosures ringed with larger stones and lava boulders. At the top of the hill is a small rocky mesa, and the larger and "richer" sites are near this top. Many of these sites have been partially excavated and the objects secured demonstrate a high degree of culture. Tripod bowls of typical Chalchihuites shape with the rim up-curved in two places, each perforated by a small hole, and with vertical legs converging to a wedge are found in plain black and in black with carved decorations, filled with red. Ornate copper ear-ornaments and shell ornaments decorated with incised circles with central dot, fine obsidian flaked and chipped blades, copper bells and other ornaments, a finely carved human figure of bone, beads of shell or bone, stone axe-heads and larger objects of carved stone, conical and biconical pottery spindle whorls and a figurine of black pottery have been found here. The culture was evidently of a high grade, and all its details connect it with that of Chalchihuites. No sherd or object of the typical red-on-buff painted ware was seen but we were told that painted pottery had been found there; nevertheless, it is certainly not characteristic. The site is obviously, however, typical of one phase of the Chalchihuites Culture.

The town of Zape lies at a distance of some 225 km. northwest of Durango City. It was the northernmost site examined by the expedition, not far south of the border of Chihuahua. Three late Pre-Columbian sites were examined in this region. The site reported on by Guillemin Tarayre in *Exploration Minéralogique des Régions Mexicaines,* Paris, 1869, is at Santa Ana, a few miles south of Zape. Owing to the fact that this site has been the only one known between Chalchihuites in Zacatecas and Casas Grandes in Chihuahua, undue importance has always been given it. Tarayre's report is not incorrect, if read critically, but his plan of the site in his plate 3 is greatly idealized, especially as regards the regularity and height of the mounds. We were much disappointed in this site. The ploughings of the last seventy years may have altered it considerably, however.

A plan of the present appearance of Santa Ana (Zape), accurately drawn by Mr. Robert H. Merrill, is shown as fig. 3 *b* [in the original publication]. This should be compared with the plan of Tarayre. The site of Santa Ana is, like all sites in this region, a high hill partly surrounded by a bend in the river; the slope is slight. As one nears the top he becomes aware of low terraces and of lines of interred stones like those seen further south. The unbroken lines at present are never more than a few feet long nor the terrace fronts more than two feet high. One line of nine stones in a row is 2.5 m. long. Some of the terraces appeared to be about 7.5 m. in length. The stones used in this region are always elongated water-worn river boulders.

The most important features are at the crest of the hill. Here is a rectangular court about 15 x 20 m. in size, surrounded by mounds of about 1.5 m. maximum height, more or less as indicated in Tarayre's plan, but it is not clear whether there were four separate mounds or whether some of these coalesced. Considerable excavation had been done in these mounds, but apparently no masonry was revealed. The masonry structure noted by Tarayre in the center of the court had disappeared, and it is impossible now to determine whether it was Pre- or Post-Columbian.

Several other sites of similar nature were examined in this region, all on hills partly surrounded by bends in rivers. All consist of rectangular enclosures outlined by lines of stones buried vertically and projecting slightly above the surface. One such, containing a few such sites, is across the river from the town of Zape Chico. The largest and most undisturbed site found is on the Arroyo Quelites, about two hours' walk northeast of Zape. About twenty such rectangular sites were observed here; most of them are small, from 3 x 4 to 4 x 6 m., but a few as large as 10 x 12 and 10 x 17 m. were observed. In most, the soil level within is slightly raised, but even in the case of the largest mounds the height is not over 1 m. The largest mounds often have transverse lines of stones, especially one dividing them into equal halves. Most of the stone lines are parallel and in all cases but one the long axis is approximately north and south. There is one depressed plaza or court about 16 x 12 m. in size with a low mound at the west side, higher ground to east and north, but the same level to the south. At the corners of certain stone lines tall upright stones had been placed; similar stones were placed at shrines much further south near Azqueltan in Jalisco.

Excavations were made in one mound that had already been partially dug, and potsherds were collected here and on the surface. In the excavation several broken large metates were found and quite a number of metate manos; these must have been purposely interred here. The metates are trough-shaped and large, about 50 x 40 cm.; the manos resemble the type of the American Southwest, relatively rectangular and thin with one convex surface. Two of these measured 25 x 11 x 5.5 and 18 x 10 x 6.5 cm.

The potsherds found in all of these sites are distinctly inferior to those of Hervideros and further south. No examples of cloisonné, carved, incised, or of fine red-on-buff ware were found, and we may be certain that this region is beyond the limits of those wares. Most of the sherds are monochrome, gray or buff with a minority of bright red. A few painted sherds were found. The colors are the same as at Chalchihuites, red-on-buff, but the designs are much ruder and the proportional quantity much less. Several objects that are apparently the legs of tripod vessels were found; these are solid, rude, and quasi-cylindrical. The stem of a tobacco pipe was found very similar to that from Pueblito, but larger and with a much larger orifice, and a half of a broken, black, quasi-hemispherical pottery spindle whorl was given to us as having been found at Santa Ana. Tales were of course heard of finds of fine unusual objects, such as gold ornaments, but these are not credible. No noteworthy artifact from this region was seen. Beads were made of tubular pieces of hollow bone. Excellent stone bowls and fine grooved axeheads were made.

The type of the house sites, rectangular and outlined by deeply interred vertical stones, is almost identical throughout the entire region visited, indicating that the basic culture is the same. The presence of tripod vessels and hemispherical spindle whorls in the Zape region indicates that the culture there was basically Mexican. We may therefore deduce that the general Chalchihuites-La Quemada Culture extended north to the region of Zape. At this point, however, it had become attenuated and peripheral, and had lost much of its fine quality.

Probably the culture did not extend far, if any, north of the Zape region. It is only about 350 miles, air line, from here to Casas Grandes, a region of certain Puebloan affinities, and only about 100 miles to the southern boundary of the Medanos phase of the Chihuahua Culture, as given by Sayles.[5] At this latter point Sayles saw no clear evidences of Mexican influences. Nor does the culture extend far to east or west. To the east it has disappeared long before one reaches the city of Torreon, two hundred kilometers to the northeast, and to the west it is only a short distance to the high mountains, where a slightly different and lower culture must have obtained.

Some researches were pursued in the high pine-covered mountains of the Sierra Madre Occidental to the west, in the region of Sotolitos, about 120 km. northwest of Durango City. Sites are rare and small in this region. Two small ones were seen, on both of which are rectangular small low mounds outlined by stones interred vertically, and extending just above the surface, like those seen at all other sites, and presumably of the same basic culture. At both places, however, structures of another nature were observed. These consist of an open depressed oblong court or plaza bounded on each long side by a long mound of stones. The ends of the court are open and the level depressed area extends as an apron beyond the flanking stone mounds. The resemblance to a primitive type of Mexican ball-court is obvious. Potsherds are rare on these sites, but a few were picked up, all small and weather-worn. The shapes are apparently all simple, and none shows at present any trace of painting or decoration. While the culture, judging from the stone-lined sites, must have been somewhat similar at basis to that of Chalchihuites, it must have been even more peripheral and simple than that of Zape.

Technological Ceramic Analysis and Deductions

A THOROUGH qualitative analysis of the pottery fragments secured was made by the Ceramic Laboratory of the University Museum, sponsored by the Works Progress Administration, Project No. 2232, and a complete technical report was submitted by the leader, Mr. Donald Horton. Naturally only a digest of this report can be given here. Of several hundred sherds available, half of the total having been retained by the Mexican government, some sixty-three were analyzed qualitatively. The selection included sherds of all obviously different wares from all of the sites visited, not only the ten open sites above described, but other open sites and many caves, about twenty-five in all.

From a general point of view the study was disappointing inasmuch as it revealed no clear-cut distinctions between any sites or any types of ware, no criteria by which any geographical or cultural boundaries or divisions could be established; no sherd could be assigned to any site or category on the basis of its technical peculiarities. However, certain peculiarities suggest that, had the study been pursued on a larger scale, and with more specimens, and particularly had the quantitative phase been investigated, such criteria might have been deduced.

The paste is composed of clays of sedimentary origin, generally bentonite, containing minute fragments of volcanic glass in different stages of alteration. Quartz, feldspar, and fragments of volcanic rock are common intrusive elements, and all are abundant in most specimens. Quartz is present in proportions of 5 to 13 percent. Feldspar occurs in two forms: plagioclase, which is more common in the mountain sites, and orthoclase in the valley sites. The temper employed is pulverized potsherds in the open sites; sherd temper is generally lacking in pottery from the caves. About 60 percent of the sherds have black cores, indicating incomplete oxidation or firing; with very few exceptions the sherds have not been fully oxidized. The typical colors of the paste, the unoxidized black cores, are mouse gray and drab. The oxidized band between the surface and the dark core is narrow and of the same color as the surface, unless paint has been applied. The paint colors vary from brick red to ferruginous. The oxidized bands and unpainted surfaces show a color range from testaceous to mouse gray. Typical colors are wood brown and cinnamon. Exceptional colors are ocher red and terra cotta.

The average surface hardness is remarkably high, 5.5 to 6, the range being from 3 to 7. The inclusions (quartz, feldspar, and volcanic rock) are moderate to sparse in quantity and of medium size; the texture would be considered as medium and the surface texture smooth. The core is dull, the surfaces dull to lustrous; many are polished. Relatively few of the sherds have a true slip, although most of them have the superficial appearance of such, due to thorough smoothing and polishing.

A possible reconstruction of the technology of the sherds may be outlined as follows: The sedimentary clays were tempered with moderate to coarse sand, composed of the debris from volcanic rocks and, except at some of the mountain cave sites, with crushed sherds of local or trade ware. The wares were mostly well polished. They were fired at an intermediate temperature, which brought the surface very close to complete oxidation. The dark cores which are characteristic in this pottery may have been due to firing conditions, but there is a possibility that the low fusion point and density of the clays prevented oxidation of the core. Certain of the wares were slipped with a coat of unrefined clay and subsequently painted. A dark line marking the contact of slip and body in several cases suggests that the ware may have been fired both before and after application of the surface coating. Where the slip is of fine texture the applied paint has penetrated only slightly; in other cases the paint has penetrated through the slip. Certain sherds are entirely painted, although it is difficult to decide whether the applied surface should best be described as a thick ocher paint, or a relatively fluid ferruginous slip.

More specifically, a comparison of the sherds from Antonio Amaro with a few secured at the type site of Chalchihuites shows a close technical resemblance. The sherds from Antonio Amaro can be divided into two groups on the basis of composition. The red-on-buff ware, which is both slipped and painted, seems to be composed of a clay slightly different in character from that used in certain other sherds. The latter are less dense, more flaky, are not clearly bentonitic in character, and contain few if any microorganisms; the inclusions differ in quantity. The sherds from Pueblito are not bentonitic in character and contain non-microorganisms. The unique white-on-red pottery differs only in having a slightly finer texture; it was presumably, therefore, a ware of local manufacture, not imported. The sherds from Zape (Santa Ana and Quelites) are relatively homogeneous and not very different from those further south. They are of relatively coarse texture, of a flaky clay without clear bentonitic structure. The birefringence is relatively high, in which characteristic they differ from the sherds from the southern sites. A specific characteristic of the Santa Ana sherds is the presence of thick plates of biotite, and occasional grains of other ferromagnesian minerals.

The sherds from the caves are characterized by a moderately coarse texture, flaky clay, an average hardness of 6, and an absence of sherd temper, with a few exceptions. Those from caves in the high Sierra are very similar to those from the caves near Zape; these have a high birefringence, and an abundance of plagioclase, rock fractures and tuff. One from a cave near Torreon has a low birefringence, and lacks rock fractures and tuff.

7

A Brief and Succinct Account of the Events of the War with the Tepehuanes, Government of Nueva Vizcaya, from November 15, 1616 to May 16, 1618

Charles Wilson Hackett

Between the years 1923 and 1937, Latin American historian Charles Wilson Hackett published three volumes of manuscript materials relating to northern Mexico and the Spanish Southwest. These volumes, appearing under the title *Historical Documents Relating to New Mexico, Nueva Vizcaya, and Approaches Thereto, to 1773*, were part of a corpus of material extracted from Spanish archives by Adolph F. and Fanny R. Bandelier in the years 1913–14 and (following A. F. Bandelier's death in 1914) by F. R. Bandelier in 1914–15. The collection covers a vast range of subjects and is a rich source for the history of this large area. In bringing out the material, Hackett added valuable annotations and translated the documents, using parallel pages of Spanish and English.

One of the Bandelier documents is a chronological account of the great Tepehuán rebellion that flared up, violently and suddenly, in late 1616, and kept the Nueva Vizcaya area in turmoil until mid-1618. The account, though written completely from the Spanish point of view, and with a great deal of righteous indignation, gives the only reasonably complete account of a rebellion which, for a year or so, threatened Spain's insecure hold on her Northwest Provinces. Other Indian groups, however, failed to rise in concert with the Tepehuán and the latter were crushed after considerable loss of life on both sides. Nueva Vizcaya was pacified and Spanish rule in Northwest Mexico was not seriously threatened again until the borderland revolts of the late seventeenth century.

B. C. H.
C. L. R.

IT IS now a year and a half since this war began, and it is perforce true that since it had such severe and deliberate beginnings it will not be easy to conclude. These Tepehuanes were induced to apostatize through instinct and the persuasion of the devil. They set up an idol; they were governed by wizards; and, in order better to establish their new project, although they are numerous and extend over many leagues of New Spain, they at once attempted, for greater security, to convoke all the other nations of that jurisdiction. They were so astute and clever in this movement that there scarcely remains in the entire government (which is almost 250 leagues long and nearly as wide) anyone who has not taken part in the uprising.

As soon as this occurred investigations were made of the situation, from which it appeared that for three or four years they had been formulating revolutionary plans, which afterwards they put into execution on November 15, 1616. Their first scheme was to attack all the ports and towns of the government at the same time, and if God our Lord had not distracted them from this design by the prospect of stealing a quantity of clothing and merchandise which they came upon on the road to Topia, which served to give warning of the day set, there is no doubt but that the damage would have been irreparable. Indeed on various occasions and days they committed many murders and robberies and burned villages; for six or seven months they kept the field, attacking in all directions, until finally the viceroy of New Spain was able to send sufficient assistance in the form of some captains and soldiers who aided those who were here. As a result the war has gone against them.

The governor, Don Gaspar de Albear, as soon as he heard of so great a movement, learning by investigations which were made that the chief purpose of the Tepehuanes was to destroy the villa of Guadiana, capital of the jurisdiction, for which purpose the Tepehuane villages round about Guadiana were united and agreed, adopted a plan to forestall them, and thereby gained an advantage over them. In order to do this he concealed his design, and under pretext of fortifying the government buildings, had the principal Tepehuanes called together before they should declare the revolt. On Monday, November 21, 1616, in consideration of the seriousness of the situation, he called upon the factor, Rafael de Gascue, appointed on the preceding day *maestro de campo* and lieutenant-captain-general—he being the most experienced person available—to seize craftily the governors, caciques, and principal men of the Indians. This he did very cleverly, securing seventy-five of the most warlike ones, all of whom confessed that it was true that on the following Tuesday, November 22, they were to attack and destroy Guadiana. These Indians were apprehended at about six o'clock in the afternoon. Most of them were [placed] in the government buildings, some in stocks, others bound, while a few were [placed] in the jail.

About nine o'clock that evening a very loud alarm was sounded in Guadiana, a town of about one hundred Spanish settlers. The confusion was terrible, for those who came in from the outside said that more than two thousand Indians with bows and arrows were coming. The few Spaniards who were there took the forewarning and killed nearly all the prisoners, only five or six being left alive, and these were hanged the next day, Tuesday, at the hour appointed for their uprising. Some of them died as Christians, confessing the projected general uprising. One chief named Don Marcos, one of the principal leaders of the revolt, would by no means make a confession, and voluntarily sprang from the gallows. Their bodies were placed upon all the roads, and the remaining Indians lost courage and counsel and fled to the mountains.

By this means the danger which threatened Guadiana was relieved somewhat, and the governor was enabled to take the field, which he did, with the largest number of men he could muster; these were poorly armed, because the idleness of peace had resulted in neglect of the weapons. He set out on December 19 of the same year, having first hung a spy who was caught on November 27, as he was coming to reconnoitre the villa and ascertain its condition in order that a troop of eight hundred Indians on foot and fourteen mounted, led by an Indian named Pablo, might attack it on the morning of the next day, the twenty-eighth. These Indians were in ambush at El Jaral, a secret rendezvous two leagues from Guadiana. However, upon the death of their spy they gave up the plan.

On the twentieth of the same month, before dawn, the governor reached the *estancia* of La Sauceda without being seen or his presence being known by the enemy. At this *estancia*, which is nine leagues from Guadiana, many people were gathered and these were many times attacked furiously by the enemy. On the twenty-first, eight hundred Tepehuanes, believing that the governor had not reached the *estancia*, came to pillage it. Our men on seeing them and thinking that they were few, went out to meet them without order or plan. The Indians for their part cautiously retired toward the mountains, where, having the bulk of their number in ambush, they attacked the Spaniards. As a result the fighting was without system and our men were subjected to considerable risk. A Spaniard named Herrera was killed; he was carried off by the Indians, there being no help for it, since he was not missed until some time after he was gone. Seven or eight other Spaniards were wounded. Our men killed fourteen of the vagabonds but did not wound many. With this, the Tepehuanes for the time being disappeared.

Bad news of murders, robberies, and incendiarisms came from all sides, especially from Guanacebi, the most important mining camp in the kingdom of Nueva Vizcaya, and situated in the centre of the Tepehuane country. There the citizens of that town were in great danger from the horde of Indians, who diabolically attacked them many times. These citizens asked for the most prompt assistance, announcing that they could hold out for only twelve or thirteen days, since they had no food or munitions of war. Whereupon the governor held a council of war with the captains and the most experienced soldiers, all of whom were of the opinion that help should be sent, but that under no circumstance should the governor take it to them on account of the risk he personally and his people would run; for, if he should have misfortune, as was likely on account of the few men which he had, and the governor and his soldiers should be lost, the kingdom itself would be lost. But the governor, realizing that if he did not go in person there would be no one to take the assistance, and that it was a great pity that one hundred persons in Guanacebi, in such great danger, should perish, resolved, quite properly, to go himself. And some persons, who until then had held an opposite opinion and who had given weak excuses for not going, no longer opposed accompanying him. It therefore turned out that those who went did so because they saw that the governor was going.

He set out from La Sauceda on December 30 to go to succor San Juan del Río, the mines of Indehe [Indé?], and those of Guanacebi. He arrived at San Juan at nine o'clock on the night of the same day. Leaving eight soldiers to garrison this town, he set out on January 1, 1617, and arrived at the mines of Indehe [Indé?] on January 7. There he collected victuals and cattle to take along, and flour which the *alcalde mayor* of Santa Bárbara, with the help of one hundred Conchos Indians, brought to him.

He set out [from the mines of Indehe] on the twelfth and reached Guanacebi on the fifteenth with the arms and ammunition. Cutting his way through the midst of the enemy he found all of the people assembled in the church and in four adjacent houses in the last stage of resistance, for the enemy had already burned all the place and the equipment for taking out silver. Their provisions had failed, and they were eating the dogs and cats. The governor comforted them all, praising them for their endurance, and gave them three hundred quintals of flour which he had brought them, six hundred cows, and four hundred fanegas of corn. Leaving them a presidio with twenty-five soldiers, powder, and munitions, he set out on Sunday, January 22, for a town named San Ignacio, otherwise known as El Zape, five leagues from Guanacebi and in the district assigned to the religious of the Company of Jesus. He found the church and [parish] house burnt, the town deserted, four religious of the Company [of Jesus] shot with arrows and dead, and one hundred other persons with them, whom he buried. From here he returned by way of Santa Catalina, Santiago Papasquiaro, and other towns, where he found dead four other religious of the Company [of Jesus], one Franciscan friar, and another friar of the Dominican order whom he had left behind; in addition many other corpses numbering over one hundred and sixty were found. On these roads he had frequent encounters with various Indians.

Near Santa Catalina on February 12 there came out to attack the governor and his men a great number of Tepehuanes. It was not possible to know for certain how many there were, but they advanced to attack, thinking that our men were the settlers of Guanacebi who were deserting the town and fleeing. They were quickly disillusioned when they saw the spirit with which our men—although few, there being not more than thirty soldiers—made the attack. Our men killed thirteen of the vagabonds and captured one alive named Andrés López, who told where part of the enemy forces were concealed in a stronghold, at a place named Tenerapa. The Indians fled through the hills, which gave admirable opportunity for flight.

This day the governor marched and reached the town of Atotonilco at about nine o'clock at night. Here he called a council of the captains and told them, as they already knew from the above-mentioned Indian, Andrés, that the enemy was fortified in Tenerapa, and that it would be well to march that night and surprise them at dawn before they should have news of his coming. All said that it was not possible that night to march the ten leagues from that point to Tenerapa, over mountains difficult to traverse, and that in addition to having fought the Indians that day they had marched six leagues, and that if this had not been the case and they had been rested, the night would not be long enough to march ten leagues, which would require at least twelve hours. To all these difficulties they added many others, but in spite of them all the governor decided to set out at once after some light refreshment. He therefore set forth the same day, going in addition to the six leagues another ten, over intricate, rough roads, on which the pack animals could make no headway after midnight, and the Indian allies moved slowly, being tired and having little spirit. But the governor encouraged them all until morning, when, about an hour after sunrise, they caught sight of Tenerapa, which is in a very strong natural location. The road to it being difficult, they were detected upon it by an Indian who sounded the alarm, so that it was necessary to make the attack at once. This our forces did with such spirit that it was as though the Spaniards and Indian allies alike had not traveled half a league. The battle lasted about an hour before the enemy fled. Sixty Tepehuanes were killed, and the prisoners, including women and boys, numbered two hundred and twenty persons. These were taken, chained together, to Guadiana on March 4.

Meanwhile, the affairs of war of the kingdom and the defense of Guadiana remained in charge of the lieutenant general, Rafael de Gascue, who defended the place very well. Four or five days after the governor had left Guadiana the Tepehuanes considered that the lieutenant general was practically alone in the place because the governor had gone away with almost all the men. They therefore convoked some two hundred Indians, a number which they thought would be sufficient to take the place and destroy it. So they came with great secrecy to a place called El Tunal, about a league from this villa. The lieutenant general heard of this and not wishing to await them in the settlement, sent in search of them Captain Gonzalo Martín de Soria with fifteen companions, with the orders which they were to follow. They marched half the night, going around four leagues in order to come upon them from behind, and at dawn attacked with spirit some sixty Indians who were going in advance, reconnoitring. At the first shots two of their captains who were leading them fell, which filled the others with so much fear that they turned about and fled, many of them breaking their legs as they fell down the rocks. Their right hands were brought to Guadiana, where the soldiers were very well received, since the victory had relieved the town from the danger which threatened it.

On March 4, as has been said, the prisoners arrived at Guadiana, and on the next day, the fifth, their camp was placed about a league distant at a place which they call Pacheco. The prisoners were sentenced and apportioned. Here orders were given concerning what the other captains had to do in the other parts of the government, where revolts had been declared. Captain Bartolomé Juárez, captain of the presidio of San Hipólito, among the Xiximes, was ordered to go on a campaign by way of the Tepehaune towns to the west of Guadiana. He set out at once in compliance with this order, and had some successful encounters with the Tepehuanes, killing and capturing a number of them, and punishing some of the towns of the Xiximes for having revolted and confederated themselves with the Tepehuanes.

An order was sent to Diego Martínez de Urdaide, the captain of Sinaloa, one hundred and fifty leagues from Guadiana, to leave a strong detachment in those provinces and go out to meet the Tepehuanes whose mountain range overlooks Sinaloa on the west. The said captain began to put this order into effect, but the disturbance of the Indians of Sinaloa was so evident, particularly among the towns neighboring upon the Tepehuanes, that he had to take contrary counsel and await developments in the territory which was under his charge. Still, this captain executed justice on more than sixty persons, and although many of those Indians have declared war and attacked our towns, the damage has been slight, because we were well forewarned.

During this time the fire of revolt had sprung up in some of the towns along the South Sea belonging to the government of the Audiencia of Guadalajara. Being advised of this, and requested by the audiencia to furnish help, the governor declined to place confidence in anyone save himself; therefore, making preparations during March 1617 for this journey with a fair number of Spanish soldiers and some Indian allies, he set out on the twenty-second of the same month. He first went to Chiametla to pacify that province on the way, for in it there had also been many towns which had revolted. It was necessary to exercise great diligence in finding the Indians, particularly those of the place called El Rincón de Zamora, because the natives were favored greatly by the roughness of the land, it being necessary to go down almost on all fours over part of the road, in places even using ropes to let themselves down into places where the animals could not enter, nor even men completely armed. Finally, although with great labor, the governor accomplished the pacification of those people. From there he went to the towns of

[Nueva] Galicia, and gave assistance to the presidio of Acaponeta, where the Indians had burned the village, and drove the enemy away. As a result of this journey, the peace of that land was assured, as has been demonstrated, for since that time there has been no rumor of enemies. The Audiencia of Guadalajara thanked the governor profusely for this, and he returned from Chiametla to Guadiana, whence he had gone some five months before. Neither did the factor, Rafael de Gascue, neglect to urge the aid which was asked for from the viceroy of New Spain; on the contrary he went in person to the city of Mexico and arranged to have some companies brought, for the men whom the viceroy finally sent from Zacatecas and San Luis were not sufficient for the pursuit of the entire forces of the insurgents. This assistance, consisting of three companies, paid for eight months, their leader and commissary being the factor and lieutenant of the general, on September 22 reached Guadiana, whcre the governor was already awaiting it. The governor distributed the three captains and the rest of the men where they would serve the best purpose.

At this time the enemy, who until now had been campaigning extensively, began to retire. It was learned that they had separated into six armed congregations or groups, many leagues distant each from the other, so that they had come to embrace the entire government, the Tepehuanes having mingled with many other nations.

Captain Bartolomé Juárez was ordered to take charge of the conquest of the Mesquital, the Guazamota, and their allies. He has been engaged in this task for six months, and has had three or four brushes with the natives of those parts in which he was successful, killing a few. On the day of our Lady['s Conception] in December 1617, he hanged twelve of them. Although the latest news of him was a plea for help, saying that the enemy was pressing him seriously, nevertheless it is known that the principal cacique, called the Nayarit Gentile, was treating for friendship which was by way of being achieved, and that he was a person with whom his neighbors would be likely to act in concert.

Captains Ontiveros, Castañeda, and Aguirre have worked toward Santa Bárbara, also with success, killing and imprisoning many, and reducing some towns which had been perverted by the Tepehuanes, who have now entered the valley called San Pablo, whither it is known that many of them have retired.

Captain Montaño took the road toward Guanacebi, in the direction of the pass called El Diablo, and toward Tecuchiapa, in which place many of the principal offenders have taken refuge. He will not fail to do a good job, because he has on two or three other occasions had good fortune with the enemy.

Captain Mosquera has operated against the Indians called Salineros and two other nations, the Conchos Tobosos and the Noñoques. He has effected two important captures among them, executing justice upon some and reducing others.

The governor remained three or four months at the seat of his government, Guadiana, arranging the affairs of the war in the manner described. But inasmuch as one of the most warlike captains of the Tepehuanes, Gogojito by name, after committing many assaults and making great ravages on the herds of the country, had gone into hiding forty leagues from Guadiana, and inasmuch as it was considered certain that he was there conducting negotiations to return when he thought wise, the governor planned that Captains Soria and Tomás García, after some successful actions in which they had engaged near here, should reconnoitre the passes. They complied with the order, and when they reached the place where Gogojito and his people had ensconced themselves among the rocks, they judged, after having made a reconnaissance and compared notes, that it would be necessary to have a larger force than what they had before they could obtain any success against the Indians. They were, then, able to kill only four or five of the enemy and to catch a little Negro who had gone with them. They therefore returned to Guadiana, whereupon the governor was forced to take this task upon himself.

Setting out upon this task early in February of this year, 1618, by marching at night after he had reached the vicinity of his destination and going into ambush during the daytime, he brought it about within fifteen days after his departure that the Tepehuán Gogojito fell into his hands, and atoned with his death for all the outrages which he had committed. With him died some others, among them two of his cousins. His people, who were fortified among the rocks at a little distance from there, were able to take refuge in flight. The governor pursued them, although without effect as far as this body of Tepehuanes was concerned. Yet his labor was very fruitful and of considerable importance, for, influenced by the death of Gogojito, the Xiximes, Acaxees, and other towns belonging to various nations living within that district, came to surrender to the governor. Thus he left the Xiximes who had revolted, at peace, as well as some other towns which had favored them.

The entire government has been made very joyful by all this, and by the hope that the remaining situation will be easily adjusted in the future. The governor and his men carried provisions for only twenty-five days, hence, having been out more than seventy days, they suffered from great hunger and hardships, as they had nothing to eat for forty days besides horse and mule flesh. He came down by way of the valleys of Papasquiaro, Guatimape, and Terame, dividing his troops into four parts, which have examined the country and made some captures of importance. In particular, near a place called Sombrerete, they hanged six old Tepehuanes; others of less age they took prisoners. In the valley of San Julián they killed five Indians of Coneto who a short time previously had killed two Negro shepherds near San Juan del Río.

From this time the governor expects to hold the territory by presidios and to protect the roads by escorts, two companies being kept in service for whatever may be necessary. By this means he will save expense to His Majesty and accommodate affairs in the most convenient manner.

Recently four or five towns have come asking peace. One Indian named Rafael, moved by the death of Gogojito, and especially by having seen the great damage done by an animal of the size of a tiger some months ago in a town near Guadiana, came pleading for mercy with a crucifix in his hands. He was well received, and offered to go and bring back in peace some of the insurgents, leaving as hostages his wife and sons. He went, and brought back some chiefs of various towns, who offer to settle down peacefully.

This is the course which the war had run, and the state in which it is at present, May 16, 1618.

8

EXCERPTS FROM THE

Account of the Triumphs of Our Holy Faith among the Most Fierce and Savage People of the New World . . . VOL. 3

Padre Andrés Pérez de Ribas

Father Andrés Pérez de Ribas (1576–1655) was born in Córdoba, Spain and joined the Jesuit order as a young man, after having already been ordained priest. He was sent to Mexico where he served in several important offices, including that of Provincial for the order in New Spain. In 1645, Pérez de Ribas published the *Historia de los Triunfos de Nuestra Santa Fé* . . . , an account of Jesuit mission activity in the Northwestern Provinces of New Spain. Drawing from the reports of various field missionaries, Pérez de Ribas collected considerable cultural material as well as information on the actual mission effort.

Here we translate the portions of Pérez de Ribas's account that deal with the culture of the isolated Acaxee and Xixime Indians of the Durango, Sinaloa border area and of the Tepehuán Indians of Durango. Although Pérez de Ribas published his great work in 1645, it must be remembered that his accounts of the Acaxee, Xixime, and Tepehuán represented the situation that existed perhaps two generations earlier.

In this translation, particularly, we have striven to maintain the essence of Pérez de Ribas's writing, which is rather stilted and stylistically and syntactically heavy. We have endeavored only to remove dangling clauses and a few of his more fanciful wanderings in what may be the first printing in English of a small portion of his monumental *Historia*.

For a summary of available information about the Acaxee and Xixime, see Beals (1933). Other material on the Tepehuán is presented in this volume in the documents of the Tepehuán Rebel-

lion and in the writings of J. Alden Mason. For recent summaries
of data on Tepehuán culture, see Riley (1969) and Pennington
(1963).

B. C. H.

C. L. R.

About the [Indian] Nations That Populated This Mountain Chain; and Their Peculiar Customs

ALTHOUGH there were, and are, many nations that inhabited the
extent of this mountain area, I shall mention only those that had to do
with this Mission Headquarters of Topia, because the others will be
mentioned when I write about the Missions of San Andrés and Tepeguanes which border on those nations. The main nation on whose lands
the town of Topia is found, is the Acaxee. They [the Acaxee Indians]
had their farms and small dwelling areas in the form of small villages or
hamlets not in the highest areas of the pine forests since it was too cold
in that region, but rather placed lower down [on the mountain sides]
and protected by [natural?] declivities. Ordinarily, they were perched
atop rock pillars or isolated as a defense or as a fortress against enemy
attacks. On those stone promontories they built their small houses,
some of rock and clay, others from rough mountain timber, the roof
being of straw. Aside from these, they built larger, communal buildings,
with such a small door that, in order to enter, one had to bend almost
double and duck down. This also served them as a defensive measure
when under attack by the enemy; they would open their loopholes and
fire arrows without being affected themselves. And on all of the farms
of this nation of people there were probably from twelve to sixteen
thousand souls, aside from all the others, with which we will deal later.
The main sustenance of this people, all of whom were farmers, was
maize and beans. Together with these crops they sowed more common
local seeds which they got as gifts [of Providence] and which are different from those of Europe; but they have various types of squash
which serve them as ordinary vegetable stuff, all in great abundance and
of good savor, different from those of Castilla [Spain]. Maize serves as
bread for them; they grind it by hand on a stone which each one has
in his house, and that job was only done by women for men would be

offended to perform the task. Moreover, they had as sustenance other
wild tree fruit such as plums, and those they call *zapotes* [sapodillas]
and *guamúchiles* [the fruit of a specie of acacia] which grow on their
mountainsides or on the edges of the arroyos and rivers. They always
settled their farms near a spring or arroyo where they would have water
and their tillable land at hand. Another gift which God gave these people without any effort or care on their part, is an extremely smooth
honey, white as snow, which was found in the hollows of the live oak
trees, not in honeycombs (although they have those too, unlike the
people in the province of Sinaloa) but rather formed in the concave
areas of the trees. In these hollow areas a type of large bee builds little
"jars" of wax, like mounds of eggs full of honey. The people enjoy that
fine liquor in abundance and already have the wax for their altar
[candles]. The clothing of these people is as short and scanty as that
which has been written about for other groups. The truth is that these
mountain folk use more agave-thread cloaks which their women make,
and these serve them as skirts for the women, and the men wear them
around their shoulders to be put on and taken off at random, and some
even had cotton [mantels], of which there was very little. All of them
girdled themselves with some cordlets or belts from which some hung
with flower blooms or edgings in the manner of fringing, which served
to cover them somewhat, which shows their gentility, because since they
received the Faith and entered into the mines to work, everything is
better and more muted [than before, in reference to their clothing].
They grew and kept their hair most carefully, braided with strips of
cloth—the men as well as the women. The women, and even more so
the men, adorned themselves with large strands of white, small snail
shells, greatly esteemed among them. They searched for these shells or
bought them from other coastal peoples. They also wore similar trinkets
on their arms, and in their ears and the septum of the nose, both of
which they pierced as children in order to be able to hang things from
them. For full dress they also had bands around their legs which they
made from strips of deer skin—deer which they had killed. They also
wore these bands on their ankles, and girdling themselves with the
bands, they said, gave them strength for walking through their mountains and along their rough roads; and if, perchance, they found themselves weary, they had as a cure bleeding themselves, by puncturing the
temples and the head if they had a headache. The stature of these people is middling, and much less than that of the Sinaloas. Their color is

yellowish brown, [i.e., *bazo*—brown inclining to yellow]. They are strong
for working purposes and particularly for climbing slopes, mountains
and peaks in that they are light in weight. It is worth their while for
the plains Indians to fear these people, for the mountain men are light
and the others heavy and torpid. The women are very strong for carrying loads even though the loads may be very heavy. They carry the load
on their backs, suspended from their heads or foreheads with cords or
cloth strips. From these cords is suspended a large basket in which an
Indian woman will carry a *fanega* [approximately a hundredweight] in
addition to her small child which she carries wrapped up, and her household of bowls and jugs and even the parrots and birds which she raises;
and with that load she will traipse through the hills and peaks and she
will walk four and more leagues through her mountainside, with a small
staff in her hand. And they are accustomed to this from childhood. The
nature of these people is animated and happy, not sad or melancholy,
and so they converse with the padres and the Spaniards most affably,
and the food that they have prepared in their homes is at the door for
any and all who may arrive, even though they may be from another
tribe—so long as they are not enemies. Their [mental] capacity is not
lacking, since, as happens in many cases, in one day they learn, in their
language, the Pater Noster, the Ave Maria and the Credo. They are
very tenacious and persevering in whatever they begin. Fortunately, it
was quite common among those taking catechism in preparation for
baptism to stay from morning until night, without remembering to go
to eat, learning their prayers and catechism, and that they did for several days. And that same tenaciousness they maintained during an uprising which I shall discuss later, in which they surrounded the Spaniards who were secluded and fortified in a church and kept up a steady
bombardment with arrows for two weeks running. And now I shall write
about their old wars, which were perpetual with other nations that they
came across and, at times, of the same tongue. This [warfare] was a
vice that the Devil had very well introduced among them to lead them
quickly straight to Hell, and the vice was passed down from father to
son. Some of those wars were community-wide in nature, the troops
going out to battle with their enemies; others were [conducted] with the
use of "highwaymen" on the roads or in the fields, looking for some
enemy to eat up just as they go out deer hunting. The methods of warfare and the arms they use are the same as is described for other tribes;
the bow, a mountain lion-skin quiver full of arrows, a *macana* [a wooden

weapon, generally edged with sharp flint], and small spears made of
wood colored. red with brazilwood [used by dyers for making red dyes
and for "rouge"]. And for defensive armaments, some of them carried
animal skin shields. Adornment for warfare consisted of however many
strands of snail shells and all of the plumery they could muster. Another
peculiar and barbarous thing that these people used was a tassle or tail
which hung down their backsides. It was made of many strings of deer
skin and was dyed several colors and hung from the cord or belt with
which they girdled themselves. And finally, as to what aim these wars
and ambushes had, it was to bring back dead bodies to be eaten—and
that signified gaining victory to them. And when they had won their
victory, they would let their women and children know about it a half
league before they arrived in the village and there, as the mountain lion
teaches its cubs with its catch, so these Indians fed and raised their
children on the meat of those wild and inhuman catches of theirs. The
human body which they captured was carried dead, either whole or cut
into pieces, and delivered to the elders. The latter having made it into
chunks [by dividing it] at the joints threw it into large pots which they
kept for that purpose, and cooked it together with beans (which they
used as garbanzos [in this case, a sort of pulse much esteemed in
Spain]). They were careful to keep a fire under it and cook it all night
until they could pull out the bones, clean of meat, which they kept as
trophies of their victories. And, together with all of the people of the
valley, they divided up that inhuman pottage together with the wine
they had made. The first plate was given to the one who had made the
capture and killed the enemy. They also punctured his lower lip, if he
didn't already have a hole in it from childhood, and inserted a piece of
bone from the dead prisoner, and thus he was known to be very brave
among those of his tribe. Following this wild feast was their barbarous
dance, which the elders celebrated with sermons and stories, exorting
and giving spirit to the young ones to try and attain similar triumphs
and victories and recalling to their minds their relatives and friends who
had died at the hands of their enemies. The Devil had his part in this
celebration: we might even say that the whole thing became his, since
he captured and carried away the souls of the celebrants and most particularly [he possessed them] through taking out a portion of that inhuman pottage in a soup plate or cup and offering it to the idol which
some of them were accustomed to keeping in their houses in order that
it might give them victory in their wars. Before going out to war they

instituted a fast which they all then made the responsibility of an Indian woman, ordinarily a virgin, and this fast was extremely rigorous, because it had to last throughout the entire time they were at war, and the food which she took during the fast was very short in quantity and was only a small amount of toasted maize and nothing could be eaten with salt. She had to live alone and apart from everyone and she could neither touch nor talk with anyone. Finally, in order that it may be understood to what point the Devil had introduced cruelty among these people in their feasts and inhuman butcherings, I will tell about what happened when the padres came among one of these mountain tribes to give them the doctrine. They counted the skulls of 1,724 persons which these people had killed and eaten and then hung in front of their houses. And that doesn't include others that had decomposed through age, nor innumerable bones that they still had hanging about, because they spared no one from their cruelty. And the same thing took place among the other nations of these mountains, more among some, less among others. The wild vice reigned among them and has been written about quite often in order that it may be made clear what preaching the Gospel among them does.

About the Great Extent to Which Superstitious Idolatry Reigned Among These Mountain People and about Other Different Customs

NOT OF LESS esteem, but of greater esteem among all others, has been the fruit gathered and the victory won from the Devil who, through countless numbers of idols, talked to or appeared before the people, misleading them with these same idols. There was one case where the people delivered twelve baskets of these heathen idols to the padre. The principal mediums or pseudo ministers of these idols and of the Devil (who was with them) were wizards [*hechiceros*] and relatives of his, and normally were false curers of disease. And all paid tribute to them. Consequently, it is they who have most stringently opposed the preaching of the Gospel. But thanks be to Jesus Christ that His divine word has had so much force and virtue in conquering them and overcoming those same family members of the Infernal dominions. [It is through Him] that the padres who have brought the doctrine to these mountain peoples have been able to deliver into the fire such a great number of those idols and figurines (and there have been thousands of them; and the ones which the padres have destroyed, turned into ash, or broken into pieces, are countless in number). They kept some [of the idols] to ask for and obtain victory in their wars; others they had kept their fields safe from the animals; others to bring rain or to bring fish to their rivers. And all of the idols were of various and never-seen figures [i.e., beings] and, at other times, they have no figures; nothing more than some peculiar, rough stones with which the Devil deceived them. He talked to them innumerable times, now in the mountains, again in their homes, teaching them that his name was Meyuncame, which means "he who does everything." He is still perverse in his old and damnable pretension and arrogance of wanting to be revered as God, and deceiving these people through the power which he has only through tricks and endeviled lies. In one village they had a large blade of natural stone which they worshipped in order that they might not lack stones for their arrows, because the mountain people make the points of their arrows with a sharp piece of that rock which, when it hits its mark, cannot be pulled out of the flesh without breaking open the wound. They put up a type of altar or incensory to some of these idols. There were piles of rocks [covered] with clay and they dedicated these to the idol to whom they make their offerings. And when they had nothing else at hand they put a stone on top of the pile, setting it there with straw and grass so that it would stay fixed. This is much in the manner in which the Christian pilgrims, on coming to the Sacred Cross, are accustomed to leave a stone as a sign of their reverence and desire to make even more permanent that sacred sign on which (as St. Paul said) Christ set the payment and victory of our salvation. Other times they invoked him [the Devil] with ostentation, with all parties, particularly those who took the part of priests, sitting down in a dark house deep in the night. The priests carried in their hands and played a type of timbrel. And with unknown words they invoked the Devil and he appeared to them as little figures [idols] sometimes in human form, sometimes as animals—but always savage, as is he since he disobeyed God. And there they consulted with him and told him what they wanted and they listened to his replies, some being lies and others leading them to commit wild and barbarous cruelties.

And to finish up and conclude with the customs of these people, I will briefly tell of some that were good and some that were indifferent [i.e., neither good nor bad]. Good and noteworthy customs among a

people which was so blind and deceived were their habits of not stealing or lying. And if there were any of this, it was a childhood vice, and
when someone had fallen into that situation, it wasn't necessary to look
for witnesses to make him admit his delinquency because the Indian himself confessed it, although it must have cost him dearly. And perhaps
this was the strong sentiment that, when a robbery did occur, caused
the culprit to have to move either from his dwelling place or [even]
move to another village. And, so, they did not use doors nor did they
have any closed thing. They were not very given to the vice of dishonor
and if it was known among them that a woman had been bad just once,
no one would marry her under any circumstance. And married couples
generally lived together very tranquilly and without offense to the union
or the fidelity which they owed each other. Insofar as the indifferent
customs, the happy mountain folk had the same games and entertainment that the Indians of Sinaloa have and which have been described
earlier; but even more notable and used more among them was the rub-
ber ball, which they hit with their shoulders or hips, quickly throwing
themselves to the ground with great dexterity in order to return the ball
as it flew through the air. And these Acaxees kept the court for this
game in very good condition, clean and surrounded with their fences,
something like mud walks, and many were the contests which one farm
[group] had with another with this game. And the losing group paid off
bets made on the contests with items of the value of the bet placed by
the winning group, and these bets were of the things that they most
valued. After the silver mines were discovered and they were working
there, there were times when the value of clothing or valuable items
which they bet would reach a value of five hundred pesos or pieces of
eight. And they can well get that amount out of what they call *pepenas*
[nuggets]. And I will explain here what that word means, so that one
may understand the great earnings that the Indian workers get from
working in the mines. Principally, it was the Spanish-speaking Indians
who knew metals and who were pickmen who broke up the metal vein
who worked in the mines. But aside from their daily salary which is at
least four silver *reales*, the main workers had the ability and right to
select for themselves one of the baskets (which they call *tenates* [a
basket with two handles]) full of the metal which they break and take
out of the vein every day. The metal is the richest and highly select, and
because as they know it they see to it first that their bosses keep aside
for them the most valuable, and this no one can take away from the

Indians. Because, at the point when it was taken away from them, they would abandon the mines, and both the mines and their bosses would be lost. The baskets of metal which the Indian takes out customarily is worth four, six, and perhaps ten or more pieces of eight. And this is what they call *pepenas* [nuggets] which are widely used in all of the mining towns of New Spain, and which must take place in the other dominions of the Indies. And so the Indians who are dextrous in working in the mines go about brilliantly treated and dressed, and those prizes of which I was talking, which they bet during their ball games, sometimes reached a value of five hundred pesos or pieces of eight. The mountain people also had a particular celebration for this game in which they danced for three nights before the day of their contest. And formed up as if for war, a troop of women arrived from the village and all danced together for two or three hours each night in the very plaza of [the ball] game, singing together and in loud voices they celebrated their spirit and ability in playing, encouraging the contestants with the thoughts of the honor and joy that would follow them when they won. The women spent the evening hours in preparing a huge banquet for the people who were coming to play against them, in case the visitors lost—because if they won, they wouldn't eat a bite, and the losing team got the feast. The number of contestants that played was generally six or eight chosen from the challenging team. The opponents then had no limit but could play as many men as wished to get into the game. And if they had nothing else to bet, they sometimes would bet their eyelashes, three and three or four and four, pulling that number [from each eye] if they lost. At this, some cried and others laughed as they got their entertainment from this, and they kept this custom even after becoming Christians and being baptized. It wouldn't be convenient nor is there reason to take their legitimate entertainment from them, since not even the women have any other particular games that they play. . . .

About the Fierce Customs and the Difficult Posts Among the Xixime Nation; to Which Francisco de Ordiñola, Governor of Nueva Vizcaya, Has Determined to Send a Punitive Expedition to Punish Their Insults

THE XIXIME nation has to have been the wildest, most unhuman and rebellious of all the groups that lived throughout these mountains and lived on the most difficult and precipitous parts of it; the Acaxee Indians (their neighbors) as well as the Spaniards had already experienced their treatment. And so their adhesion to our sacred faith, as well as the building of a friendship with the Spaniards, cost indescribable work, encounters, and battles. This nation of Indians lived in the heart of these mountains; and they were fortified on the most inaccessible peaks of the entire mountain range, to the point that they could not be reached, owing to the altitude and the danger presented by the depth of the gorges. Therefore, it was impossible to deal with them and pacify them. In addition to what I have recounted, that which makes it even more difficult to deal with them was their unhuman custom, which has been found more in New Spain than in any other country, of commonly obtaining their sustenance from human flesh. And when they left their mountains and gorges, it was to hunt Acaxee Indians—their neighbors— to cook potfulls of their flesh to feed upon, and to hang on their walls and doors and surrounding trees the bones and skulls [of their enemies] in order to celebrate their victories. And they were so proud, insolent, and daring with these victories and banquets that every day the number of ambushes multiplied and through these ambushes the Acaxee nation, in particular, was being reduced. The Acaxee is the principal group found in the two missions of Topia and San Andrés; they have a mutual boundary on the north with the barbarous and unhuman Xixime. And although at times the Acaxees, aided by some Spaniards, tried to defeat them with their weapons, it was with loss of life and even defeat. For the Xiximes, made confident on the one hand by the inaccessibility of their mountain peaks and on the other by being so capable of getting around in them, always came to combat highly confident, and they made their competitors withdraw with loss of life. The Acaxee Indians, being in their majority Christians and vassals of the king and under his protection, and also having the missionary fathers intervening for them and trying to raise their children whom they so dearly loved, took recourse to the governor of [Nueva] Vizcaya, requesting his favor and relief from all of the damages and evildoing. The governor adjudged that the Acaxee Indians were requesting justice and rights; and he immediately replied to them that during some attack they should try to take one or more prisoners from the Xixime Indians and bring them to him so that he could seek information from such a backward and cruel people, and thus give the remedy that seemed the most appropriate to him. The Acaxees fortunately captured two, and although one of them died a little after being wounded while he was being captured, the other arrived safe and sound in the governor's hands. He used no force with him but instead tried to make friends with him and give him gifts and, having detained him for some days so that he might know the treatment of the Spaniards, he sent him out to tell his people that it was not as they believed, not as others who deceived them would have them believe, but rather [a situation of] friendship and benevolence. And that he was very desirous that they should enjoy such friendship and benevolence, and if they would cease their actions and attacks, they would be at peace with the Christians. He added as a conclusion that wherever they didn't do as he asked, he would go personally with a powerful army to those very lands, no matter how steep they might be, to give them a memorable punishment. With this message he dispatched the Indian who returned very contented and honored with a costume which the governor had given him. And so that he might get to his home safely [the governor] asked one of the fathers who were indoctrinating the Acaxee Indians if he would accompany this Indian to the settlement of San Hipólito which was on the Xixime border. And he ordered his captain to receive the obedience and peace of those barbarians, if they were to come and pledge it, in the name of His Majesty, pardoning them the deaths and insults that they had committed to that time. And thus it was carried out, and the captain sent the Indian out from his fort, and he arrived safely among his people where he was very well received by them when they saw how happy he was with the kind treatment that he had been given. They heard his message and they decided that all of the head men and chiefs [caciques] from their villages should go to the San Hipólito and, in the name of the entire nation, to make peace with the captain, which they did in the manner that the governor had indicated, simultaneously pledging their allegiance to the king, our lord, and making themselves his vassals. The Xiximes kept this peace for some time; they entered Christian Acaxee villages and communicated with the Spaniards in their towns, with a showing of benevolence. Nevertheless, just as it appeared that things were at a point where the light of salvation would enter into them, without any reason whatsoever (although the Devil's work was enough reason) the nation rebelled with such a huge and diabolical fury that, from four different directions at one time, they began to kill all of the Christians that they found in order to eat them as they had done before. Finding themselves [i.e., the Acaxees] under so much pressure, they once again asked the governor of Vizcaya to defend them

and to support them. However, he told them to abandon their homes
and churches and to go and live in other parts. And [they also told him]
that the Xiximes had invited them to ally themselves with them and go
against the Spaniards, who would surely do them in if they would not
do so. And as proof of this latter fact they [the Acaxees] sent him [the
governor] an Indian prisoner who had just come from the Xiximes with
that message. The governor, Francisco de Ordiñola, although he was a
great soldier, an expert in warfare with barbarous Indians of the Provinces of Nueva Vizcaya and Galicia, in order to save the loss of lives
and money for the king, charged the captain of the fort at San Hipólito
to return to make new gestures to the Xiximes, to quiet them. This he
did, through a Xixime chieftain . . . who, leaving his people along with
twenty Indian relatives, had come to live near the Christian Acaxees.
On several occasions the rebel Xiximes were resolved to kill them because of their friendship with the Spaniards and the Church. And it
was a specific act of providence by God that they didn't do so on this
occasion when this chief went to deliver the captain's message to them.
They responded most arrogantly that it wasn't peace they wanted but
war, and told him to come out and fight and, if he didn't, they would
come immediately and find him [and his soldiers and Acaxee allies] and
kill and eat them because they liked the taste of their flesh. And so saying and doing, they got together a large band of people, set out for the
settlement called De las Vírgenes with the intent of destroying it and
killing anyone they found there. And such was the arrogant and prideful
determination that they had that they killed a Spaniard on his own
ranch, along with a son and five Christian Indians and their wives.
They killed all but one person who escaped them and spread the news.
They carried away the bodies of the dead to eat them, leaving behind
the entrails as testimony of what they had done. With this case, every
one throughout the land became most upset and when the governor received news of it, he sent a message to the Viceroy of New Spain, who
is Captain General of that nation and all her provinces, telling him of
what had happened in Nueva Vizcaya and the San Andrés Mountains
in order that His Excellency might give orders as to what should be
done and in order that he might provide himself with the manner in
which to carry it out and to avail himself of the expenses of war. At
that time the Marquis de Salinas was the Viceroy (whose fine government is well remembered in the Indies), and he, together with judges
from the *Real Audiencia* and theologians whom he called to judge the

cause and punishment that such insolence begged, resolved that the governor of Vizcaya, himself, should call up the people, the Spaniards as well as friendly Indians, and go to punish those damages and to put the brakes on such an insolent and arrogant people. He was also to defend and aid Christianity in that mountain area. In compliance with that order, the governor got together two companies, each one of 100 Spanish soldiers and, in addition to them, other Christian Indian troops. In total, there were 1,100 infantry who set out for San Hipólito. Arriving there, the governor selected 20 Spanish soldiers to remain as a garrison for the Acaxee Indians and the fathers, who were indoctrinating them, in the event that some band of Xiximes might fall upon them during the period of warfare. This was because those Indians [the Xixime] could run like deer through those mountains. And once he had done this, he set out again, taking two of the local fathers who knew so much about the region along with him as advisors. He also wanted them along to see after spiritual matters for the army on such a dangerous journey.

About the Tepeguanes. . . .

. . . THE NATION called Tepeguana . . . was not as numerous as those of other Christian provinces, but the tribe that was brave and fierce could cause the ravages [previously] discussed, in part where there were few Spaniards in residence. On the position, dwellings, and customs which this nation possessed in their gentility, it will be necessary to comment. . . .

The Tepeguan nation has its ferocity written in its name; for their name means hill, or from this word, "Totl," which means stone or a large rock; and either one describes the Tepeguanes who live among hills and rocks and are hard and rocky in nature, and they are like the trees that grow in those hills and rocks, which are hard and knotty live oaks. Nevertheless, that which is most marvelous of anything said yet is that among those rocks God had placed his people predestined to Heaven. These people had their gentility, their farms, and today those that have their villages have them part on the plains and part in the mountains at the springs of De Topia and San Andrés, of which we have spoken. And in that area they are neighbors to the Xixime and Acaxee nations and even to those [nations] in the deepest interior of Sinaloa; because, even though this Tepeguan nation is not the most numerous of those of which we have written, they are among the most extended in their dwelling space in New Spain, and they reach almost to New Mexico. They fall under the jurisdiction and governance of Nueva Vizcaya and under the Bishopric of Guadiana, which city is their provincial capital. At thirty leagues from this city the Tepeguan villages begin, the first of which is called Santiago Papazquiaro, being some two hundred leagues from the great City of Mexico. . . . The Spaniards entered the Tepeguan lands, some of which were deserted, in order to settle there, owing to the discovery of silver veins and mines, many of which have been found in the region and every day new ones are being discovered which are of very high quality. . . . Aside from this, the Tepeguan lands beckoned the Spaniards with their beautiful and spacious fields and heavy, fertile growth to settle large livestock ranches, especially large livestock such as cattle, horses, and mares with which many large herds and ranches have been formed. And all of this was done without offense to the native population, but rather with benefits for them: because before these things had come they did not take advantage of the mines, nor did they have livestock to feed or with which to feed themselves; and since the Spaniards came and settled, they have found sustenance, clothing, and wealth in their abundant lands without violence nor outbreaks of war. However [the Spaniards] weren't so careless as to forget their arms or to provide themselves with arms, living among people of such ferocity, unknown qualities, and in whom there was little to have faith, and who, in the beginning, menaced the Spaniards with certain acts [of hostility]. But the Spaniards tried to avoid warfare at all cost, attempting first to win over and calm the natural ferocity of the Tepeguanes with love and good treatment. They worked especially with some chiefs and captains of the Indians, among which (as it is with these tribes), no matter how barbarous they may be, there are some who are more faithful and reachable.

The nature of the Tepeguanes was always ill disposed, courageous, and warlike, always ready to lift their head to subject other peoples and make them fear their neighbors. Particularly they treated in this manner the Acaxee, the Tarahumara, and others, whom they had so cowed and so dominated that a small number of Tepeguanes would enter one of their villages, without fear of resistance, and carry off women and maidens as they pleased and take them to their lands to tyranically take advantage of them. The weapons of these Indians were the same as described for the other tribes: Bow, arrow, *macana* [flint, or stone-edged club], brazilwood pikes or spears. Such was the nature of these Indians that, after the incursion of the Spaniards and after the outbreak of warfare between them, having served as wranglers, they became so dextrous as horsemen and handled a lance or *dejarretadera* [a hooked knife] so well, that they used these weapons when they could get them, and used them so ably that they were as capable as very able Spanish cavalry. And perhaps they learned to use firearms and arquebuses that they took from the Spaniards, although they could never maintain their use, for they did not know the art of making gun powder. That is all about arms and warfare. Their sustenance was that common to Indians; maize, with other seeds that they sowed, since they were almost all farmers, although not of large fields; and owing to that lack, they also used other wild fruits as did the other nations. They also took advantage of other wild game and birds, of which there was a great abundance in their land. Their dress was like that of other mountain groups discussed. They used mantels [blankets] made of cotton which they planted and of agave which grew in the mountains. And from the same materials, the women made the skirts which they wore. From the mescal [maguey, or American agave] plant and other wild fruits they made wine and enjoyed their frequent drunks, which the Devil had introduced among all of these people. The houses were of wood or mountain saplings, or of stone and clay, and their villages consisted of some farms [which looked] like a caravan [i.e., a line-village arrangement], near water holes, arroyos, and rivers, which were in abundance. And the principal one was Santiago Papazquiaro, their main village. Insofar as the remainder of their customs, [there were] mainly the *hechiceros* [wizards, shamans] . . . in accordance with the ferocity and cruelty which these people possessed.

9

The Opata: An Inland Tribe of Sonora

Jean B. Johnson

The Opata in some ways represent one of the least understood native groups in northern Mexico. They were first visited by the Spaniards in the 1530s but contact was very sporadic until the seventeenth century when these Indians were made a key part in the Jesuit plan for missionization of Sonora and Arizona. The loyalty of the Opata and related groups to the Spaniards made it possible for Spanish influence to inch forward into Arizona and finally, in the eighteenth century into California. One result of Opata docility was the rather complete acculturation of the Indians, with the result that the aboriginal Opata have tended to be slighted in culture histories of the region. For example, in the *Handbook of Middle American Indians* (Hinton, 1969) the Opata, Pima, Papago, and Seri *together* are allotted only four pages of text.

The theme of this short monograph by Jean Johnson (published after his death by the University of New Mexico Press) is that the Opata were a sophisticated people representing perhaps the highest cultural plateau in the Greater Southwest. This point of view has been disputed, and indeed may be somewhat exaggerated, but with the increase in archaeological research in the area, especially the detailed work by Charles C. DiPeso on Casas Grandes, a new look at the Opata is now in order.

Johnson's paper was obviously planned as a preliminary report. It contains some curious gaps, perhaps the most noticeable being the failure to include Adolph Bandelier's extensive commentary on the Opata.

In this reprinting of Johnson we retain the comments of Leslie Spier, editor of the University of New Mexico Publications in Anthropology at the time of the original printing. In Spier's words:

After Mr. Johnson's untimely death, this paper was kindly offered for publication by Mrs. Johnson. A memorandum with the manuscript indicates that it was completed in July 1942, and hence contains no references to material available after that date. It is presented here very nearly as Mr. Johnson prepared it. Some of the terms given as though Opata are palpably of Spanish or Nahuatl derivation, but we have thought it best to let these stand, marking the more obvious of them by a following asterisk. A few amendments to the text—set off by square brackets—have been made by the editor.

C. L. R.

THE OPATA, a group numbering some sixty thousand[1] at the time of the Conquest, have completely disappeared today as a cultural and ethnic entity. It is doubtful whether five persons could now be found who can recall even fragments of the language. Their geographical and cultural positions are of considerable interest to those who deal with American Southwestern-Mexican cultural connections.

It seems worthwhile, then, to put together from the various sources all the scattered bits of purely ethnographic information obtainable on the Opata. Such an attempt cannot, of course, give a complete picture of the culture, but sufficient data are available to allow us to place the Opata in relation to their congeners. This paper does not include comparative data from the Southwestern area, nor from other Mexican areas; it aims only to present an ethnographic outline of the Opata.

For the Sonoran area, and particularly for the Opata, there is fortunately plenty of documentary data. Much of it contains little real ethnographic information, but gives a great deal of detail on Indian-Spanish relations; this material is very briefly summarized in the section dealing with historical change. Some of the manuscripts used here are presented for the first time; other sources are well known to specialists of northwest Mexico, who have, however, consulted them with ends other than Opata ethnography in mind.[2] The material for this paper is taken from sources that range in time from the sixteenth century to the modern field observations of the writer.

The reader will note that linguistic evidence is used to a large extent—for example, that taken from Lombardo's excellent grammar, and from other early linguistic sources. Occasionally, and when there was strong corroborative evidence, the writer has felt justified in inferring for the Opata the existence of culture elements not specifically mentioned or described in detail in any of the sources, but which are present in neighboring groups.

In certain cases it is possible to make such inferences because of the demonstrably high correlation of culture content of such peoples as the Cáhita (i.e., modern Yaqui-Mayo) and the Opata. Given, for instance, the known distribution of the musical bow in Sonora, or that of cocoon dance rattles, it seems justifiable to infer the existence of those elements among the Opata. Another case in point is the long-stick gambling game: since the Opata are completely surrounded by groups which have the game, this fact, together with the linguistic evidence, makes it extremely likely that the Opata also had the game. Such inferences, however, are not demonstrable facts, nor are they so stated by the writer.

The natural landscape and demography of the Opata have been definitively treated by Sauer[3] in a series of readily accessible papers, and hence do not require repetition here. Kroeber[4] has placed Opata as a member of the Cáhita-Opata-Tarahumar group of the Uto-Aztecan linguistic family.

It may be added that there is an abundance of Opata linguistic documentary material. This, together with recent phonetic investigations and vocabularies collected from the last speakers of Opata,[5] is more than sufficient for the preparation of a modern descriptive linguistic sketch of the Opata. The phonemic pattern of the language is such that it can be written almost phonemically in Spanish orthography; thus the Jesuits' works can be readily utilized. From the same sources, it would be possible to define dialect differences.

Under the name Opata there are actually included two language groups, the Opata proper and the Eudeve. Local and variant names which occur include the following: Aibine, Egue, Heve, Hehue (Eudeve), Tehuima, Teguima. The Jova, or Ova, were a ruder, barranca-dwelling people who apparently had a simpler culture than the Opata. Linguistically, Opata and Eudeve were "as different as Portuguese and Spanish," while Jova was probably a distinct language.[6]

[The country of the Opata (and the somewhat more southerly Jova) lay in the upper drainages of the Sonora and Yaqui Rivers in eastern Sonora. Their territory spanned the district lying immediately south of the United States boundary, adjacent to southwestern New Mexico, for some one hundred seventy-five miles southward.]

Material Culture

Houses and towns.   The Opata lived in large and orderly towns.[7] The Opata word for town, *hoira*,[8] is cognate with the Yaqui *hó'ara*.

There were apparently several house types: wattle and daub, adobe (?), and mat-covered. One source mentions arched roofs.[9] Another source lists houses of cane, of adobe, of grass, of mud, and of mats.[10] The ubiquitous *ramada*, a flat-roofed, wall-less structure with a brush and earth roof supported by tree trunks, was also present. Perhaps community houses were present,[11] but more probably the warriors used the *ramada* as a meetingplace, as do the modern Cáhita.

Some sort of storehouse for corn was used; Lombardo referred to "a storehouse of cane." Beds were made of lengths of cane tied together.[12]

Agriculture.   Maize was the staple and was cultivated according to the basic Mexican pattern; it was planted with the digging-stick, or *coa.* Lombardo gives *nat, na* "*la coa.*"[13] Lombardo also gives a full maize vocabulary, the terms of which refer to stages of development, ripening, etc., of the plant. Similar vocabularies reflecting the importance of the maize complex are found among the highly agricultural peoples of Middle America. The Opata vocabulary is so extensive as to result in some forms used with derived senses, e.g., the verb which signifies the sprouting of the corn is also used to indicate the appearance and growth of children's teeth.[14] Also noted were many lexemes like *cäuotü*, "the method of husking the corn so as to leave the leaves in place."[15] The Opata corn vocabulary is cognate with and paralleled by that of the Yaqui.[16]

Beans, including the *tepari*, were grown. Various kinds of squash were grown: Lombardo and *Fragmentary Manuscript* list four named types. Squash was dried and preserved, and the dried and toasted seeds, known today as *pepitas*, were also eaten.[17]

It is not known if chili was grown before the advent of the Spaniards;[18] but an Opata word for chili exists, (*urúk*).[19] Perhaps the word refers to the wild "chili" known to the modern Cáhita as *chiltepín*.[20] This is a small, red, and extremely fiery berry which a wild shrub produces abundantly. It is powdered and sprinkled on food. Tobacco, *macuchi*, was grown and smoked.

Generally speaking, the lands of the Opata are rich and fertile. Irrigation was practiced where necessary, and sometimes gardens were watered with water brought by hand from the river.[21] Melons and watermelons are mentioned in very early sources, but these were introduced by the Spaniards. Cotton was used to a very considerable extent, but the details of cultivation are not known.

Women assisted the men in the labor of cultivation, but unlike the Pima, the women did not have to do all the work.[22] The barranca-dwelling Jova depended more largely on hunting and gathering than did the Opata and Eudeve.

Wild foods and plant products. The Opata utilized wild plants to a very large extent. Cactus fruits, the pitahaya, the tuna, and to a much lesser extent, the fruit of the saguaro cactus, which is available only in the Pimería Alta, were important. The pitahaya produces in May, June, and July. The tuna, fruit of the nopal cactus (*Opuntia* sp.), begins to ripen in March or April. The unripe fruit is collected in March, dried, and thus preserved to be cooked later.[23]

The *palmito* was used to make mats (*petates*), and the heart, which is "like a cone of sugar," was eaten nearly raw.[24] The mescal plant was roasted and eaten,[25] and boiled to make the alcoholic drink *aguardiente*, of which the old people were very fond. This drink is now known as *bacanora*, and is, of course, distilled. Mescal fiber was used to make cordage.

The Jova had as a staple food plant, the *maqui*, which is a root the size of a *camote* (sweet potato) or potato, with a dark skin. The flesh is white and is poisonous when raw. It must be boiled several times to remove the poison. The Opata also made some use of it, although they had abundant crops of corn, and later, of wheat.[26] Two other edible roots resembling the sweet potato, called *cavor, cavore,* and *sarat, sarte,* were known to the Opata.[27]

Mezquite beans were used extensively; in April the unripe pods were collected, boiled, dried, and later used in stews. In June the ripe fruit was gathered; part of the crop was eaten raw, since the fruit is tasty and sweet, and the remainder was stored to make atoles and stews. The mesquite gum was also eaten, and the "foam" of the tree was a remedy for suppurating boils.

The *Documentos para la Historia de México* gives a lengthy list of plants and their uses, of which only a few of the most important will be mentioned here. The *bachata* (Opata *batzat*) is a plant which gives a small, black fruit the size of a chick-pea, which is very sweet. It ripens in May. The root serves as soap. The *amole* (soap plant) was likewise used as soap. *Morales* (*babiro*), the mulberry (?), ripened in June: the tree is small, as is the fruit, but is very good. The wood was used to make bows. (The Yaqui make bows of mezquite.) In short, "Sonora produces many other wild fruits useful to its inhabitants; one would never finish listing them if one wished to refer to each one of them. There is hardly a month in the year that one of them is not producing."[28] Lombardo lists well over a hundred plants used as food or medicine. The leaves of a number of plants were boiled and eaten as greens.

Intoxicating drinks were made of corn, mescal, cactus (tuna); the most effective was made from the *saúco** (elder?) tree.

Pita,* i.e., cordage, was made from mescal, and also from a plant called *so*, which also produced a very sweet fruit. Gums of several trees were collected and were used as glues or incense, e.g., the *toro* tree, the pine, and another which produces a lacquerlike rosin, used as a countervenom.[29]

Preparation of foods.　　Corn was ground on the metate and was prepared in the usual forms, e.g., tortillas, atole, pozole, pinole.[30] Lime was burned and used to leach corn.[31] Salt was traded from the coast, or was obtained from a few places in the Opata country; the *Documentos*[32] mentions a war between the towns of Bacadeguatzi and Baserac over salt-producing land.

Food was boiled in earthenware pots, or was roasted in ashes. Tortillas were roasted on the usual round *comal*. Núñez remarks that the Opata were good and fairly clean cooks, and other authorities remark on the variety of their stews. Possibly meat was cooked in the earthoven with hot stones, as is the modern Sonoran usage; certainly mescal was roasted in this manner.

Hunting and fishing.　　Deer were the most important single source of meat, and are very numerous even today. Mountain sheep, rabbits, and other small game were also hunted. Rabbits were hunted in community drives and killed with sticks or light arrows.[33] (The modern Yaqui use special light arrows for rabbits and small game.) Birds were hunted to some extent, but the methods are not known. Honey was collected.[34]

Deer were stalked and killed with bow and arrow. Blinds of branches were constructed at water holes. Hunters made use of deerhead disguises. It may be inferred that the Opata made use of cord deer-snares, as do the Yaqui.[35]

Fishing was of some importance. Fish were taken with the hand, in weirs ("*coger pescado atajando el agua*"?), with an instrument "like spoons," with hook and line, and with the net.[36] Fish were also poisoned with *mauégo* (Span. *barbasco*), which is perhaps the same as the San Juanico tree used by the modern Yaqui for fish poison.[37]

Perhaps canoes were used: Smith gives a word for canoe. *Balsas*, or rafts, were made by the Opata of Saguaripa.[38]

Household utensils, basketry, and pottery.   Cordage has already been mentioned. Animal skins were tanned, but details of the method are not given. Pottery was made in a variety of forms, judging from the names of different kinds of vessels which occur in the sources. Gourd vessels (*jícaras**) and spoons were used.[39]

Very fine basketry of *palmito* and other fibers was made in a large variety of forms as noted by Lombardo. Hats were made after the coming of the Spaniards. Three modern examples of Opata baskets in two techniques and one hat were collected by the writer in Tónichi in 1940 and are now in the collections of the Museum of the American Indian.

Basketry was woven in a semisubterranean round room with a brush roof, which was known as the *húuki*. The women wove only in the hot season and retired to the *húuki* for that purpose. The *húuki* was constructed next to the house. Informants explained the underground room as necessary to keep the weaving materials at the proper degree of humidity. Women wove both basketry and cloth fabrics.[40]

The less sedentary Jova formerly made most of the *petates** (sleeping mats) of *palmito*, which they brought to the towns and exchanged for seed and clothing.[41] Fire was made by friction.[42]

Clothing, weaving, and ornament.   Clothing was made both from cotton fabrics and from skins. Skins were cured and dyed.[43] There is a large cotton and weaving vocabulary, including such terms as cotton, combing (carding) cotton, spinning, *malacate** (spindle whorl), women spinning, fabrics, the loom, etc.[44]

Wool became available with the advent of the Spaniards and was quickly adopted. Even the backward Jova had a few sheep and made their sole, blanketlike garment of wool as early as 1760.[45]

Men wore a breechclout of cotton, and other garments of skin; women wore "cloaks" of cotton, and cotton belts or sashes were woven.[46] Painted clothing is mentioned.[47] A number of plant dyes were used. Cloth and skins were dyed with the following plants: *chunero* gave yellow dye; *añil** gave blue; *brasil** gave red; *coca,** an aromatic vanilla, gave black. Also, *issaguára* was the instrument used in dyeing, from *issagua*, to dye.[48] (The modern Cáhita know and use the same plants.)

The following description of weaving is taken from *Documentos para la Historia de México*.[49] "They weave very cleverly and in different ways; they imitate the type, but not the quality of the tablecloths and napkins of Germany." First, four stakes are planted in the ground more or less distant from one another, depending upon the proportions which the finished fabric will have. A longer, smooth stick is tied across the stakes [at each end as a loom bar] which give the width of the piece. These are tied about half a *vara* (16 or 17 inches) from the ground. Then the women begin to warp the threads on the crosspieces from a ball of thread, which they pass from one to another until the necessary number of warp threads has been reached.

Then the weaver picks up the counter warp threads by means of double threads [which serve as harnesses]. The double threads are then wound around the heald rods. Two, three, or more such rods are put in [to form sheds], depending on the complexity of the pattern which is to be woven. A batten like a sword blade is used. The batten, turned on edge [to open the shed], allows the passage of the shuttle. The weft is put in with a reel, which is a thin stick with the thread wound about it. The woven fabric is tightened [packed] by means of a small pointed stick.

Thus the loom of the Opata falls in with other Mexican looms, and is like that of the modern Pima and Huichol. The girdle-back loom, of which one end is tied to a tree or roof beam, and which is the common loom type in central and southern Mexico, was apparently not known to the Opata. The Huichol, it is noted, have both the stationary ground-loom and the girdle-back [back-strap] loom. Modern Mayo use the stationary ground-loom for weaving sashes. The women wove or plaited little bags of hair in which they kept their rosaries.[50]

The linguistic data give native lexemes for sandals, but no detailed descriptions are available. In modern times, a type of soft-soled, pointed-toe moccasin of three pieces (known as the *tegua*) is made. This may be an imitation of eighteenth-century Spanish footwear, although it must be noted that the *tegua* strongly resembles the Apache moccasin.[51]

Headgear and decorations were made of skins, and feathers were worn in the hair by the warriors. The men wore their hair long.[52] The hair was washed with a kind of mud to cleanse and dye it.[53] One source reports tatooing of newborn infants (see ceremonial sponsorship, below). Face and body painting was not practiced, and the Opata made fun of the neighboring Pima who painted themselves.[54]

Weapons. The principal weapon of the Opata was the bow. The modern Yaqui bow is the simple bow, made from a species of the mezquite; perhaps the Opata bow was similar. Arrows were made from the *souāro* tree, according to Lombardo.[55]

Stone arrowheads (*tavit*)[56] were known. Núñez says that the arrows were never made of cane, and adds that the points were of stone and bone. In his time (1777), stone was no longer used, but bone was common. Iron points were used by some, but the most common was a simple foreshaft of *romerillo*, an exceedingly poisonous plant.[57]

It seems hardly possible that the Opata failed to utilize such a first-class material as cane for their arrows, particularly since most other Sonoran peoples use cane almost exclusively. Yaqui arrows are laterally feathered with two trimmed feathers, with a cane shaft, and a foreshaft of hard mezquite, which itself forms the point. Three arrow-point types occur: single barb, double barb, and no barb. Modern Yaqui also have a light wooden arrow with no foreshaft and no barbs, which is used to hunt small game. The latter are fire hardened. Feathers and foreshaft are affixed with sinew.[58]

Núñez states that the Opata used axes to fell trees. The ax was the same shape as the Spanish iron axes, and was hafted in a split wooden handle, attached by sinews.[59]

The Opata were famous for their arrow poisons. Apparently several poisons were used in addition to the *romerillo* mentioned above. A poison was extracted from a tree known as *mago*, and another was used to poison coyotes and dogs.[60] The Jova used such a powerful arrow poison that not only did the wounded man die, but the curer who tried to remove the poison by suction as well.[61] (The Yaqui also use arrow poison.) People were also killed among the Opata by poison administered in food, the women being especially prone to this practice.[62]

Skin quivers were used by the warriors, as well as light lances and light round shields.[63] The club was used, although it was stated to have been a weapon more characteristic of the Pima Bajo. (The Yaqui also used clubs.)[64]

Games.   Judging from the number of terms referring to gambling, the Opata were very fond of play and gambling, e.g., *tzémegua*, "to play"; *patole*, to bet"; *himá*, "to win what is bet"; *ové*, "to bet against"; *datu*, "to collect the bets."[65] From these data, together with the fact that the modern Yaqui recall a long-stick gambling game, it seems legitimate to infer the existence of a long-stick game, probably with counters, for the Opata. Betting also ran high on the ball games and races, but "without disputes, and with great amusement," according to Núñez.

There is some evidence for races and ball games. Núñez states:

Their common game was called *Goquimari*, which . . . is to bet on who will run [faster] with a ball which they kick with their feet; the other [game] was running races in pairs, the runners starting two by two, naked, with their heads decorated with sashes of dyed and colored skins, and with waist-bands of the same material. Today [1777] on very festive days, they still play it.

Zúñiga,[66] writing in 1835, describes the games as follows:

Sundays they play *Guachicori*. The town is divided into *barrios* of above and below [i.e., moieties], which are opposed contestants. Each group names a Captain, and they "fight a race" with two bones tied together, which they call *maneu*. The women follow the players of each moiety. It is a very strenuous game, in which strength, . . . agility in running, suffering and audacity are necessary. No arm is permitted other than a small, weak stick, which serves to strike the pair of bones; the stick may not be used to defend oneself or to strike another. Frequently a push and the resulting fall cause the death of a player, but this does not result in quarrels or fights.

Another game is called *gomi*, which is played with two wooden balls the size of an orange, which are kicked along by two or more players, always in even numbers. The race continues for one or two leagues.[67]

The modern Yaqui, although they no longer play these games, still remember the details; the dirts [darts? first?] game (in Yaqui *wokhi mári*) was played between two towns. Tight waistbands were worn by the players to strengthen them.[68]

Social Life

Warfare.   All sources unanimously attest the warlike prowess of the Opata. Indeed, during most of the period of their recorded history, they were the principal bulwark of Sonora against the incursions of the hated and feared Apache. This warlike reputation was equally enjoyed by the Jova, who, although peaceable enough in their relations with the Opata and the Spaniards, were indefatigable Apache fighters.[69]

Perhaps the most important Opata functionary was the War Captain. Each town had its War Captain, who commanded the warriors. Normally, every able-bodied man was a warrior, and together they appear to have formed a Warrior's Society, perhaps like that of the Yaqui. The details of how a Captain was selected are not available, but it seems that the most important requisite was success in planning and leading raids against the Apache. There are also some indications that the War Captain possessed supernatural powers, "*que presume de hechicero.*"[70] Núñez states that the people were ruled by their War Captains and the old men.

On occasions of ceremonial intoxication, the older men and the Captain were privileged to recite their war deeds. On these occasions, there were songs and dances, which lasted all night. The War Captain acted in matters of public safety only; a council of elders (*ancianos**) decided other civic matters.

A neophyte warrior had to go out several times with a war party. If he successfully passed this novitiate, he was initiated. The Captain gathered all the warriors, one of whom acted as sponsor for the initiate. The sponsor, who faced the initiate, with his arms on the boy's shoulders, was armed with bow and arrows, light lance, and a light round shield. The Captain addressed the novice, telling him what he must do in order to become a successful warrior; that he must be brave, suffer hunger and thirst, cold, fatigue, and the like, without complaining. Then the Captain took from his quiver a hard, dry eagle's foot, and scratched the novice's chest, arms, and legs with it until the wounds bled freely. The novice was supposed not to flinch or show signs of discomfort. Then the Captain gave him his arms, a bow and arrows. The witnesses and the sponsors each gave the boy a pair of arrows.

Following this initiation, the novice still had to undergo special tests and hardships when on a war party. He had to keep watch, discharge the dangerous function of spy on the enemy camp, and generally execute all the unpleasant tasks to which the older warriors assigned him. He remained in this unenviable status until another neophyte was initiated.

War parties were attended with considerable ceremony; preparations were made during the eight days preceding the day of proposed departure. The night before the party left, the Captain "talked all night." Scalps were customarily taken.

If a war party returned defeated, the warriors crept into town at night, trying to avoid notice. If they were successful, they arranged it so as to make a triumphal entry by day. An old woman from the town was armed with bow and arrows, and acted as mistress of ceremonies in the subsequent victory dance. The old woman, accompanied by the Captain's wife and the other women of the town, went out to meet the returning warriors. The old woman formally welcomed them, seized the scalps which they had taken, and began to dance with them. At the same time, she insulted the scalps and abused them with special songs. Thus they entered the town. The warriors did not take part in this celebration, but stacked their arms and looked on.

Captives were tortured, especially by the women, who burned them on the thighs with brands. Not all captives were killed; children were kept and apparently adopted or treated as slaves.

The booty which had been taken in raids was given to the old men and women: if the warriors were to have used it, it would have resulted in their death on the next war party. The wilder Eudeve and Jova sometimes took the hand of the enemy as well as the scalp. They used the hands to stir the pinole they made for the victory celebration.[71]

Zúñiga describes a dance called the *Taguaro*, in which they pretended that the Apache had come to steal the donkeys and the women. The warriors left the town to attack them and to recover what they are supposed to have stolen. Then the warriors returned to the plaza, where a tall pole had already been erected. On the top of the pole was a figure which is called the *Taguaro*. The old men approached singing, with rattles, while the warriors loosed their shots at the figure, and received praise or vituperation depending on the quality of their marksmanship.[72]

When on a war party, the direction in which the enemy lay was divined by means of a freshwater crayfish (called in Opata *hupitui*). It was held by the head and questioned; the answer was divined from the movements of the creature's legs.[73] (The Yaqui divined the approach and direction of the enemy by observing the fall of small sticks balanced on the fingertips.)[74] The Opata warriors liked to attack at dawn if possible; such an attack was called an *albazo* < Span; *alba*, "dawn." It was the duty of the War Captain and his men to scout the territory around the town daily, to make sure that it was safe for the people to go to their work in the fields.

As has been emphasized, the enemy of the Opata during the eighteenth century (and part of the seventeenth as well) were the Apache. In the sixteenth century and earlier, however, the Apache do not appear to have been such a problem. Probably the Opata fought among themselves before they had to present a solid front to the Apache menace, or traded raids with their neighbors, the Yaqui, Pima Bajo, etc. The fight between Baserac and Bacadeguatzi, both Opata towns, over salt, has already been mentioned.

Dances, musical instruments, and ceremonials.   The Opata had a number of public dancing performances and ceremonies. These lasted all night, and in some cases were accompanied by ceremonial drinking and sexual license, in which wives were apparently exchanged. The latter was called *diabro* butuhurss,* "for the devil" [*sic*].[75]

Gourd rattles are mentioned by the sources, and Núñez, in addition to mentioning the Scalp Dance, refers to, but does not describe, a "dance of the Drums," accompanied by singing. Perhaps the drum was like that of the Yaqui. Probably flageolets were used. Leg rattles made of cocoons of the *attacus orizabi* were used, as among the Yaqui and Mayo. Rasping sticks of bone or wood (also Yaqui) were used for dances, and mothers used them to quiet fretful children.[76] Probably the Opata had the musical bow. (The Cáhita form is of thick cane, and has no resonator.)[77] European instruments—the violin, harp, and guitar— quickly became popular. Lombardo mentions guitar and harp.[78] Núñez states that there were more than forty violinists in Santa María Baserac in 1777.

As early as 1730, aboriginal dances and ceremonies were well suppressed by the Jesuits. They had, however, a dance called *torom raqui,* which was performed to assure rain and abundant harvests. It was performed in the spring (Opata *cuque*), and lasted from dawn to dusk. It was attended by everyone. They sowed the entire plaza where they danced with every kind of seed and branches, and at intervals with the hooves of animals, cow horns, and other similar things.

In the four corners of the plaza they erected *ramadas* of branches, from which the dancers emerged in turn, "with howls and a terrible clamor," to the sound of bone (rasps?) and rattles. They were masked in "abominable costumes and headgear." They danced to each one of the places (where seeds, etc., were sowed) in the plaza, and danced before them with the "saddest of groans, weeping, and diabolical ceremonies." The good father adds that the dance had not been performed for ten years, since he strictly forbade it.[79]

Another rain dance is reported in 1764. At night a number of girls left the house, where their musicians—old men and women—remained. These made a great noise with hollow calabashes and bones (rasps?). The girls went to a place which had been well cleaned and swept, and danced there, dressed in white, or clad only in a shirt. This was done in the rainy season, when the rain would not fall. They believed that by these means the clouds would halt (their flight), and give the rain which they needed for their fields.[80]

Zúñiga describes the following dances which survived into the nineteenth century. *Dagüinemaca* (< *daguia*, "to dance"; *ne-maca*, "I give") was a dance which made public a formalized friendship and obligation between two persons.[81] One would dance before a person toward whom one felt friendly, and would give him a gift, such as a horse, cow, or chicken. The honored person would then embrace the other, and dance a few turns. This sealed the alliance of friendship, and these two were called *noraguas*, that is, friends. (See also ceremonial sponsorship below.) In a year's time, the gift and the dance were returned by the recipient.

The *Taguaro* has already been mentioned. Zúñiga[82] mentions another dance, called the *Jojo*, which he describes as an historical dance, commemorating "the passage of the Aztecs, and the coming of Moctezuma, whom they await as the Jews await the Messiah." "This dance," he says, "appears to be abusive and superstitious to those who do not see in the allegories more than witchcraft or idols; but basically it is purely historical." The modern Easter dances, the Deer and Pascola dances, will be discussed in detail in the section dealing with historical change.

Marriage and sex relations.   The Opata were monogamous, but unions were extremely brittle, according to Núñez. The wedding ceremonies are of considerable interest. First, the marriageable girls were placed in a line, and the marriageable boys in another. At a given signal, the girls commenced to run. At another, the boys pursued them. The boys had to overtake the girls, and each boy, choosing his girl, had to catch her and seize her by the nipple of her left breast. Thus the betrothals were made and confirmed. Then the dance commenced.

The Jesuit author was told that the nuptial pair, or pairs, danced naked. Each pair was then put in their sleeping mats, and the rest of the party continued dancing and singing all night, or until they were tired. The author states that such functions were still held in his time, but out of sight and hearing of the priests.[83]

Loose women were known as "flower-women." The word *guisai* described the manner of slipping about stealthily at night to meet secretly with lovers.[84]

Kinship.   The sources give what may be considered almost a complete list of Opata kinship terms as follows:

Parent-Child Group

Father (son spk)	*massiguat*	possessive	*no mas*[85] "my father"
Father (daughter spk)	*mariguat*		*no mari*
Mother (both)	*deguat*		*no de*
Son (father spk)	*noguat*		*no no*
Son (mother spk)	*miriguat*		*no miri*
Daughter (father spk)	*maraguat*		*no mara*
Daughter (mother spk)	*aquiguat*		*no aqui*
Children (both parents)	*nonotziguat*		*no nonotzi*

Grandparent-Grandchild Group

Paternal grandfather	*posiguat*	possessive *no posi, no po* "and in this manner they also call the brothers and sisters of the grandparent"
Paternal grandmother	*cariguat*	*no cari* "also her brothers and sisters"
Maternal grandfather	*paoguat*	*no pao* "also his brothers and sisters"
Maternal grandmother	*xüguat*	*no xü (su)* "also her brothers and sisters"
Paternal grandchild	*posimariaguat*	*no posima*
Grandchild of paternal grandmother	*camariguat*	*no camari*
Maternal grandchild	*paomariguat*	*no paoma*

Grandchild of maternal grandmother	*xumariguat*	*no xumari*
Great-grandfather	*voponiguat*	*no voponi*
Great-grandmother	*vipiniguat*	*no vipini*
Great-grandson	*vapatziguat*	*no vapá*
Great-granddaughter	*cocotziguat*	*no cocó*

Sibling Group

Elder brother	*vatziguat* possessive	*no va*
	pl. *vapatziguat*	*no vapá*
Elder sister	*cotziguat*	*no co*
	pl. *cocotziguat*	*no cocó*
Younger brother	*voniguat*	*no vo*
	pl. *voponiguat*	*no vopon*
Younger sister	*viniguat*	*no vi*
	pl. *vipiniguat*	*no vipin*
Sisters (brothers spk)	*vuúgua*	
Brothers (sister spk)	*doriguade*	
Blood-cousins	*maguat*	

Uncle-Nephew Group

Father's elder brother	*cumúguat* possessive	*no cumú*
Father's younger brother	*teviriguat*	*no teviri*
Father's elder sister	*soróguat*	*no soró*
Father's younger sister	*vavoguat*	*no vavo*
Mother's elder brother	*cutziguat*	*no cútzu*
Mother's younger brother	*taiguat*	*no tai*
Mother's elder sister	*tepóguat*	*no tépo*
Mother's younger sister	*deriguat*	*no deri*
Children of elder brother	*tevitzimariguat*	*no tevitzima*
Children of younger brother	*cucumariguat*	*no cucumari*
		no cucuma
Children of elder sister	*taimariguat*	*no taima*
Children of younger sister	*cutzimariguat*	*no cutzima*
Children of elder brother (woman spk)	*vaomariguat*	*no vaoma*

Children of younger
   brother (woman spk)   *sorómariguat*   *no soróma*
Children of elder sister
   (woman spk)   *detzimariguat*   *no detzima*
Children of younger
   sister (woman spk)   *tepomariguat*   *no tepóma*

Affinal Relations

Husband   *cunágua*
Wife   *hubigua*
Father-in-law,
   mother-in-law   *guasseguat* possessive *no guasse*
Son-in-law   *monéguat*   *no mone*
Daughter-in-law   *modeguat*   *no mode*
Brother-in-law,
   sister's husband   *mutziguat*   *no mutzi*
Brother- or sister-in-law
   and sister of the wife *mutzimariguat*   *no mutzima*
Brother's wife
   (woman spk)   *mocatziguat*   *no mocá*
Husbands of two sisters
   (reciprocal)   *cussiguat*   *no cussi*
Foster-parent   *chigua*   *no chi*
Foster-child   *chimariguat*   *no chima*

Other Terms

Brothers, sons of   *seni tui* "of one belly"
   one mother
Twins   *toui, tovi*
Close relatives   *naita*
Distant relatives   *verassihua*

The following abstract terms are of interest:

himaragua[86]   the kinship as a whole
maguaragua   < maguat, no magua, etc; the close kinship
                     between brothers, sisters, and cousins
vuchúguat   the relationship between uncles, aunts,
                     nephews, and nieces

Barcastro gives the following terms which vary from those given by Lombardo above: male cousin, *taigua*; female cousin, *derigua*.[87] It must be remembered, however, that almost a hundred years separated Lombardo from Barcastro, and probably by the latter's time the kinship terminology had already begun to break down badly.

The element -*ru*, suffixed to a kinship term, indicated that the relative was dead, e.g., *no de-ru*, my deceased mother; *no massi-ru*, my deceased father; *no mara-ru*, my deceased daughter, etc. The suffix was also used with certain other types of nouns, generally names of objects considered personal or inalienable, e.g., house, field, etc.[88]

The Opata had the following three terms indicating female physiological growth: a girl whose breasts had not yet developed; a nubile girl, i.e., with developed breasts; a woman who had given birth. There was a term for virgin, which applied to both male and female.[89]

The bases of kinship reckoning were: 1] blood as contrasted to affinal relatives; 2] age differences; 3] sex differences. Reciprocal terms and other features of interest, e.g., great-grandparent-sibling terms, may readily be seen in the foregoing arrangement of the kinship terms. A further bit of evidence of sex division is found in the occurrence of a small but important woman's vocabulary, especially in the affirmatives and negatives. For example, *háve*, "yes," man speaking; *heé*, "yes," woman speaking, etc. (The same phenomenon occurs in Cáhita.)[90]

It must be added that aunts and uncles called sons of their nephews and nieces by the term for grandsons; also, grandparents' brothers and sisters called grandparents' nephews' and nieces' sons by the term for grandsons.[91] It is stated that brothers- and sisters-in-law were extremely prone to marry each other,[92] i.e., *sororate* and *levirate*.

Sponsorship.   In addition to the social ties which devolved naturally upon the individual through birth and sex status and marriage, there were a number of formal social relationships with otherwise unrelated persons into which every Opata entered. These have aptly been called ceremonial sponsorships by Spicer, who has studied them exhaustively among the modern Yaqui. Sponsorships were perhaps the most important single factor, outside of actual kinship itself, in the integration of Opata society.

Each type of sponsorship was clearly accompanied by definite obligations and privileges. These were binding not only upon the two individuals primarily concerned, but included their kin as well. By a legal fiction, relatives acquired through sponsorships were regarded as blood kin.

The Opata acquired his first ceremonial sponsor shortly after birth, with a ceremony called *peri*. In some parts of the Opatería, at least, the infant was tattooed around the eyelids with a black pigment, although this was specifically denied by Núñez, speaking of Santa María Baserac in 1777. The *peri* was primarily a name-giving ceremony: a sponsor was chosen for the infant, and it was he who gave the name. The sponsor became the child's ceremonial father, and the sponsor's kin stood in the same relation to the infant and its family as they did to the sponsor's true son.

The Opata watched the lines of kinship carefully when marriages were being arranged. Unfortunately no detailed information is given regarding preferred and prohibited mating. It is fairly clear, however, that two families united only by the *peri* relationship could intermarry. It was regarded as a tie of alliance and friendship.[93]

The sponsoring of an initiate into the warrior's group has already been mentioned. Probably other changes in status, e.g., marriage, were also accompanied by ceremonial sponsorship. Thus the individual automatically established bonds of friendship and reciprocity with many otherwise unrelated family groups.

The Opata sponsoring system blended early and easily with the introduced Catholic complex of baptismal and marriage godparents. But there were important adaptations: the Opata adapted the new complex to the old, and there was a tremendous extension in the application of the Spanish godparent terms, which were naturally equated with their aboriginal correspondents. The Jesuits found this extremely confusing, as can well be imagined. Lombardo[94] cautions his colleagues that sons of *compadres*[95] call each other brothers, and are also *compadres* to each other. The true parents' brothers and sisters automatically become *compadres* and *comadres* of the godparent. If a man or woman acts as godparent, then his wife or her husband becomes a godparent automatically, even though the latter may not have been present. When the priests were investigating marriages submitted for their approval, they found that the Indians did not distinguish between true and ceremonial brothers and sisters.

In any Opata community, then, an individual was normally bound by these ties in one way or another to the majority of his neighbors.

(The same general pattern exists today among the Cáhita, where details of the functioning of the system can be studied.)[96]

In addition to the foregoing ceremonial sponsorship, formalized friendships were of great importance. Presumably an individual could enter into as many of these friendships as he chose. Both parties had strictly defined duties and privileges. The manner of setting up such a relationship has already been described (*Dagüinemaca:* see dances and ceremonies).

In Opata, such a friendship between men was called *noragua* (< *no,* "son," *-ragua,* abstractual nominal suffix, hence, literally, "sonship"). *Mararagua,* "daughter-ship," was the similar relationship between women. The institution was operative only between persons of the same sex.[97]

The sources state that there was nothing that a man would not do for his *noragua;* he had to grant his every request. Should the *noragua* be about to start a dangerous trip, his friend would leave his own affairs and family to be with him and aid him in every way he could. It is unfortunate that the sources supply no further information on this most interesting point.[98]

Religion and Knowledge

Shamans and curing.   Shamans were present in each community, and were respected and feared. The sources mention only male shamans. Intrusive objects caused disease. The shaman first fanned the patient with a fan of large feathers. Then he sucked, practiced sleight of hand, and removed the object from the patient's body. The intrusive object— a thorn, pebble, worm, hair, etc.—was then thrown into the fire. A fire was always kept burning brightly in the patient's house, no matter how warm the weather might be.[99]

Arrow wounds were sucked and filled with powdered peyote. This was left for two days, and the treatment repeated several times. Poultices of various plants, such as maguey, mescal, date palm, and *romerillo,* were also applied. Those suffering from thirst owing to the temperature caused by the wound were given the root of the *pochote* tree (silk-cotton tree, *Ceiba*) to chew.[100]

The Opata herbal was very large, and evoked the unqualified praise of the author of the *Rudo Ensayo.*[101] *Pipichagui* (Opata *tairago*) is a "wild lettuce" which is good for stomachache, and for delayed menstruation of several months (abortifacient?). *Toloache* (*taguaro*)[102] is good for bites and fevers, aches and pains, and catamenial difficulties. There are plants which confer virility and fertility. *Uña de gato* (*jussi*), "cat's claw," a spiny desert plant, is good for stoppage of the urine. A number of plants used to treat the *mal gálico* (syphilis) are mentioned. Pine needles (*ocosaguat*) and other aromatic plants were burned as parturifacients, the smoke being applied to the parturient.[103] The cocoon of a certain worm was reputed to be an effective remedy for the *mal de aire*; it was burned, and the patient exposed to the smoke. Every Indian used different herbs to treat a particular sickness. The sweat bath was used extensively as a treatment for certain illnesses.[104]

Epidemics were of frequent occurrence among the Opata. The yellow vomit (*saguai dodo*) was especially feared, and was common among the neighboring Pima.[105] *Toloache*, i.e., the plant called *cupitzio*, not the *taguaro* above mentioned, was the remedy. *Tuparo* was a plant used to kill bedbugs.

A person bitten by a rattlesnake catches the snake, stretches it out, and bites it. Then the bite on the person does not swell, but the snake swells and dies. The wound may also be burned, or gashed, and toasted deer horn applied. But more commonly, rattlesnake bites were treated by taking human excrement dissolved in water.[106]

Religious concepts and death.   The concepts of rain and fertility were important (see dances, above). The data indicate that four was the ceremonial number, as among the Yaqui.

The Opata venerated the sun and the moon as brother and sister respectively. They greeted the new moon by throwing handfuls of pinole in the air. The sun likewise received offerings of pinole when it appeared each morning. The sun was commonly called *tät* (i.e., *táat*), but the elders called it *tecassa*, the son of *taumissa*, but they did not mention the name of the mother of the sun. The moon was called by the elders *aquit*,[107] although the common name was *metza*, which is also the word used to indicate a month.[108]

The Opata welcomed the appearance of the moon with dancing, shouts, and cries. They said that during eclipses the moon was shielding itself from its enemies, and thus called the eclipse *inamerai*, that is, "he who has a shield." In order to frighten away the enemies of the moon, they shouted and played instruments.[109] (The modern Yaqui do likewise at eclipses.) Today pregnant women run three times around the house during an eclipse; otherwise the infant "would lack a part."[110]

The dead are interred in a sitting position, with new clothing and offerings of pinole, *quelite*, and other foods. A dead warrior was interred with his weapons and insignia.[111]

At death, the souls go to a large lake, on the north shore of which is a little man, a dwarf called *Butza Uri*. He receives the souls and transports them in a large canoe to the south shore, where a revered old woman called *Hoatziqui* lives. She swallows the souls one by one, save those she finds with painted faces, like the Pima. These she rejects, saying that they are spiny like the cactus, and throws them into the lake. Those she swallows live a life of plenty in her belly.[112] Such little men were much respected and feared, and the people were careful to treat them well and not offend them.

Núñez records the tradition that in the east dwelt a woman (deity) whom they called Mother, and in the west a man (deity) whom they called Father. This pair dressed like Indians, and the man always carried a green staff. When these two were about to leave their homes to visit mankind, messengers appeared to give notice to the people, so that they might prepare to receive them; "but since they never arrived at this settlement [Baserac], the people never met them."[113]

Shamans were addressed by spirits in the form of pumas, dogs, or more commonly, in the form of a snake.[114] The ancients had a belief in a double-headed eagle. The warrior bird (Opata, *guegue*) presaged war when it cried, as did the cry of a certain fox. The cry of the owl meant death for a sick person or presaged the approach of war.[115] A sudden strong wind betokened the approach of the Apache.[116]

If one was bit by a snake, and recovered, then he was likely to be killed by lightning. When one was bit by a snake, one threw away all the clothing he had on at the time; otherwise, he would be liable to be bitten again. So that lightning would not strike one, at the end of the year he poured a jar of water over his body from head to foot.[117] At Christmastime, the men of Tónichi go to the higher mountains to fetch a large pine tree to the town. As they carry the tree through the town and the plaza, the women dash jars of cold water over them.[118]

The Opata rejoiced in a thunderstorm, and gave every sign of pleasure. But when hail fell, the people caused it to cease by placing thick lengths of cane in their doorways. A person struck by lightning was allowed to remain where he fell. His family brought food, etc., to the spot. If he died, they held the death celebration on the spot, but did not bury the body for two or three days. They believed that the soul had been frightened out of the body by the lightning, i.e., soul loss, and that it was wandering about nearby. If, however, the soul did not return within two or three days, they buried the body there.[119]

Heaps of sticks, stones, and bones were piled at certain spots along the roads. Some said that they did this in order to leave their weariness there; others said it was because someone had died there of cold, and that the sticks were left so that the dead person might warm himself with the fuel.[120]

The Opata had a deluge myth in which the ancestors of the Indians, a few boys and girls, saved themselves by entering a stick, "hollow like a drum."[121] Individuals with webbed fingers, and hunchbacks, were named, but no details of associated beliefs are recorded. In certain ceremonies, and at Easter it was prohibited to cut the finger nails or trim the hair.[122]

Time reckoning, seasons, and directions.   The hours of the day were reckoned by the sun. The summer solstice was named, and perhaps there were observances of the occasion. The rainy, hot, and cold seasons were named and delimited; spring was the season of drought.[123] It seems that a lunar calendar was in common use. Seasons and calendar were oriented in terms of agriculture, i.e., the growing season, planting, harvesting, etc., of the corn. Venus and the constellation known in Spanish as the *Tres Marías* were known and named, but no further astronomical details are given by the sources.[124]

Lombardo was amazed at the extensive vocabularies of directions and cardinal points: even the children used the terms in common conversation. People referred to the parts of their houses in terms of cardinal points, and one would not say, e.g., "I am going to Matepe," but "I am going northwest to Matepe" or something similar.

Examples are:

sivi	east	*tena sivi*	southeast, "between south and east"
uru	west		
vate	north	*tena uru*	southwest
teno	midday(?)	*va sivi*	northeast
		va uru	northwest

Lombardo gives forty-four additional directional terms, including up and down, and their application.[125]

Historical Change

FROM THE time of the first Spanish *entradas* into northwestern Mexico, say in the earliest part of the seventeenth century, the Opata were in continuous, close contact with the whites. Missionization by the Jesuits commenced shortly thereafter. The record of baptisms commences in Onavas, an important Pima Bajo mission, whose limits included some Opata, in 1622. The records of the neighboring Opata town of Santa María de Pópulo de Tonilce (Tónichi)[126]—located later on the banks of the Yaqui River about two leagues above Onavas—commence in 1628.

The Opatería contains some of the most fertile lands of Sonora. Moreover, precious metals were early discovered, and mines were opened. The Indians wandered off in considerable numbers to work for the Spaniards in these enterprises, although the Jesuits stoutly opposed their leaving the mission territories. Spanish settlers quickly became numerous. The whole story has been one of ever-increasing encroachment upon Indian lands with consequent cultural disintegration. Yet the Opata never rebelled against Spanish domination. All sources unanimously praise "the firm loyalty of the Opata and Eudeve nations"[127]

The Opata were permanently allied with the whites in the bitter struggle against the Apache. Indeed, the Opata troops were commissioned by the viceregal government, and as late as the 1850s one finds references to the "Opata soldiers and their War Captain."[128] This picture is diametrically opposed to that of the Yaqui-Spanish contacts, where the independent Yaqui first rose in rebellion on account of increasing white encroachment in the years 1735–40 and have vainly repeated the procedure at very frequent intervals.

It was true, nevertheless, that the Opata complained bitterly of being imposed upon by the whites, but they never did anything about it. They were unjustly and inconsiderately called on to furnish escorts for officials and priests at the latter's whims, and had to undertake long, arduous campaigns in the mountains, all without remuneration. Sometimes they even had to furnish their own food and supplies for such campaigns, while their own fields went unattended during their absence. Zúñiga in 1835 wrote of the likelihood of an Opata uprising because of these and other similar injustices. But it was too late—the uprising never came.

The importance of the Apache in the history of Sonora cannot be overemphasized. In the eighteenth century, their depredations had become so general that much of the country was unsafe, even for large parties. Whole territories, towns, ranches, and even mines, were abandoned by the Spanish and Opata. At one time the abandonment of the entire province was under consideration. Had it not been for the Opata, it would have been impossible for the Spaniards to have held the province.

As early as 1730 the priests had been able to suppress many of what to them were objectionable features of the culture of their docile and obedient converts. These include such features as rain and fertility rites. We have the explicit statement of the priests that, while they suppressed certain dances, etc., they taught the Indians new ones to take their places![129] We are in the fortunate position of being able to determine what these new dances and ceremonies were that the Jesuits introduced with unusual astuteness, since the new elements still survive among the Cáhita, the remnants of the Pima Bajo, and even among the modern descendants of the Opata.

The new elements were, of course, blended with aboriginal elements, resulting in a curious hybrid complex from Spanish and Indian sources, with, perhaps, the latter predominating. The main [one] introduced dances, which were connected with Christian religious observances, were the following: Matachín, Moors, and Christians, and the hybrid complex of masked performers and ritual of the Easter season.

The Matachín dance is so widespread and well known in Mexico that a detailed description would be out of place here. Spicer gives the details for the modern Yaqui.[130] It may be parenthetically noted, however, that the small boy dressed in lacy feminine garments, and who dances in the center of the dancers, is none other than the "Maid Marion" of the English Kerry-Dancers and of similar European forms of the dance. Among the Opata of the southernmost town of Tónichi, both men and women danced the Matachín, unlike the Yaqui, where men alone dance.

The pantomimic battle of the Moors and Christians is likewise so well known that a mention of it suffices. In Tónichi it was performed some twenty-five years ago with an interesting variant. The defeated Moors finally tried to flee the field, but were brought back by the Christians, who turned them over to the women. The women were divided into two groups, the Moorish women and the Christian women.

Each Moor soldier was seized by his sash, in front by a Moor woman, in back by a Christian woman. A veritable tug of war ensued, but the Christian women won, and triumphantly dragged the unresisting Moors into the church, where they were baptized anew.[131]

Details of the lengthy and incredibly complex Easter performances of the Yaqui are well known.[132] The Opata had almost identical observances. Points in common between the two groups include a series of processions in which several ceremonial groups took part and small boys, acting as military police, disciplining the masked Fariseos, etc.

The Fariseo Society, which may be roughly defined as the forces of evil and the enemies of Christ, is comparable in every way to the Fariseo Society of the Yaqui. The performers carry a wooden dagger in one hand and a long stick in the other; these they clash together to mark the marching rhythm of the procession. The Opata Fariseos are kept circling the outskirts of the procession, while small boys, with naked torsos painted with spots, keep them in order with switches. Being evil, they may not enter the procession of Christians. On *Sábado de Gloria* (Holy Saturday), which is the culmination of Holy Week, the Fariseos are finally brought into the church. (The present church in Tónichi, completed in 1772, is now a battered and eroded adobe structure.)[133]

The similarities to Yaqui usage are so evident as to obviate lengthy comment. Among the Opata, anyone may serve as a Fariseo who wishes to, or one may serve a year or two because of a vow, or to do penance. The organization, unlike the Cáhita, is loose and informal. But the Opata Fariseos take advantage of the occasion, and of the disguise afforded by their masks, to commit all manner of petty crimes, such as chicken-stealing, etc. Many are drunk, and serious brawls have occurred. Because of the unpleasant features, the local authorities in many of the former Opata towns condemned and completely suppressed the society as a public nuisance.

In Tónichi the Easter observances are almost entirely secular, and everyone takes part in them: "they are a sort of a drama or comedy," the people say. A dramatic presentation of the Passion of Christ is performed in Spanish, from a traditional play, the parts for which are handed down and preserved from year to year with occasional recopying.

The secular, informal, profane, and almost trivial character of the Tónichi Lenten observances contrasts strikingly with the severely formal and religious nature of the Yaqui observances, hedged about as they are with ceremonial restrictions and penances.[134] Here, obviously, we have a remarkable instance of differentials in rates of acculturation and disintegration from the traditional norms. Yet both Opata and Yaqui were exposed to Spanish influences for the same length of time, and, initially at least, under almost identical circumstances. The sole difference was that the Opata contact was not attended by friction, while this was overwhelmingly the case with the Yaqui. These facts serve to explain in large part the differences between Cáhita and Opata acculturation processes and their end results. There are, on the one hand, ethnic survival and a feeling of nationalism on the part of the Yaqui in the face of the common enemy, namely, the whites and mestizos, and on the other, the complete disappearance of everything resembling an Opata culture and cultural milieu.

Modern informants in Tónichi stated that the Opata also performed some kind of Pascola and Deer Dances, which are rightly considered as characteristic of the Cáhita. It was not possible to obtain further details from the Opata. It may be inferred that they probably had similar performances, although these probably differed considerably from the Yaqui-Mayo type.

The masks of the modern Opata Fariseos are not without interest. A collection of thirty-nine masks was obtained in Tónichi in 1940 by the writer.[135] Their occurrence has not hitherto been noted. The masks are carved from *chilecote* (balsa) wood, which is abundant in the vicinity. It is also used to make crude stools, etc. The masks are painted with a variety of colors and pigments, and some show a decided depth of artistic feeling. The characters represented are all traditional, and most are named. It may be noted that some fifteen of these are animal representations, while nine represent monsters. The remainder are human or anthropomorphic and include such Holy Week characters as Judas, etc. Some have crosses painted in the forehead, as do the Yaqui Pascola masks.

At the conclusion of Holy Week ceremonies, i.e., on Holy Saturday, the Yaqui Fariseos burn their masks and other regalia on a straw figure of Judas in the churchyard. While these burn to the merry explosions of firecrackers, the erstwhile Fariseos—their vows fulfilled with the conclusion of their ungodly work—are led into the church by ceremonial sponsors, and are there received into the rejoicing congregation. Only two of the Yaqui Fariseo masks, which are of hide, are preserved until the following year, when a complete new set is made. Like the Opata, the Yaqui masks represent a traditional series of characters.[136] The Opata, however, do not burn their masks: the Fariseos give them away to small boys, or keep them to be used again or loaned to friends. Men who give their masks to boys often redeem them a year later for a few cents, if they decide to take part as Fariseos again.

On the basis of material presented here, as well as evidence from other Sonoran groups, the extensive ceremonial use of masks is quite clearly an aboriginal tradition. The Jesuits were accustomed to masked mummers in their own culture, and so did not find them objectionable. Spanish culture, however, influenced the aboriginal mask tradition in two important ways: first, in the nature of the beings represented, the *dramatis personae*, and second, in the technique of manufacture. Obviously it must have been a much more difficult task to carve balsa wood satisfactorily before the introduction of metal knives. Perhaps wood was little used in pre-Conquest times, masks being made mostly of skin, as are the Yaqui Fariseos types. Certainly a much higher degree of artistic virtuosity was attained when good knives became available. An analogous case is found in the wood-carver's art of the Northwest Pacific Coast, which reached its culmination in many respects after the artifacts of the whites had become known.[137]

On the subject of political organization, the sources only state that under aboriginal conditions the Opata were governed by the War Captain on the one hand and by the council of elders on the other. The council of elders was highly respected, and old men were generally deferred to on account of their age.

During colonial times, each town had the following officers:

Ecclesiastical

Fiscal mayor, who was also the church notary; in Opata, *mador*. One or two assistant *fiscales*, depending on the size of the town.

Temastiones (*Temastames*), sacristans.

Maestro, lay priest who conducted the services in the priest's absence. He could not administer the sacraments.

Civil

Governor, *Alcalde, Alguacil*, and *Topile*. These officials were elected yearly, according to the laws of 1716, under the priest's supervision. We may be fairly sure that the latter manipulated town politics to his own liking. All the offices are Spanish institutions, save that of *topil* (< Aztec *topilli*). The *topiles* were boys who served as messengers and men-of-all-work for the municipal authorities. The institution is found throughout Mexico.

The remaining officer, perhaps more important than the foregoing, was the War Captain, whose functions have already been described.

In colonial times, crimes were punished by whipping with one or two dozen lashes. Sometimes Indians who were remiss in attending mass were also whipped.[138] Each town had a municipal house, in which was located the jail. Stocks were also used.[139]

Under aboriginal conditions a War Captain could rise to dominate a wider extent of territory than was comprised by his own community. "The Jesuits on the Yaqui were visited by the great *cacique Sisibotari,* from his town of Sahuaripa, and were told that he controlled seventy settlements.[140] Probably these *caciques'* spheres of influence were temporary, and depended entirely upon the personal qualities of the leaders themselves. The tradition, if such it was, was continued and strengthened by the Spaniards in colonial times by the appointments of successive Opata "Captains General," i.e., War Captains, to keep order and chastise the Apache. This office persisted until the middle of the nineteenth century.[141]

As has been hinted, the Opata very quickly adapted themselves to the Spanish colonial way of life. They are invariably reported as "very fond of the Spaniards," "most loyal subjects of H. M.," etc. The sources dating from the period 1770–80 all speak of the use of, and fondness for European clothing, even shoes, and stockings, tools, arms, etc., by the native population. Zúñiga remarked in 1835 that the majority of the Opata knew Spanish, and did not pretend that they could not speak it, as many of the Yaqui do today.

The Indians were very devout Catholics, and were extremely fond of religious exercises. They "loved to adorn their houses with pages from old breviaries, and prints of Saints," which were brought in from Michoacán. They eagerly took up European music and instruments, which they played very well. The men were fond of painting, and exhibited a good deal of artistic feeling. In 1764 the author of the *Rudo Ensayo* was able to point out some mechanics, carpenters, tailors, etc., among the Opata. The Eudeve were more conservative, while the Jova were never entirely formally "reduced" in the missions.[142]

It is clear that the rate of the acculturational process was extremely rapid, and was attended by little friction. Small wonder, then, that travelers at the close of the last century and the early part of this, such as Pinart, Lumholtz, and Hrdlička, were unable to find an Opata population and culture, but were forced to admit that the Opata were in every way indistinguishable from the Mexicans.

ESPECIALLY WORTHY of note are the large numbers of wild plant products upon which the Opata were dependent to a surprisingly large extent for such a highly agricultural people. Fishing techniques were rather highly developed for a semidesert dwelling people. Cotton, weaving, and dyeing seem to have been more important than some previous writers have felt.

Nature was bountiful in the Opatería: there was an abundance of highly varied foodstuffs. We should like to know more about the poisonous tuber called *maqui*, which was a staple of the Jova, as well as many other wild foodstuffs mentioned in the sources. The problem of chili, and many other similar problems, need work in the field by an ethnobotanist.

The Opata did not live on that ecologically narrow shelf of existence by which Kroeber characterizes the Pueblos peoples of the American Southwest.[143] Perhaps for this reason Opata culture and society, so far as we can judge from the sources, seem to have been as correspondingly uncrystallized as Pueblo culture was crystallized.

Opata warfare has a decided Plains flavor. It may be supposed, however, that warfare did not loom all-important before the Apache menace became serious. Dances, ceremonial intoxication, sexual license, rain and fertility practices strike a familiar note. The possibility of mass marriage or betrothal is interesting. Shamans and curing are good basic North American traits. There is no hint of a peyote cult among the Opata, although there are indications that there was such a cult early among the Pima Bajo.[144] Opata emphasis on cardinal directions, etc., is most suggestive.

Incidentally it may be mentioned that the Opata looked down on their Pima Bajo neighbors, regarding them as savages, inferior in bravery, culture, and industry. In this opinion the Spaniards concurred.

Ceremonial game moieties were to be expected in the region. The kinship system, and what information is available on social organization—contrary to expectations—shows no trace of any kind of sib system. (Nor do the Cáhita data indicate sibs.) The sororate and levirate occur. The use of the *-ru* suffix to indicate a deceased relative is a rather rare feature, although similar mechanims occur among the Twana and some Algonkian tribes.[145] Ceremonial sponsorship is a most important feature of social organization.

The Opata, then, fit pretty well into the pattern that would be expected of them, if one judged only on the bases of their geographical location, and from what is known of their neighbors. They show a very high cultural correlation with their close neighbors, the lowland Cáhita. Nevertheless, the data reveal some rather unexpected trends and developments. By and large, the total Opata cultural inventory impresses one as being larger and infinitely richer than that of their Southwestern American neighbors.

Little has been said regarding trade; but the principal trade routes leading to the Pueblos passed through the Opatería. Most important items of trade were parrots and parrot feathers. The parrot occurs in numbers only in the southernmost part of the Opata territory, and grows increasingly more numerous in Sinaloa, etc.[146]

Among others, our sources are silent on the following items: boys' puberty rites, couvade,[147] human sacrifice, cannibalism, fetishes or idols, priesthood, temples or kivas, and tree worship.

It has long been the tendency of American ethnologists, whose views understandably exhibit a Southwestern bias, to regard northwestern Mexico, and especially the Sonoran region, as culturally peripheral to the Pueblo peoples of the Southwest. This view was inevitable before some of the salient ethnologic facts of the Mexican northwest were disinterred from the sources and made available to the Americanist.

Now, however, with the publication of such studies as those of Sauer and Beals, this view no longer seems tenable, or at least must undergo serious modification. It does not seem at all likely that the numerically small and environmentally restricted Pueblo people could ever have been the focus of a larger culture area including such peoples as the Opata, who alone were numerically much larger than all the Pueblo groups together, and whose rich cultural inventory indicates that they suffered no ecological restrictions. By this statement the writer does not wish to imply that there was a radical difference in basic orientation and content between the two cultures.

10

The Hunting-Gathering People of North Mexico

Paul Kirchhoff

Paul Kirchhoff's succinct summary of the various ethnohistorical sources on the "Chichimecs" of the north of Mexico is a valuable reference work not only to the ethnologist and historian but, perhaps even more so, to the archaeologist. As more and more archaeological work is done in the arid north of Mexico, life patterns of great stability are beginning to emerge. The historic hunters and gatherers were the descendants of archaic peoples who in some cases seem to have lived almost unchanged for long periods of time—hundreds or even thousands of years. Of course, with the restricted information available to archaeology, specific information on social, political and religious organization cannot be recovered. It is here that a synthesis of ethnohistorical materials is valuable. It provides the archaeologist with the ethnographic analogy that can give new dimensions and depth to the archaeological picture.

C. L. R.

THE HUNTING-GATHERING cultures of the North Mexican zone indicated on the [following] map suggest a basic unity, not only in contrast with the surrounding cultures of peoples of greater or lesser degree of agriculture, but also in contrast to other nearby hunters and gatherers, for example those of lower California or of the Great Basin and Rocky Mountains.

Throughout the area collecting and hunting was the basis of existence with fishing secondary, although [see map] quite important in some places. The three activities, as a general rule, gave good results and all sources commented on the good physical condition of the Indians.

The unequal distribution of natural resources was reflected in the uneven distribution of population; in some cases regions especially rich in food, such as the *Gran Tunal* of San Luis Potosí, were divided among several adjacent tribes.

Collecting.   The basic vegetable foods were tunas [prickly pears], mesquite [screw beans], agaves [*Agave Americana*] and palms, together, in some regions, with other fruits, roots and, occasionally, seeds. From the different types of tunas they ate the fruit (raw; made into "wine" or as raisins), the leaves, and flowers. The mesquite ground in a wooden mortar was consumed in the form of "wine" or made into bread that is described as a large white twisted loaf that could be kept for months or perhaps a year. The shoots and the prickly leaves of the agaves, and in various regions also certain roots, were cooked in underground ovens. The fruit and flowers of the palm tree were eaten. Canary seed [*Phalaris canariensis*], the use of which is mentioned only in the region of La Laguna, was made into bread. Bread was also prepared from the roots of tule [a type of rush or reed; Juncus].

For gathering-tools an earth-scratching stick and a net fastened to the end of a pole for gathering certain fruits are mentioned in Nuevo Leon. Everywhere bee honey was collected and in La Laguna the juice or syrup [*maná*] of the agave flowers. The main beverage was the juice found in hollow nopal cactus; when this was lacking, agave juice was drunk.

We know very little about the methods of preparing the so-called wine of the tuna or mesquite. The Indians of the region of San Luis de La Paz (mainly Guamar) stripped off the outside of the tunas, straining the juice through straw sieves and put it to heat in the sun or over a fire. Mesquite wine was prepared by cooking the flour. We do not know in what type of vessels these intoxicating drinks were prepared and stored, for outside of the ceramic ware of the south of Tamaulipas, only the water proof basketry (mentioned among the Guachichil and Guamar Indians) are noted. Hot stones were put in the baskets [for cooking], although using this method [for preparing wine] is not mentioned in the area. An intoxicating drink made of agave juice (pulque) was known only among the Guachichil and Guamar. The classic stimulant of this area is peyote, which is used, in cooked form, as a drink. The use of wild tobacco (if, indeed, it appeared in the area) was unknown.

Collecting activities followed a fixed annual cycle according to when certain plants ripened. In Nuevo Leon and probably also in other areas, the vegetable part of the diet during summers was based on fruits and during winters on roots. Dried tunas (although perhaps known only in the eastern part of our area) and, above all mesquite bread made up, in certain seasons, for the scantiness of fresh plant foods. It is said that the Indians frequently let themselves be guided by wild turkeys to places in which the fruit was most abundant and they explained, thus, their custom of not eating these birds.

Hunting.   The main wild animals hunted for food purposes were rabbits, hares, and deer. But a special characteristic of this area is that the Indians ate almost all the animals (mice, *tuzas* [rodents related to the guinea pig], etc.), exceptions being very uncommon. Hunting of birds was important in some regions. Certain quadrupeds were hunted only, or principally, for their skins, for example the squirrel, wild cat, etc.

The ubiquitous hunting weapon was the bow, of which we know only that it was not reinforced and that the cord was always of fiber. The arrows, differing in regard to detail from tribe to tribe, were made of a shaft (with groove and feathers) and of a foreshaft with the point fire-hardened or, more frequently, with a stone point. The quiver was known throughout the area (in contrast with the southern part of Lower California). The only other hunting weapon was the sling, perhaps used only for aquatic birds. A very common method of hunting was the drive by means of which the game was surrounded by a circle of men or by fire. The converging inclosure type of drive is mentioned only for southern Tamaulipas. For duck hunting there was the custom not only of using bow and arrow and sling, but also a method of catching the ducks by the legs, whereby the hunter swam among them, his head inside a gourd that floated on the water. There is no mention of certain weapons and methods of hunting known in the surrounding regions, such as the throwing stick [*palo arrojadizo*], the spear thrower [*propulsor*] and the hunting net.

The hunter never brought back the game himself (this was the task of his wife) nor did he eat of the meat, which was divided among the members of the group, the hunter receiving only the skin. The sole method of preparing meat mentioned in the sources was roasting. Even so, it was cooked only until half-done.

Fishing.   Fishing, important only in certain areas, was done with bow and arrows, fish traps, nets (only in the north), and by gigging the fish. There is no mention either of fishhooks or poisoning the water. In Nuevo Leon the fish were cooked in underground ovens.

In a number of regions the Indians were not acquainted with the use of salt, while in other regions they used the ashes of certain herbs for salting purposes. One characteristic trait in food preparation throughout the area was that each food was prepared and eaten alone.

Cultivation.   Only in the south of Tamaulipas and in the Pame sub-region was agriculture known, due to influences from Mesoamerica. The existence of pre-European agriculture in La Laguna, affirmed by several authors, is still doubtful.

Utensils and vessels.   It seems that in all parts fire was produced by rubbing two sticks together. Axes or hatchets are never mentioned and probably were absent, as in lower California and the Great Basin. Use of a mortar of wood instead of the grinding stone common to all the neighboring hunters-gatherers seems a characteristic of our area. Concerning vessels, there is mention only of impermeable basketry among the Guachichil and Guamar; sacks or bags used in other regions for transporting goods and, as a result of influence from the south, pottery and stone vessels in southern Tamaulipas.

Transport.   In La Laguna, reed rafts were known and in Nuevo Leon carrying was done with nets fixed inside a wooden frame. Portable cradles (*portaniños*) were known only in certain regions. In Nuevo Leon, the custom was to carry children seated astride the neck of horses, as in certain primitive tribes of the Continent [Old World?].

Habitations.   In many areas it is affirmed that there was no knowledge of construction whatever, and that the Indians, moving around continuously in search of food, slept in the open air or in caves. For other areas dome-shaped straw huts are spoken of; in Nuevo Leon these are grouped in a semicircle.

Clothing.   It was not the custom in this area for the men to cover their genital organs; there is a single isolated example of a Guachichil leader that wore a bundle of herbs in front. In some parts of Nuevo Leon the men wore on the shoulder a skin or blanket of rabbit or hare skins sewn together. The Zacatecas [Indians] wore short trousers of dog skin and on the forehead a band of leather. The Guachichil and Guamar used buttons of red leather, and when sandals are mentioned they have leather soles.

The women wore as a minimum a little apron of "herbs" but generally they also wore, front and back, two deerskins that were sometimes decorated.

Both sexes wore the hair long and in certain regions, braided. The Guachichil and Guamar colored it red and painted the body in various colors but preferably red. The tribelets of the north were distinguished by different stripes, painted or tattooed, with certain secondary differences between the sexes, placed on the face or on the body or on both. Necklaces and earrings are mentioned with some frequency; nose ornaments only in Tamaulipas. Tools ("combs") made of mice teeth served as instruments for tattooing. Brushes of roots are never mentioned.

Warfare.   Weapons of war were the bow and a two-edged dagger fixed with bitumen cement on a wooden handle and, in Nuevo Leon and in the north of Tamaulipas were carried stuck in a strip of skin in the form of a spiral to protect the left arm. The warriors were also accustomed to defending themselves from enemy arrows by means of arrows that they always held in the hand (over and above those that they had in their quivers). In this area there is no mention of darts, clubs, *macanas* [a wooden weapon generally edged with sharp flint], and shields.

Warfare was common only among tribes of completely different languages; tribes that spoke similar dialects almost always were united through alliances. Such allies in La Laguna were accustomed to coming together for purposes of war in the fourth phase of the moon. Arrows of a particular class or with certain characteristics (for example bloodstained or stripped of feathers) signified, according to the region, declaration of war or peaceful intentions and also served as an invitation to festivals.

They always tried to recover their own battle dead, and at the same time to carry off as many of the enemy, either dead or as prisoners. Some were scalped and the scalp was placed on a post for the victory celebration. The Guachichil and Guamar always carried these scalps with them. The northern tribes used enemy skulls as containers from which to eat and drink. The Guachichil and Guamar pulled out certain bones and nerves of the living captive and also, it is said, the enemies were eaten for "vengeance's" sake. As a general rule in the whole area an effort was made to completely destroy the dead enemy's body. The Guamar carried with them a bone with marks that indicated the number of dead enemies.

Social Organization.   In the north the tribes were very small, while those in the south were fairly large. In several regions there existed the customs whereby an ambitious person might become chief by killing the old chief; in the southern part of Tamaulipas this was done by challenging the chief to a duel.

In Nuevo Leon intertribal or intergroup marriages were known as well as marriages with women of other, and hostile tribes, with the aim of making peace. Such marriages between members of different tribes were, in turn, in many cases the cause or the pretext for new hostilities.

Throughout the area the suitor brought a deer to the home of his betrothed; the details of this custom varied from region to region and probably from tribe to tribe. Marriage ceremonies are not mentioned in the sources and in some cases it is expressly stated that none were known.

While in Nuevo Leon the postmarital residence was patrilocal, among the Guachichil and Guamar it was matrilocal. Only in the north was there marriage of a man with several women at a time. Among the Guachichil and Guamar, on the other hand, it was the women who had the most freedom, especially in having love affairs after marriage. The public recognition of homosexual relations between men appears only in the extreme northeast of our area, that is, in that region nearest to the sedentary groups of Texas [Indians] that had this custom.

Religion.   The religion of this area was characterized, negatively, by the absence of idols, offerings and sacrifices; only in La Laguna is there a single mention of an idol and also of a live toad living in captivity "that was their god" and it is in this region where there were burnt offerings and sacrifices of blood. The presence of idols, offerings and sacrifices among the Pame is clearly due to Mesoamerican influences. In all the region (including the Pame area) the sun was considered a deity. There is no mention, however, of the religious importance of the moon. Throughout the area the Indians were accustomed to look into the sun or to raise their arms to it, although it is also said that "they looked at certain stars."

Blood had a certain ritual importance although in a way very distinct from Mesoamerica. Only in La Laguna was the blood drained from one's own body to offer it in a ceremony to drive away comets. In the rest of the area one person took blood from another. At the birth of the first child of whichever of his wives, the relatives and friends scratched the father's body with a sharp instrument until he was covered with blood. In a ceremony to cement peaceful relations between two tribes, all the members passed a sharpened piece of bone through a hole made in the ear of a man chosen for this purpose, and rubbed their bodies with the blood that was produced.

Taking peyote and dancing at night around a fire was somewhat characteristic of the entire region. Also the few special rites mentioned, as for example the La Laguna rite of driving away comets, took place at night around a fire.

In La Laguna, deer heads were kept and used in a number of ceremonies. The best of these heads was burned a year after death of its owner. For defense against bad spirits and epidemic diseases the camp was encircled with stakes or spines or the whole group retired to a place full of spiny plants. There was great fear of witchcraft and objects, even skins of tunas, were not thrown away while passing through enemy territory. To acquire the qualities of animals they were painted on the body, or the ground bones of the animals were consumed. In one case the Indians killed a very successful witch and ate him in order to share his qualities.

Death.   Throughout the majority of the regions the dead were buried. Only among the Guachichil and Guamar and in a certain part of Nuevo Leon, perhaps in that area that was adjacent to the above groups, was there a custom of cremation. Among the Guachichil and Guamar even the bodies of enemies recovered from the field of battle and those who died as prisoners were cremated. These two groups always carried with them the ashes of dead relatives, while they scattered those of enemies to the breezes. In Nuevo Leon the ashes were buried.

In Nuevo Leon and the north of Tamaulipas there existed the custom of eating the bodies of dead relatives "in order to keep relationship with them." The custom of eating dead enemies had reached the region of the mouth of the Rio Grande, although it has also been pointed out that the Guachichil and Guamar did this "for vengeance."

There are only two methods recorded for curing certain illnesses: one consisted of scarifying the painful areas, the other the use of "fire buttons" [hot coals?]. Not only were moribund individuals abandoned but, at least in one tribe of the La Laguna area, persons not yet dead were buried.

Games and musical instruments.   Typical of the region seems to be a ball game [*chueca*] which at times was played between two tribes. A game with bouncing balls and the game of *patolli* are mentioned only among the Guachichil and Guamar. With regard to musical instruments, timbrels and musical rasps are mentioned and, among the Guachichil and Guamar, also the *teponaztli* [a type of rattle].

Division into subareas.   Together with the basic unity of this region that makes it necessary for us to consider it a single culture area, there exists a series of regional differences that permit division into subareas (see map). It is clear that the scarcity of data can lead to many errors since that which seems to be a special characteristic of the area could well have existed also in other areas. But in spite of these doubts, the facts relating to the special characteristics of the subareas taken together are sufficient to give this division a certain validity.

The subarea "Guachichil" is characterized by the following traits: painting of the body; coloration of the hair; head gear; matrilocal residence; freedom of the married woman; special forms of cruelty to enemies; bones with marks to record the number of enemy dead; cremation; presence of traits that are foreign and, at least in part Mesoamerican (*teponaztli*, pulque, ball game).

The scarcity of data on the Zacatecas makes the formation of a subarea "Zacateca" very tenuous, we establish it principally because almost all that is known about this tribe, outside of traits basic to the whole area, has a special character; short trousers of dog skin; leather bands on the forehead.

The subarea of the "Rayados" is, in turn, divided into three sections, of which the central "Nuevo Leon-Northern Tamaulipas-South Texas" represents the basic culture of the subarea: very small tribes; painted or tattooed strips as tribal marks; mouse-tooth combs for tattooing; skin or a blanket of interwoven skins worn over the shoulder; religious importance of smoke; the mourning custom of pulling out the hair.

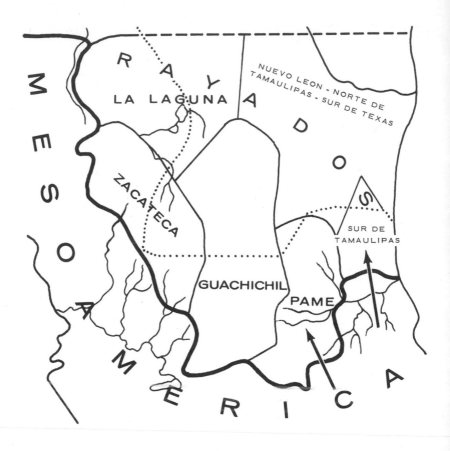

The section of "La Laguna" adds to the basic characteristics of the subarea the following traits: cultivation (?); flour and bread of canary seed [*alpiste*] and of tule root; the ritual importance of deer heads; burnt offering of food; sacrifice of one's own blood; major importance and cooperation of shamans; idolatry; importance of ritual numbers (4, 6, 7).

In the section of "southern Tamaulipas" the following traits can be added to the basic characteristics of the subarea: dancing on one foot without musical accompaniment; betrothed couples going alone for a time through the bush without copulating (Mesoamerican influence?), and a series of foreign traits, probably of Mesoamerican origin, though details about them are lacking: cultivation, permanent villages, pottery, stone vessels. Materials on the importance of cultivation in the religious system are lacking.

The data that oblige us to create a subarea "Pame" refer on the other hand, almost entirely, to religious ideas and customs that seem to be part of a Mesoamerican agrarian complex: idols, among them the mother of the sun; "paper" offerings; ceremonies of sowing and reaping in which the priest sprinkles the field with blood drained from the calf of his leg; temples on the summit hills, with a stairway for climbing them, and guarded by priests; sepulchers of important persons near the temple.

11

The Fiesta of the Pinole at Azqueltán

J. Alden Mason

One of J. Alden Mason's early visits to Tepehuán country took place in 1912 when he visited the Tepecano village of Azqueltán in Jalisco. Even at this early date Mason found the Tepecano very acculturated but he did succeed in obtaining various ethnographic data particularly of ceremonials of the Tepehuán *mitote* type.

In the more than half a century since Mason's visit the Tepecano have lost much more of their aboriginal culture as indicated by Jones (1962) and Phil C. Weigand, Southern Illinois University Museum, who visited Azqueltán in 1968.

C. L. R.

BY THE first of January 1912, I had already spent nearly three weeks in the little pueblo of Azqueltán, and had been accepted as a permanent resident. This little village lies at the bottom of the barranca, or cañon, of the Rio de Bolaños, in the northern part of the Mexican State of Jalisco, and on the edge of the Huichol country. Here dwell the remnants of the Tepecanos, or, as I prefer to call them, the Tepehuán of Azqueltán, for they claim, and probably with justice, to be an isolated branch of this greater nation.

The little pueblo, reported to be so aboriginally clannish, so absolutely isolated, by Hrdlička in 1903, has since greatly changed. The village is now full of mixed blood, the houses are mostly of adobe; nothing but Spanish is ever heard in the houses, and most of the older customs are entirely forgotten. Only in the isolated little ranch houses, situated within a five-mile radius of the pueblo, are found the conservative persons of the older generation who still cling to the customs of their ancestors.

Following information obtained from natives with whom I had

established relations of confidence, I started out about dusk with Eleno, and following a winding trail that led toward the Cerro de la Niña Encantada, arrived an hour later at the isolated ground which had already been prepared for the ceremony.

The square, or patio, according to my observations, was about thirty feet in width, the size of all patios which I noticed in this part of the country. It was a roughly circular enclosure, cleared of all plant life and free form stones. On the northern side several trees marked the outer limits, but on the south a ring of stones was placed. Approximately in the center was a pile of flat stones covering a heap of ashes, this being the fireplace necessary to all ceremonies. In a rough circle without were placed seven large stones partly sunk in the earth, these forming the seats for the communicants at the ceremonies. This circle of seats was approximately fourteen feet in diameter, leaving an outer circle, or path, about eight feet in width for the dancers. To the east the circle became elongated, like the neck of a pear, and here, just beyond the outer diameter, lay the altar. This was a rough structure of stone, five feet in width and a foot in height, roughly circular and flat on the top.

A fire was burning in its proper place in the middle of the patio and several figures were gathered around it. Without stopping to notice details, however, even without depositing our bundles, we performed the five circuits of the patio required by ceremony, pausing before the altar at the completion, where Eleno delivered one of his Tepehuán prayers. Then we were at liberty to take observations. Just outside of the patio itself was another fire, around which a group of several women and children were gathered. Within, around the central fire, were four elderly men and two middle-aged ones. Only these of all the Tepehuanes had gathered to celebrate their ancient custom. The *cantador mayor*, or chief singer, the highest functionary of Tepehuán religion, a simple, gentle old soul, greeted me kindly, lamenting to Eleno that so few of their brethren cared enough for the health and the safety of the pueblo to come and aid in the ceremonies so beneficial to them all. One of the other old men was well known to me, but the rest were strangers. It was evident that, while not invited to the function, yet, having arrived, there was no objection to my presence. A glance at the altar showed me that it was covered with the *chimales*, ceremonial arrows, decorated *jícaras*, and other objects. The men were conversing unrestrainedly, generally in Spanish, but oftentimes in Tepehuán.

Presently the chief singer approached the altar, where he busied himself for a time. Though it was too dark to see, I learned afterward that he put some peyote in a cup of water, meanwhile reciting a prayer and offering the peyote water to the four cardinal points. This peyote is an object of great religious importance to the natives of the north of Mexico, the rite extending even to our own Indians in Oklahoma. It is the root of a small cactus, *Lephora*, and contains a narcotic principle much valued by the Indians. The cult is particularly well developed by the Huicholes, among whom the procuring of the plant constitutes a religious duty. As it does not grow in this part of Mexico, it is necessary to make a long pilgrimage far to the east, a journey of thirteen days, and during all this time, from the time of setting out from the pueblo until the last rites are performed after the return of the party, a period of forty-seven days, nothing but the peyote itself may be eaten by the peyoteros. This duty is still considered obligatory by the Huicholes, but in these decadent days it is permitted that the *cantador* of Azqueltán purchase his peyote from the Huicholes. It is still considered, however, an object of great power, almost supernatural, and its use is everywhere hedged with custom and restriction. When it is offered to the cardinal points, the *cantador* must recite the formula, ná varictö′ do′ ö′ hi va′mörör a′midör napuivo′p̄miƚda hö ga navaruhmi ′ komak, "It-is-green beautiful lake-in whence thou-wilt-send that which-is-thy-cloud."

Soon the *cantador* came up to us and requested us to occupy the stone seats close to the fire. Producing a large bow with a tightly strung sinew string, he prepared two short sticks. Then, in response to a request from one of the elder men, he went to the altar and gave the asker a small piece of peyote, rubbing the rest on his leg where he had a bad sore. Turning to me, he requested to know the hour. Upon my replying that it was seven-twenty, he asked how many minutes to eight. Nevertheless, with a glance at the stars he remarked that it was well to commence. Then, approaching the altar, he took from there five ceremonial arrows, wound with colored yarn and with feathers of the royal eagle attached. One was placed in the ground just to the west of the fire, two others were given to two of the elder men, while the *cantador* retained two. Then he seated himself on his proper seat, the one nearest the altar, facing to the east, the other two men on either side, and we others in a row a trifle behind him.

Following the lead of the *cantador*, the arrows, grasped by the pointed end, and with the eagle feathers hanging loose, were slowly raised, pointed to the east above the altar and slowly swung around to the north, the west, and the south, while the *cantador* slowly recited the formula, ci'ar vwö' ta, ba' barip, hu'rnip, o'gipas, vwöc ci'kōr hö' vwan, "East-beneath, North, West, South, entire horizon through." When the initial position to the east had been reached, the arrows were held stationary there while the *cantador* recited the *perdón mayor*, or principal prayer. It was recited in a low tone, almost inaudible, and in long sentences, requiring a full breath at the beginning, the tone dying out toward the end. The *perdón* is too long to be given here, requiring about five or six minutes to complete. At the end, the arrows were again pointed to the four cardinal points and another shorter *perdón* recited, followed by an even shorter one. Following the last pointing of the arrows, they were replaced on the altar and the fiesta had been opened according to ritual.

Then commenced the real work of the evening. Scooping out a little depression in the earth immediately in front of his seat, between him and the altar, the *cantador* inverted over this a *jícara*, or half-gourd, and on this rested his bow, holding it firm with his naked left foot. Then, striking the bow with the two sticks so that it gave a clear note, he commenced his evening of song. Thus he sang, alone and unaccompanied, except for the monotonous note from the musical bow, with but four short intermissions between songs, from eight in the evening until after daybreak. Five songs occupied these ten hours, making, with intermission, an average of an hour and a half to a song. The first song is, ta' ta ha' rikama cihainud'u dukama, "the song to the morning star"; the second, tö' do' ō'hi u'vikama cihaindu' dukama, "the beautiful green woman," now identified with Maria Santísima; the third, uf tuta' vikama cihaindu' dukama, "the song to the water woman"; the fourth, ci' ciarto' 'tikama cihaindū' dukama, "the song to the sun's rays"; and finally, to' nor so' so'ptio' 'tikama cihaindū, dukama, "the song to the sun bead-man." Each of these songs has a different tune, with innumerable verses. Each verse consists of two lines; the first, the line by which the song is here named; the second, differing more or less for each verse, but similar in each song. The sentiment itself is really beautiful and worthy of a poetical translation, speaking of how the great gray clouds pile up from the beautiful blue east, how the lightning begins to appear and all the heavens reply to its voice, how the welcome rain commences and the whole world is refreshed by its coming.

Meanwhile, while the *cantador* was performing his task, we others were expected to aid the efficiency of the prayer by dancing the *mitote*. This is performed by dancing singly around the patio, just outside of the circle of seats, in the usual anticlockwise direction, pausing at each cardinal point and facing out for a moment to dance to the north, the west, the south, and particularly to the altar at the east. It was not required to dance throughout the entire song, but during a part of each song, and particularly during the latter part, it was expected that all male attendants should take part in the *mitote*. The dance is done by taking three steps alternately by either foot, the last step being stamped. Some performers took three short steps forward, others one step forward, one a trifle back, then a longer step forward, repeating with the other foot. During the intermissions between the songs, and even during the singing, we lay around the fire, smoked, dozed, and chatted in a low tone. The fire was under the charge of my other old friend, the father of Eleno and son of the Nestor Aguillar mentioned by Hrdlička, who evidently saw no antagonism between his two offices of *ci'ciartio"t*, or guardian of the fire, and of sexton in the little church.

As the night wore on and daybreak approached, the *cantador* commenced on his last song to the sun. This had not a plaintive tune like some of the others, but a gay, happy, and triumphant air almost like a song of victory or of deliverance from tribulation. Its continuous burden of tonori', tonori', tonori', "the sun, the sun, the sun!" made a deep impression on me as the moon gradually gave way to the morning star and the latter to the sun. One who has experienced nights passed in the open in the rare air of Mexico cannot wonder at the joy with which the natives greet the first warm rays of the sun.

After the last song had been completed, some of the communicants, including a woman and child, approached and knelt at the altar, making certain motions in following the lead of one of the elder men who pointed with a long cane on which some decorative designs had been incised and the tail feathers of the *cuiss* or *aguililla* attached. All were then given *pinole*, or pulverized corn, to eat.

Following the administration of the pinole, as the dawn brightened, the *cantador* approached the altar and again removed the four ceremonial arrows. Giving one to each of the two eldest men and holding the other two in his right hand, he again seated himself on his *banco* with his assistants on either side of him and prepared to end the fiesta according to ritual. Slowly the arrows were circled from the east to the north, the west and the south, while the formula was repeated as before. Pausing on the return to the east, the *cantador* recited another prayer of a minute or more in duration, giving thanks to heaven for benefits and begging pardon for sins. Then the arrows were ceremoniously circled again, replaced at the altar, and the fiesta was ritually complete.

It yet remained, however, to cleanse and bless the communicants. Going to the altar, the *cantador* took a basket and from it distributed to all present five or six *chuales*, or tamales, made of the black corn. Then, standing at the altar, he broke one into six parts, throwing one part to each of the four cardinals and to the zenith. Another bit was thrown to the center of the group of men. Then, standing at the altar, with the cup of water in which several pieces of dried peyote were floating in his hand, he called us, one at a time, to the altar to be cleansed of all evil and sickness and blessed and rejuvenated by the power of the arrows and the peyote. Standing there by the altar, our hats in our hands, the *cantador* slowly and with a peculiarly graceful motion waved the feathered arrow over our heads, finishing the motion to each of the cardinal points and the zenith and thereby exorcizing all our troubles to the corners of the earth. Then by means of a feather dipped in the cup, water of peyote was sprinkled on our heads and in our hands, imparting to us its magic power. Then the remainder of the peyote water was sprinkled over the altar, the seats, the fire, and the attendants, the last few drops being applied to the head and hands of the *cantador* by the guardian of the fire.

At this point I asked for a delay of a short while, explaining that the sun was not yet high enough to enable me to photograph. With customary courtesy and deference my request was granted without question, and I busied myself by observing the arrangement of the altar. This was decorated with all the paraphernalia requisite to the religion of this region. At the back, to the east, was a large, embroidered cloth, possibly two feet square, supported by two upright sticks with a cross stick, and directly in front of this, four *bastoncitos*, or sticks, decorated with cotton, arranged in two groups. In the center of the altar, evidently merely resting there, were the *petaco*, or box, in which the paraphernalia were kept, a cloth, and a string of dried peyote. The principal objects of religious ceremony were all gathered at the front of the altar or on the ground immediately in front of it. Placed on the front of the altar were ten *jícaras* of various sizes, some decorated with beads inside and out, others plain; in these, resting on cotton representative of the clouds, lay the little objects, archaeological, modern, and natural, which are significant of natural phenomena, animals, local places, or almost any conception of interest to the Tepehuán mind. With much pride the *cantador* displayed to me his valuables, remarking their power for good in protecting the pueblo from sickness and all ill. Immediately in front of the altar, planted in the earth, were two large *chimales* emblematic of the face of God, large hexagonal objects of colored yarn and cotton, and to either side of these were other objects of ceremonial importance, *bastoncitos, algodones,* both made of sticks and cotton and one or two ceremonial arrows. In a row in front of these, evidently to protect them, were placed the four new ceremonial arrows already used by the *cantador* and his responders. Again, immediately in front of these, was placed the little china cup with its peyote water. Against the altar rested the long cane of *aguililla* feathers which seems to be emblematic of the authority of the *cantador*.

The *cantador* packed all his paraphernalia in the wooden box, except his feathered cane, which he carried in his hand; the Guardian of the Fire carefully replaced the flat stones over the ashes of the fire; all hands took up their belongings and we were ready to start. Led by the *cantador*, all present, this time including the women, solemnly performed the five ceremonial circuits of the patio. On reaching the altar on the last circuit, the men reversed and retraced their footsteps, going this time in a clockwise direction to the entrance to the patio at the north. The women did not step in front of the altar this last time, but, waiting till the men had turned, fell in at the rear of the little procession.

12

The Tepehuán of Northern Mexico

J. Alden Mason

The Tepehuán Indians have been one of the more neglected groups as far as anthropological studies are concerned. This has, indeed, been true of all the peoples of the Sierra Madre Occidental, one reason being the considerable difficulty of access to this very wild and rugged region.

J. Alden Mason for many years was interested in various aspects of Tepehuán work, archaeology (see this volume), linguistics, and general ethnology. Mason made several short trips into Tepehuán territory and though his main interest was in linguistic studies he did make a variety of ethnographic observations. This present paper, originally published in a German publication, has never had wide circulation in the Western Hemisphere. The paper is of particular historic interest for it represents an excellent concise summary of our knowledge of the Tepehuán, North and South, before the more recent work of the last decade (Riley: 1959, 1963, 1969; Pennington: 1969; Service: 1969).

Two valuable points were made by Mason in this pioneer work with the Tepehuán. Reacting against the tendency of most earlier writers to lump all Indians called Tepehuán, he stressed the very real differences between the Northen and Southern Tepehuán, differences that are linguistic as well as cultural. On the other hand, previous writers had tended to differentiate sharply between the Tepehuán and Tepecano and Mason demonstrated that the Tepecano are almost certainly an offshoot of the Southern Tepehuán, very similar in language and culture but far gone in cultural decay.

C. L. R.

IN SPITE of their original large numbers and extensive habitat, and their importance in the colonial history of northern Mexico, the Tepehuán are the least investigated Indian group of the Sierra Madre Occidental, far exceeded by the more numerous Tarahumar and the smaller —at least in area—Huichol and Cora. No comprehensive monograph on them exists, and only a few short articles. Apart from myself, only Lumholtz, who visited them in 1895, gives much firsthand information; almost all other articles are based on his observations, or on colonial records, census reports, and similar data. This neglect can be ascribed mainly to their present small numbers, isolation, and especially to their relatively high degree of acculturation to the Mexican peon pattern. But the rapid progress of this acculturation demands their detailed study before many more of the old cultural traits are forgotten, for the Tepehuán culture in many respects forms the connecting link between those of the southwestern American states and those of Mesoamerica.

My observations on the cultures of the several existing Tepehuán groups were incidental to linguistic studies, for the languages are the principal element that differentiates them from the rural Mexican without tribal affiliation, and which connects a number of Indian groups from the Pueblo region to that of the higher cultures of Mesoamerica.

The Tepehuán are members of the Piman or Pima-Tepehuán linguistic family, which includes also the southernmost group, the Tepecano or Tepehuán of Jalisco, and the Papago, Upper Pima (Pima Alto), and Lower Pima (Pima Bajo) to the north (Kroeber; Mason, 1936, 1940). These occupied most of a long north-south extension of almost a thousand miles from the Gila River in Arizona to the Rio Santiago in Jalisco. In addition to this unusual range, the family has two other remarkable characteristics: it is the most variant of the Uto-Aztecan linguistic families, and the differentiation between the languages is extremely slight, probably no more than that between the Romance languages. This has important connotations as regards aboriginal history— migration and separation. Glottochronology suggests that the separation of the Tepecano from the Pima was of the order of 695 years ago (ca. A. D. 1265).

Considering, as does Sauer, probably the best authority—and as we may, the Tepecano to be but the southernmost group of Tepehuán, and formerly contiguous with them, in prehispanic days the Tepehuán occupied a habitat in the mountains and foothills of the Sierra Madre Occidental nearly five hundred miles long northwest to southeast from the southern headwaters of the Rio Fuerte in Chihuahua to the Rio Santiago in Jalisco, and in places over a hundred miles in width. Today the groups are isolated in small enclaves, but the total north-south distance is but little less. The population was probably rather sparse, without urban settlements of any size, and the colonial reports of twenty-five thousand Tepehuán warriors attacking Durango City in the great uprising of 1616 may be dismissed as a great exaggeration, especially since they were repulsed by a Spanish garrison of about six hundred, leaving, according to report, fifteen thousand slain Indians. Nevertheless the population must have been considerable; as everywhere, it was reduced tremendously by epidemics in the days immediately following the conquest.

All the Tepehuán are mountain Indians, accustomed to rather long, cold winters with snow and ice. Only one crop of corn can be raised annually. The Spanish chroniclers recorded that they suffered when removed to the seacoast. Other groups occupy the barrancas where more tropical food plants are grown. All are ranchería rather than village Indians, living in houses some distance apart; the villages are administrative centers with a few public buildings of adobe, and a church. The Tepehuán tend to be physically large and strong, intelligent, friendly, proud, independent. Lumholtz considered them much superior to the Tarahumar, more valiant, less phlegmatic, more impressionable and impulsive, not so abject-looking.

In his psychological investigations among the Southern Tepehuán, where he gave Goldstein's and Scheerer's modifications of the Kohs Block Design test, McConnell placed exactly half of his subjects in the next-to-highest category: "IV. Able to get all of the designs correctly with demonstrations on most, but with models used only on the first two or three designs."

The origin of the name Tepehuán is uncertain, but probably it is of Nahua derivation. Most likely it contains the root of *tepe* (*tl*), "mountain," but another possible etymology is "conqueror." Simeon gives *tepeuani*, "vainqueur, conquérant. R. *peua.*" Under *peua* he gives *Nitepeua*, "vaincre, soumettre, subjuguer."

Today the Tepehuán live in three isolated groups, the Northern Tepehuán around Baborigame and Nabogame in southwestern Chihuahua, the Southern Tepehuán in southern Durango and northern Nayarit, and the remnants of the Tepecano—who call themselves Tepehuán—in northwestern Jalisco. The two Tepehuán groups are separated by over two hundred miles, have no knowledge of each other, and differ considerably in language and culture. The Southern Tepehuán and the Tepecano are less than one hundred miles apart, and are very closely related in language and culture. The Tepecano at least are aware of the existence of the Southern Tepehuán. It is strange, therefore, that the Spanish chroniclers differentiate Tepecano from Tepehuán—though admitting the close connection—but do not seem to distinguish between the two Tepehuán groups. The time of separation of the Southern Tepehuán and the Tepecano cannot have been more than several centuries, possibly even post-Conquest, and they may have both been known as Tepecano to the earliest Spanish, the Northern Tepehuán as the Tepehuán. The Tepecano are reported to have a tradition that they formerly occupied the lands of the Huichol. Possibly a western migration of the Guachichil-Huichol separated them from the Southern Tepehuán.

The Tepehuán habitat seems to have been continuous, and is so marked on all maps (Johnson; Mendizábal and Jiménez Moreno; Sauer; Tamayo) of their aboriginal distribution. The division between Northern and Southern Tepehuán may have been between Guadalupe y Calvo and Guanacevi. Lumholtz (1902, 1: 447) describes this as a very cold, high, uninhabited region; they met no people in two days' travel. In earlier days the Northern Tepehuán and the Lower Pima or Nebome probably were also contiguous. Sauer (p. 82) suggests that they were separated by an incursion of the Opata-Tarahumar.

However, in spite of the linguistic and cultural differences, and the distant geographical separation, almost all recent writers on the Tepehuán err in failing to differentiate the Northern and Southern groups, treating them as a single entity, and making statements that are applicable solely to one or the other group. Only Lumholtz, who after sixty years is still the best source, and who visited both groups in 1895, differentiates between them in separate chapters (Lumholtz, 1902, chapter 23 [Northern]; chapters 25, 26 [Southern]). Thus Basauri (Basauri, tomo 1, pp. 353–63) describes the Tepehuán house as made of logs (these are unknown—at Xoconoste at least—in the southern region), says they dance the *mitote* (unknown in the north), and engage in ball races (unknown in the south). Only Southern Tepehuán towns are mentioned in the habitat. De la Cerda Silva's article refers exclusively to the Southern Tepehuán, although the existence of the Northern group is mentioned. His map, however, is of the northern region (and does not include the principal Northern Tepehuán area), and the linguistic section, based on Rinaldini, applies only to the language of the Northern group. Like him, Professor Gamiz's monograph is supposed to apply exclusively to the Durango Tepehuán, but he also digests Rinaldini's grammar of the Northern Tepehuán, and quotes from Lumholtz's accounts of both groups without distinguishing them. Tamayo's "Carta etnográfica de la República Mexicana" shows a large Southern Tepehuán area, but no Northern region.

The Tepecano or Tepehuán of Azqueltán, Jalisco (Hrdlička; Mason, 1912, 1913, 1917), were reduced to a small population of about one hundred in 1911–13 when I made two visits to them, and no Tepecano or Tepehuán were reported in Jalisco in the 1930 census. They are probably now almost completely acculturated, the language remembered by few. In 1913 they differed outwardly from the typical Mexican peon only in dress, the men wearing the white *calzones* typical of the Indian of the Sierra Madre. The houses had walls of field stone and thatched roofs. All spoke Spanish in ordinary conversation, and the younger generation did not know the native language and had no interest in the old religion. However, the conservative elders could speak Tepecano and, while all were nominal Catholics, practiced the old religion, with calendrical ceremonies at night in sacred patios, under the direction of a *cantador mayor*, with ceremonial objects much like those of the Cora, and set traditional prayers (Mason, 1918).

Important elements of the ceremonies were a fire, an altar on which ceremonial arrows, "god's eyes" (here his face), prayer sticks, fetishes, and peyote were placed, singing and drumming on the musical bow by the shaman, and dancing by the other participants. Rain and corn were the central features of the ceremonies. The four cardinal points were important, and each had its particular color. The shaman observed periods of fasting and sexual abstinence, as did others on special occasions.

The Southern Tepehuán occupy a considerable area in the mountains of southern Durango and northern Nayarit. The census map of 1930 (Departamento de Asuntos Indígenas) records 2,081 in the municipality of Mezquital, Durango, amounting to about 50 percent of the population; 826 of these, three-quarters of them women, spoke only Tepehuán. There were 545 in the municipality of Pueblo Nuevo, all bilingual, and 420 in the municipality of Huajicori, Nayarit, of whom 61 spoke only Tepehuán. Indians were less than 20 percent of the total population in the latter two municipalities. Mezquital is largely Indian. The total Southern Tepehuán population is therefore about 3000.

The region is mountainous and isolated, without vehicle roads. The houses—at least those at Xoconoste, a peripheral region—are like those of the Tepecano, built with stone sides and thatched roof; the men wear white trousers and blouses. While conditions must be closer to the aboriginal pattern in the center of the Indian area, at Santa María Ocotán, nevertheless on its outskirts in 1948 the natives seemed to differ in few elements of economic life from their "Mexican" neighbors. One Indian characteristic is the small knitted bag carried by the men. The *mitote* is still celebrated in local hillside patios, but apparently has today more a social than a religious aspect. The "altar" holds food rather than ceremonial objects, though "god's eyes" are displayed. However, the *cantador* sings as he drums on the musical bow, and the people parade and "dance" in a circle around the fire. Venison, if procurable, plays a part in the ceremony, but peyote seems to be unknown. The *cantador* observes sexual continence, and the people a limited fast for a short time previously.

Sixty years ago, naturally, more of aboriginal culture was retained. According to Lumholtz, the men wore ribbons and flowers in their hats, and some had long braided hair. They did not make the native beer, popular farther north. He gives a description (Lumholtz, 1902, vol. 1, pp. 474–79) of a *mitote* at Pueblo Viejo, a mixed Tepehuán and Nahua village. Even then it was a social more than a religious event, given by one person or family; there are no public community *mitotes*.

Lumholtz goes to great length (six pages) (Lumholtz, 1902, 1: 463–68) in describing the extreme puritanism of the Tepehuán of the pueblo of Lajas. While one may suspect that some of the information given was exaggerated for its effect upon him, punishments—exposure in the stocks, floggings, and imprisonment—were inflicted for rather trivial offenses, sins, and deviations from the strict social and moral code. Other pueblos seem to have been less puritanical in these matters, and this strictness may have been at its height at that time; nothing such was noted by me in Xoconoste in 1948, though perhaps not specifically questioned.

The Northern Tepehuán are fewer, occupy a smaller region, and are much more acculturated; the towns of Baborigame and Nabogame southern Chihuahua are their centers. The census map of 1930 records 1,597 Tepehuán in the municipality of Guadalupe y Calvo, less than 20 percent of the total population, of which only 153 spoke only Tepehuán. In 1951 few of the natives wore the white *calzones*, most of the men wearing the blue jeans of the typical Mexican peon of this region, and outwardly differing in few respects from the latter. But a photograph taken by Lumholtz (1902, 1: 427) in 1895 shows the men wearing *calzones*, and hair of shoulder length, held back by large handkerchiefs or scarfs.

Houses are of horizontal pine logs with interlocked corners and gable shingled roofs, almost exactly like American frontier log cabins except for the lack of chimneys. That resemblance is so great, and the houses so untypical of Mexico, that one naturally suspects such influence and origin. However, they were characteristics sixty years ago in Lumholtz's time. Corn beer, *tesgüin*, is enjoyed, but peyote seems to be unknown. One aboriginal element that is retained is the ball race which is performed today almost exactly as recorded by Lumholtz (1902, 1: 430, 431). Men, women, and children have separate races, the women running with a stick and a ring instead of kicking a ball. The language of the Northern Tepehuán is that of the only published Tepehuán grammar and dictionary, that of Rinaldini, copies of which are extremely rare.

Religious ceremonies may still be performed in isolated places, but were rare even in Lumholtz's time. They differed markedly from those of the Southern Tepehuán, Cora, and Tepecano, being given in sacred temples, log houses with flat roofs (Lumholtz, 1902, vol. 1, pp. 432–34). Here the men and women gathered monthly at night, it is reported. They sang and drank native beer until the god Tuni, their brother-in-law, stamped on the roof. Entering, but visible only to the shamans, he drank the beer and, in a merry mood, gave them advice on how to procure rain and avert evil. Then the female deity, Mother Moon, took his place and delivered homilies to the women. Outdoor *mitotes* were unknown. Lumholtz reports that their customs differed from those of the Tarahumar in complex observations of rules with regard to puberty. As among all these groups, many aboriginal features are preserved in the practices of the curing shaman.

About 150 miles north of the Northern Tepehuán are the Lower Pima, Pima Bajo, or Nebome, with one group centered at Maicoba on the Sonora-Chihuahua border and another near Onavas on the middle Yaqui River. The latter group has lost practically all its tribal character, and only a few of the natives can speak or remember anything of the language. Around Maicoba the conditions are apparently very much like those of the Northern Tepehuán, the language still spoken, and probably many elements of the aboriginal religion and customs remembered if not still practiced. Some Lower Pima may be still unilingual. The language may be closer to Tepehuán than to Pima-Papago; in fact they were sometimes called Tepehuán of Sonora in the old records, and there are recorded statements to the effect that the Nebome spoke Tepehuán. The census map of 1930 apparently calls them Papago, and records 340 in the municipality of Temosachic, Chihuahua; no Pima or Tepehuán were recorded in Chihuahua or Sonora, according to the map, though Basauri states that, according to the census, there were 860 Lower Pima.

According to Beals, the culture of the aborigines of the Sierra Madre in early days was of two types: the northern, principally the Tarahumar, and the southern, Tepehuán and others. Corn, beans, and squash were cultivated, both sexes doing the work, mainly with a hoe. Irrigation was unknown, and the easternmost Tepehuán probably were nonagricultural. Caves were sometimes used for dwellings, and community hunts were engaged in. They may have lacked pottery.

Further ethnological researches on the Tepehuán and the Lower Pima are urgently needed before more of their vanishing culture is forgotten. Fortunately this has already begun and we may soon expect more published data on them. Ethnological and linguistic studies have been made this year (1958) on the Lower Pima, and ethnological investigations among the Southern Tepehuán. Moreover, trained linguists of the Summer School of Linguistics are learning the languages of both Tepehuán groups.

13

The Genetic Model and Uto-Aztecan Time Perspective

A. Kimball Romney

The following article by A. Kimbell Romney outlines an approach to historical reconstruction by combining linguistic, cultural, and physical data on related peoples. This "genetic model" of Romney can be used in many areas of the world; Romney himself suggests that it might be applied to the Muskogian speakers among others and Evon Vogt has utilized the method to hypothetically reconstruct Maya culture history.

In delineating the model Romney uses the Uto-Aztecan speakers as type examples and certain conclusions that he draws are, of themselves, of very great interest. For example his conclusion that proto-Uto-Aztecan speakers had the bow and arrow is significant in view of the controversy over the antiquity of that implement in the New World. This particular conclusion may or may not be valid but it demonstrates the potentialities of the approach.

C. L. R.

SINCE THE stratigraphic discoveries of Nelson and Kidder in the Southwest, the task of historical reconstruction has held an ever-increasing fascination for American archaeologists. In linguistics, however, during the same period there has been increasing emphasis upon structural interests. Among social anthropologists, personality-and-culture and functional approaches have been prominent. In these areas, then, there has been a decrease in emphasis upon historical reconstruction. Consequently there have been few recent attempts to relate the findings of all branches of anthropology to specific problems of historical reconstruction.

This paper outlines a suggested model for historical reconstruction in which archaeology, ethnology, linguistics, and physical anthropology all contribute their methods and findings to the solution of historical problems.

The method may be introduced by the use of a hypothetical situation. Suppose, for example, that there are a number of tribes which are set off from their neighbors by the fact that they constitute a recognizable physical type and speak genetically related languages which have been well studied. Let us further suppose that all of these tribes, except a few who live in a peripheral region, practice agriculture. Some of their neighbors also practice agriculture, but generally not as intensively. Finally, let us assume that the tribes differ greatly among themselves as to house types, social organization, pottery styles, and ritual.

In such a hypothetical situation, few anthropologists would hesitate to infer that these tribes developed from a common ancestral group. There is probably insufficient evidence to make the inference that agriculture was a feature of the ancestral group.

Let us ask ourselves the question: Why do we feel safe in inferring a common ancestral group for the tribes of our hypothetical example? The answer lies in the nature of the two variables on which we based the inference, physical type and language. Physical type and language, we would say, have no causal relationship; there is no functional reason why a given physical type should occur with a given language family. Therefore, when these two variables do show significant concordance in their distribution this may well represent an important historical fact, namely that the explanation for their concordance can be traced to a common point somewhere in the past. A demonstration that these two factors are also uniquely accompanied by a systemic culture pattern, agriculture, for example, would strengthen the belief in a common origin.

The fact that we make this inference of common historical tradition despite considerable differences in house type, social organization, pottery styles, and ritual, indicates our belief that physical type, language, and systemic culture patterns are generally more stable through time than such features as pottery styles and architecture.

The next question we might ask is: What type of evidence do we need to infer with confidence that agriculture, as an example of a systemic pattern, is present in the ancestral group? Since the language family of our example is well studied, the most direct evidence can be obtained through an analysis of the vocabulary associated with the agricultural complex. If we find a series of cognate terms running through the major linguistic divisions referring to identical agricultural items, we would have very strong inferential evidence of agriculture at the ancestral group time level. This would be true, of course, only if the cognates show all the regular sound shifts from the reconstructed protoforms thus insuring that these agricultural terms are of greater antiquity than the operation of the distinctive phonetic laws shown in the cognate terms.

The genetic model is designed to capitalize upon situations which approximate the conditions of the hypothetical example. In situations where physical type, linguistic affiliation, and systemic patterns coincide we have a ready-made opportunity to bring all branches of anthropology to bear upon problems of historical reconstruction. In addition to outlining the genetic model we will illustrate its application on the Uto-Aztecan speaking peoples.

The genetic model takes as its segment of cultural history a group of tribes which are set off from all other groups by sharing a common physical type, possessing common systemic patterns, and speaking genetically related languages. It is assumed that correspondence [of] these three factors indicate a common historical tradition at some time in the past for these tribes. We shall designate this segment of cultural history as the "genetic unit" and it includes the ancestral group and all intermediate groups, as well as the tribes in the ethnographic present. The genetic unit represents a substantive segment of cultural history while the term "genetic model" refers to the conceptual framework which serves as a tool to order the data.

We shall use the term "origin" as a shorthand way of indicating the incipient stage at which any particular constellation of features is first presumed to occur. Thus we may speak not only of the origin of the genetic unit, but also of the origin of various subdivisions in the later stages of development.

The term "genetic" is intended to imply nothing beyond a concern with origin, in the above sense, and mode of development of the unit of culture history. It is not assumed, for example, that all the people in the genetic unit necessarily descend from the ancestral group in a strict biological sense. Biological mixture is to be expected wherever people of the genetic unit are in intimate contact with other groups. What is required is a distinguishable physical type which converges rather than diverges as one goes back in time.

Drawing upon well-known methods of historical reconstruction the genetic model focuses attention on the task of locating the region and time in which the ancestral group lived and in tracing their migrations, developments, fusions, and differentiations up to the present. The data are ordered according to tribes which we infer to share a common historical tradition at some time in the past and thus focuses attention on the fact that people are in the last analysis the creators and carriers of culture.

The genetic model complements current tendencies which make interpretations upon an area based framework. For some problems we must go beyond an area-bound construct. Where meaningful historical units extend outside a traditionally defined area a change in perspective may lead to new results.

Rather than assuming that people have always been pretty much in the same place the genetic model directs attention to such questions as: When did the people who occupy a given region arrive there, from what direction did they come, and what cultural equipment did they bring with them? Meaningful questions about developments within subgroups may then be posed.

For illustrative purposes let us see how closely the Uto-Aztecans, who are spread from Idaho to Central America, approximate the ideal conditions of a genetic unit, which we have defined as correspondence between language, physical type, and some systemic cultural pattern. The purpose here is only to present the potentialities of the model, not to report a complete reconstruction of Uto-Aztecan history. In the interests of simplicity the Tanoan groups have not been included. They properly belong to the unit and to include them would introduce little modification in the overall picture other than to push the date of the ancestral group to an earlier period. Zuñi and Keresan speakers are seen as arriving in the region later and as taking over subsistence patterns from the Uto-Aztecans. This opinion is derived from internal linguistic evidence.

That Uto-Aztecan consists of genetically related languages has been clearly established by the work of Sapir, Kroeber, Whorf, Mason, and others. The sound shifts and other linguistic processes have been worked out in some detail and are adequate for comparative work.

No physical anthropologist has worked on the problem of whether there is a reasonable degree of fit between the distribution of a single physical type and the Uto-Aztecan stock. Much work remains to be done—the summaries provided by someone who is not a specialist in the area can provide only rough approximations. Tentatively we would suggest that there is a notable degree of correspondence between the "Southwest Plateau type" described by Seltzer and the Uto-Aztecan stock. To demonstrate correspondence between a physical type and Uto-Aztecan we need to examine the correspondence between the physical type of Uto-Aztecan peoples in Central Mexico and the Southwest Plateau type. William Saunders has compared fourteen measurements made on a series of Pueblo tribes by Hrdlička and a series of Central Mexico tribes from Comas's *Compendium*. He found that, excepting stature, the measurements coincide almost exactly. There was very little difference on head length, head breadth, minimum frontal, nasion-menton, nose breadth, cephalic index, and facial index. Some differences were found in stature, cranial height, and nasal height. This suggests the probability that the Southwest Plateau type and the Central Mexico type derive from a single racial stock. Available data, elsewhere, does not exclude the possibility that Uto-Aztecan speaking peoples derive from a common physical type.

So far we have indicated that the tribes of the Uto-Aztecan genetic unit could trace to an ancestral group homogeneous as to physical type and language. Can we attribute a common systemic culture pattern, namely, agriculture, to this ancestral group? We have both linguistic and distributional evidence.

We consider the linguistic evidence first. In a paper on the "Historical Implications of Some Proto-Uto-Aztecan Plant Terms," Romney, Kelly, Harvey, and Nicholson have compiled a list of plant cognates which are common to the whole linguistic stock. This list contains only terms which show regular sound shifts from the protolevel and whose associated meanings can be reconstructed with confidence. Terms which deal with agriculture and which trace back to a protoform are: Planting-stick, mano, metate, two terms for maize, and one for planted field. The two terms for maize, taken in conjunction with the other terms, indicate a high probability for the presence of agriculture in the ancestral group.

Distributionally we find that, with the exception of most of the Shoshonean-speaking groups, virtually all Uto-Aztecans practice agriculture. The work of Beals, Sauer, Kroeber, and others shows that in Northwest Mexico north of the Tarascan area, all, or nearly all, Uto-Aztecan peoples practice agriculture while no non-Uto-Aztecans of the area are agricultural. In the Basin area which was occupied by non-agricultural Shoshoneans, there are archaeological remains which indicate the presence of agricultural Shoshoneans, there are archaeological remains which indicate the presence of agriculture between, roughly, A. D. 700 and 1200. Furthermore, Steward found irrigation, without planting, among the Owens Valley Paiute. Some of the groups in the Basin practiced broadcast sowing. Could these features be interpreted as remnants of a past agricultural tradition among Shoshonean people? The high degree of correspondence between the distribution of Uto-Aztecan and agriculture, together with the linguistic evidence, suggests that this is most probably the case.

So far we have seen that significant concordance between language, physical type, and a systematic pattern, agriculture, indicates that the Uto-Aztecans trace to an ancestral group who were living in a common environment, speaking a common language, and planting maize. The next step in the application of the genetic model is to locate the ancestral group in space and time. The application of Sapir's criteria of locating the origin of linguistic distribution on the basis of linguistic differentiation, shows the origin to be somewhere in the traditional Southwest. Within this region they would be located in the southern rather than the northern area.

We can add further evidence on the location of the ancestral group by a study of the wild plant terms which occur in proto-Uto-Aztecan. Drawing again from the work on proto-Uto-Aztecan plant life we find the following plants to be present at the ancestral group time level: pine, juniper, oak, *phragmites communis*, prickly pear, and beargrass. This specific assemblage of plants occurs in the Southwest at an intermediate altitude zone. It is typical of the upper Gila drainage in southern New Mexico and Arizona and of the northern Sierra Madre. It is certainly not a desert environment as is found on the lower Gila, nor does it indicate a high altitude, say above 7000 feet. The assemblage checks with that found in Tularosa cave, for example, at the early time levels there.

The first estimates as to the dating of the undifferentiated ancestral prototype will of necessity be somewhat rough. A very tentative result obtained by Romney and Kelly using the Swadesh technique shows an age of three thousand years for the linguistic divergence within Uto-Aztecan proper. The results also show that Pima-Tepehuán was the first to break off. This agrees with previous inferences of Kroeber and Whorf on phonological grounds.

For the non-Pima-Tepehuán Uto-Aztecans it indicates a continual divergence with neighboring groups in contact with each other until fairly recent times, that is, until about A.D. 1000.

We are suggesting that all tribes presently speaking Uto-Aztecan derive from a common location somewhere in the upper Gila or northern Sierra Madre and that the divergence from this common group began not longer than three thousand years ago.

Now, cognate terms are found throughout Uto-Aztecan for tobacco, bow, and arrow which show all the regular sound shifts that have taken place since the divergence of ancestral proto-Uto-Aztecan. This gives us strong presumptive evidence that tobacco, bow, and arrow were present at the ancestral group level and we will add these items as part of their cultural equipment. Pottery, it seems, is not present.

So far we have said almost nothing about the results of archaeology in relation to the Uto-Aztecan genetic unit. In the past the implicit assumption of many workers has been that, by and large, people who occupy an area have always been there. If the inferences we have made so far are correct, one important implication is that wide dispersions of people take place within relatively datable periods. Though it would be going too far to attempt to make a one to one linkage between the various branches of a language stock and specific archaeological phases, it is frequently possible to make limited types of inferences of a very helpful sort.

The Uto-Aztecan ancestral group cannot, for example, be equated with the very widespread early food-gathering and grinding complex of the Greater Southwest because there is no correspondence in their distributions at the time level around 1000 B.C. Whether the Uto-Aztecan peoples differentiated out from such a base is not the point at issue— they probably did—the important point is not to equate the two. One implication of this point of view is that the cave sites in Nevada and Utah in which there is evidence of seed-gathering peoples with mano, metate, atlatl, and basketry which date at and before 1000 B.C. could not be interpreted as being occupied by Shoshonean-speaking peoples, since at the time the Shoshonean languages had not yet evolved from proto-Uto-Aztecan and the ancestral group was living in a different region with different cultural equipment practicing agriculture.

On the other hand, for example, it seems reasonable to make a tentative correlation between the Hohokam manifestation in general and the Pima-Tepehuán language family. Here there is good evidence that agriculture, the bow, and the arrow all come in together at a time consistent with the divergence of the ancestral group. The evidence on physical type is scanty but seems to indicate some mixing with local population elements rather than wholesale replacement. Linguistic evidence is clear in indicating that the Pima-Tepehuán language group is the most divergent within Uto-Aztcan and it seems reasonable to hypothesize that one segment of the ancestral group moved down the Gila River carrying maize and the bow and arrow with them and, in adjusting to the altitude and their Hokan-speaking neighbors, developed a distinctive cultural tradition.

In this paper we have outlined a model for the study of cultural history and attempted to indicate its usefulness when applied to the Uto-Aztecan speaking people. It is suggested that it may also provide possible crossties between archaeological traditions already worked out in detail.

In conclusion we might point out some other areas of possible application. I will limit my remarks to North America.

The Eskimos come to mind as an obvious example of correspondence between language and physical type. More challenging in complexity is the apparent correspondence between the so-called centralid physical type, the Mississippian archaeological manifestation, and the Muskogian languages, including Natchez. Another intriguing possibility is the concordance between Algonquian speakers and a distinctive physical type. There are certainly clear-cut differences in physical type between the Algonquians, the Athabaskans, and the Siouans. The Siouans have, incidentally, an agricultural tradition of respectable antiquity, as revealed in vocabulary. Hans Wolff's work shows squash, beans, potato, and tobacco at a proto-Siouan level.

The application of the genetic model to these and other cases should throw additional light upon the time perspective of North America.

NOTES / BIBLIOGRAPHY

NOTES

2 Notes on the Geography and Archaeology of Zape, Durango

[1] Officially "El Zape," according to census of 1930, but commonly referred to as "Zape." In etymology, possibly akin to Zapuri (place in Chihuahua), supposed to mean a "fight" or "combat."

[2] At the time that the first draft of this paper was prepared (September, 1936), there had not yet appeared "Late Archaeological Sites in Durango, Mexico, from Chalchihuites to Zape" by J. Alden Mason, in "Twenty-fifth Anniversary Studies," vol. 1, *Publications of the Philadelphia Anthropological Society* (Philadelphia, 1937).

[3] See climatic maps in Rouaix, *Geografía*.

[4] Dates given by primary and secondary sources vary from 1563 to 1569. Mecham, *Francisco*, pp. 127, 188–89, prefers the date of 1567. There is room for reasonable doubt concerning any specific year within this seven-year period. It is interesting to note that Arlegui, *Crónica* (written about 1736; first printed, Mexico, 1737; citation from reprint, Mexico, 1851), p. 41, quotes Torquemada to the effect that Franciscan missionaries had discovered, between 1555 and 1564, such *reales de minas* as "Indé, Topia, Guanazeví, Santa Bárbara," etc. Matías de la Mota Padilla, in his *Historia* (written 1742; first printed, Mexico, 1843; citation from 1856 edition, Guadalajara), 3: 200, practically repeats this statement.

[5] Alegre, *Historia*, 1: 415 (probably written between 1767 and 1780), "Con acuerdo de los mismos indios eligió el padre el sitio del Zape, valle hermoso á la falda de una alta roca, y estendido á las riveras de un río." Tomo 2: 54, "Del Valle de S. Pablo [Balleza] recién descubierto, se veían bajar de ciento en ciento á poblar en sitios cómodos para su instrucción, y eran aún muchos más los que de las serranías de Ocotlán [west and north of Zape] habían venido al partido de S. Ignacio y pueblos del Zape. En ninguna otra de las naciones de la América se hacía admirar más el poder de la gracia de Jesucristo y la suave fortaleza del yugo evangélico. Acostumbrados á vivir en el pillage, sin casas, sin hogar, sin sementeras, y á la continua carnicería de los acaxees, de Carantapa y de la cordillera de Baimoa, parece que con alojarse en el pueblo dejaban con las quebradas y las breñas toda la fiereza é inhumanidad que les inspiraban los montes." Alegre's characterization of the Tepehuanes as being pure nomads without homes or cultivated fields does not agree with other descriptions of

235

this people, e.g., "Del Anua del Año de 1596" in Documentos para la Historia Eclesiástica y Civil de la Nueva Vizcaya," *Documentos*, Cuarta Série, 3: 21–22, "ahora bastará solamente decir en general que los tepehuanes hacen grande ventaja á los de la Laguna para recibir la fé, así por ser de naturales mas blandes y llegados á razon como por tener algun rastro de política humana de que carecen todos los de la Laguna. Andan vestidos de lana y algodón; tienen cosechas de maíz; habitan de asiento en sus casillas ó chosas; crían con amor y cuidado á sus hijos y lo que mas hace al caso parece que Nuestro Señor les llama é instiga á sus hijos y lo que mas hace al caso parece que Nuestro Señor les llama é instiga á su fé y en algunas ocasiones *compellit cos intrare.*"

[6] Alegre, *Historia*, 1: 415; 2: 54.

[7] Ibid., 2: 54–55.

[8] Geronimo Ramírez, first Jesuit apostle to the Tepehuanes (worked 1596–ca. 1600), and Juan Fonte (in this area ca. 1608–16) at different periods made El Zape their residence and headquarters for work among the northern Tepehuanes and southern Tarahumaras. Juan Ortiz Zapata, in his "Relación" of 1678, *Doc. Hist. Mex.*, 4th ser., 3: 310–14, states that in 1678 the Jesuit province of Nueva Vizcaya included the "Misión de Tepehuanes," which was composed of four *partidos:* Santiago Papasquiaro, Santa Catalina (Tepehuanes), Çape [*sic*], and Tizonazo, with a population of 1,105 Tepehuanes. In actuality, the Tepehuán Indians extended north as far as Huejotitlan and the Valle de San Pablo (modern Balleza) in southern Chihuahua. The *partido de Tizonazo* was mainly non-Tepehuán, since the town of Tizonazo was inhabited by transplanted Cáhita Indians from Sinaloa and Sonora, and only Santa Cruz (east of Zape, between the Sierra de Canoas and the Rio del Oro) was Tepehuán. The southern Tepehuán missions were administered by the Franciscan order.

[9] Alegre, *Historia*, 2: 83–86. Tamarón y Romeral, *Demostración*, edited and titled by V. Alessio Robles, pp. 85–92. Bancroft, *History*, 1: 319–26.

[10] Pérez de Ribas, *Historia*, chap. 10.

[11] Tamarón, *Demostración*, pp. 86–87, "La iglesia es de adobes y techo de azotea ya viejo, y las paredes también y chorreadas, anidada de murciélagos y golondrinas, en abundancia, de que resultan inmundicias, y como carece de medios para el reparo de estos daños, ha sido precisco fomentar este célebre santuario, para lo que se trabaja ya en nuevos techos y en fortificar las paredes, desterrar aquellas pernicios aves, tengo allá tres oficiales que labran un precioso retablo que seguidamente se ha de dorar, para colocar la santísima imágen de Nuestra Señora, cerrarla con su gran vidriera para su seguro resguardo, y vestido precioso porque los pocos que tenía eran anticuados, bien quisiera se levantara nueva iglesia, como pide tan importante santuario, pero se ofrece el inconveniente de la cal que se habría de traer de larga distancia, pues allí no se descubre piedra que la pueda dar."

[12] Ibid., p. 420.

¹³ Ibid, p. 86, "este pueblo del Zape tiene vientisiete familias de indios, y en ellas setenta y ocho personas, pobrísimas y mal aplicadas al trabajo, aunque tienen agua en abundancia no se aprovechan de ella y se van acabando aquellos naturales, es un paraje solitario y árido, los árboles frutales, que son pocos, malogran la fruta por los fuertes hielos, como está a la falda de la sierra, son los fríos continuados y grandes, el río Nasas pasa por sus goteras, y al frente de la iglesia, como doscientas varas está un ojo o manantial muy copioso, de agua caliente, tanto que quema, y en su mismo origen hay una casa y dentro de ella un tanque o pilón de piedra que sirve de baño al que concurren paralíticos y otros enfermos que buscan su salud, la que consiguen por medio del patrocinio de la Santísima Virgen del Hachazo y todos generalmente se bañan y sudan bien, como aquello está muy recogido y decente, de noche tomé tres baños y no conseguí sudar."

¹⁴ Attempts had been made by Kidder in 1922, Brand in 1931, and Sauer in 1933, to visit Zape, but sickness and poor road conditions interfered in each case.

¹⁵ Tamarón, *Demostración*, pp. 99–101. The editors of this work (V. Alessio Robles, and Alberto Castillo H.) have quoted (in their note 2, on Zape) Rouaix, Alegre, and Guillemin Tarayre. Actually, these editors did not realize that they were utilizing material published by Guillemin Tarayre, for they preface the material: "Sobre las ruinas arqueológicas que se encuentran en las inmediaciones del Zape, el inteligente investigador durangueño Alberto Castillo H. encontró un precioso M. del sabio Orozco y Berra, que había permanecido inédito y aquí se reproduce íntegro. El original se guarda en Tacubaya, D. F., Dirección de Estudios Geográficos y Climatológicos, 1428–8 [*sic*]. Colección Orozco y Berra.

"*'Descubrimiento de una ciudad agrícola cerca del Zape.* (M. inédito.) Traducido para *El Renacimiento, por Manuel Orozco y Berra.*'" The material quoted on pp. 99–100, and the Plan of the Ruins, is translated almost word for word from pp. 183–86 in Guillemin Tarayre, *Exploration*, which was an extract from tome 3 of the *Archives de la Commission Scientifique du Mexique* (Paris, 1864–67), which, in turn, was incorporated in the *Archives des Missions Scientifiques et Litteraires* (published in three series of thirty tomes, Paris, 1850–90). It is possible that Guillemin Tarayre may have left a draft of his report, in 1866, with Orozco y Berra.

¹⁶ The following is a chronological list of works on, or references to, the archaeology of Zape.

AUTHORITY	WORK	AT ZAPE	WRITING DATE	PUBLICATION DATE
G. Ramírez	Anua 1604	1604	1604	. . .
D. Larios	Anua 1612	1612	1612	. . .
A. Pérez de Ribas	*Historia*, 583	?	1644	1645
F. Alegre	*Historia*, 1:415–16, 2:54–55	?	1667–80	1841–42

M. Orozco y Berra	Geografía, etc., 318	...	?	1864
E. Guillemin Tarayre	Exploration, 183–86	1865–66	1866	1869
H. Bancroft	Native Races, 4:600	...	?	1882
C. Lumholtz	Unknown Mexico, 1:448	1894	1901	1902
Anonymous	Estado Actual, etc.	...	?	1928
I. Marquina	Estudio Arquitectónico, etc.	...	?	1928
P. Rouaix	Geografía, 84	?	1929	1929
D. Brand	Amer. Anth. 37:294, map 1	1936	1934	1935
J. A. Mason	Amer. Ant. 2:56, 150–51	1936	1936	1936
E. Hewett	Ancient Life, etc., 59	1906	1936	1936
J. A. Mason	Late Arch., 137–43	1936	?	1937

[17] Pérez de Ribas, Historia, p. 583.

[18] Alegre, Historia, 1: 415–16.

[19] Ibid., 2: 54–55. It is worthy of notice that, on June 30, 1936, a small head (about one and one-half inches high), apparently broken from a human figurine, was found in the loose dirt and leaves beneath a mesquite on the Cerro de la Cruz, near one of the stone house ruins. This head is remarkably European in its features, the disposition of hair especially being like that of a bearded Spaniard. It is quite possible, of course, that this figurine is actually of European origin.

[20] This mention of the Cocohiomes (or Cocoyomes) as the builders of the structures on the Cerro de La Cruz is most interesting in view of the different interpretations that may be made of the name. Guillemin Tarayre probably learned, by hearsay, of the recent death of an old Cocoyome woman. The Cocoyomes were a small band or tribe, usually considered as part of the Toboso group or nation, which ranged from the Big Bend of the Río Grande into the Bolsón de Mapimí. Due to their participation in the attacks, that began about 1680, on Spanish settlements, the Cocoyomes are mentioned frequently in the military history of Durango, Chihuahua, and Coahuila. What became of this tribe by the nineteenth century is not known, as yet. It is possible that some Cocoyome stragglers or captives may have been placed by the Spaniards in such Indian communities as Tizonazo, Santa Cruz, and El Zape. Alcedo, in his Diccionario, 1: 222–23, speaks of the Valle de San Bartholomé as being the "antiqua residencia de los Indio Infieles Cocoyomes." However, it is almost certain that Guillemin Tarayre confused this actual tribe with another, and legendary, people believed in by the Tepehuanes and Tarahumaras. Lumholtz, in Unknown Mexico, 1: 192–93, records the Cocoyomes as being considered, by the Tarahumaras, to be their legendary enemies, or ancestors, or—at any rate—the first people to inhabit the world. Many of the walls of loose rock found on eminences and in caves throughout the northern Sierra Madre are attributed to

this legendary people. Another interesting side light is provided by Alegre (*Historia*, 2: 45) who mentions that among the tribes of northern Sinaloa (related linguistically to the Tarahumar, and, somewhat more remotely, to the Tepehuán) Cocohuame was the God of Death, and was the most venerated member of the native pantheon.

[21] Guillemin Tarayre, *Exploration*, pp. 183–85.

[22] Lumholtz, *Unknown Mexico*, 1: 448.

[23] Hewett, *Ancient Life*, p. 59.

[24] The Tepehuán nation, once the most feared of Sierra Madre peoples, is now but a small and timorous remnant, which needs to be worked ethnographically before it is too late. Less is known of Tepehuán ethnography than of the Tarahumar, Acaxee, Huichol, and Cora. To check this statement, inquire of any American ethnologist what he knows of Tepehuán ceramics and weaving.

[25] Mason, *American Antiquity*, 2, No. 1, pp. 55–56; 2, No. 2, pp. 150–51. "Late Archaeological," pp. 138–42.

[26] Not sufficient work has been done at any of these three sites to justify many conclusions as yet. Doctor J. Alden Mason, assisted by Mr. Robert Miller, of Grand Rapids, Mich., and Mr. Richard Martin, of Boston, Mass., trenched the floors of the larger caves in the Zape Chico group, but the results have not been published. The party from the University of New Mexico (Mr. Wesley Bliss, graduate fellow and photographer, Mr. Julian Olmsted, senior student and chauffeur, and the writer) compared potsherds and other artifacts from the surface of the above mentioned three sites. These items gave little evidences of cultural differences. See below, under discussion of pottery types, for further details.

[27] Hrdlička, *American Anthropologist*, n.s., 5: 431–32. Case, J., oral information given the writer at El Fuerte, Sinaloa, March, 1930. Holt, E. B., letter to the American Consul at Durango; published in somewhat altered form in *Bulletin of the Pan American Union*, 60 (1926): 1090–96.

[28] There have been outlined previously, pp. 89–90, reasons for believing that most or all of these *loma* ruins represent a people other than the Tepehuán.

[29] Good examples are on the north side of the Rio Humaya a few miles east of San Darío, Durango (eighty miles WSW from El Zape), and near the old Hacienda Rincón de Ramos Durango (some forty miles ESE from El Zape). The latter group was reported to the writer in 1931 by an American cattleman who had run cattle at Ramos before moving to Chihuahua. He compared the Durango mounds and stone lines with the *montezumas* and *cimientos* of northwestern Chihuahua.

[30] See map I and pp. 288, 294 in Brand, *American Anthropologist*, n.s., Vol. 37.

[31] Mr. Malcolm Rogers, of the San Diego Museum, a number of years ago brought to the writer's attention the unverified report of a small stepped pyramid of masonry a number of miles east of Guaymas, Sonora, in the foothills.

[32] Obregón, *Historia*, p. 185. Guillemin Tarayre, *Exploration*, p. 176.

[33] Seemingly, the basis for the belief, current among some ethnologists, that the Pima used to cremate their dead was the practice of sometimes cremating the bodies of Pima warriors killed away from home.

[34] Determinations of paste, temper, dimensions, and hardness, were made by Mr. Douglas Osborne, senior student and member of the 1936 party in northern Mexico. A total of 2,369 shards were examined.

[35] Mason, "Late Archaeological," p. 141.

[36] Some differences in paste exist. Such paste differences have little bearing on cultural relationships, as they reflect local resources rather than cultural history. To illustrate this point: one can find considerable paste differences within the same pottery type from a modern New Mexico Indian pueblo, e.g., Sia, Acoma, and Zuñi. Paste is of importance only when its constituents could not possibly be obtained near the place where the shard, vessel, or ware was found. This, of course, would suggest trade instead of local manufacture.

[37] A few possible exceptions to this statement exist. Doctor Sauer found a red on buff ware, in the Sahuaripa area, which may be a peripheral extension of the Hohokam complex. Shards of various Chihuahuan types are reported from cliff-houses between Guaynopita and Urique, Chihuahua. The writer has seen a plain polished redware, from the *monte* of the Guasave-Ahome lowlands, which was locally attributed to the ancients. This is probably an early Cahita ware.

[38] Among known historic wares in areas not distant from northern Durango are: Mayo Red on Bug, Fuerte to the Mocorito; Mayo Cream, and Mayo Red, valley of the Fuerte; Tarahumar Polychrome (red and white on yellow); Tarahumar Red on Yellow or Buff; Tarahumar plain wares— Cream, Buff, or Brown; Conchos Red on Brown; Conchos Plain Brown.

[39] Sauer and Brand, *Prehistoric Settlements of Sonora*; Vaillant, *Ceramics of Central and North America*; Brand, *American Anthropologist*, n.s., 37: 287-305; Sayles, *Some Southwestern Pottery Types*.

[40] Sauer and Brand, *Aztatlán*, letters from Doctor Sauer to the writer, August 16, 1933, and December 24, 1936; Mason, "Late Archaeological."

[41] Sauer and Brand, *Aztatlán*, fig. 5, pp. 21-30, 63-68. These five types might be termed: San Felipe Red on Buff Incised (Aztatlán Ware, p. 63); Aztatlán Red-rimmed Buff (Plain Red-rimmed Red on Buff, p. 63); Aztatlán Red on Buff (Decorated Red-rimmed Red on Buff, pp. 63-64); Chalchihuites Red on Buff (Mason's Chalchihuites Red on Buff, or Red on Brown); and Zape Red on Buff (Mason's inferior Red on Buff from Durango).

[42] News note from Doctor Isabel Kelly to *American Antiquity*, 2 (1936): 151-52; and letter to the writer, August 5, 1936.

3 The Chalchihuites Area, Zacatecas

[1] Very succinct references about such remains can be found in the *Crónica* by Arlegui; in "Crónica Miscelánea de la Provincia de Xalisco," by Fr. Antonio Tello, and in *Historia Antigua y de la Conquista de México,* by Orozco y Berra. In the *Bosquejo Historico de Zacatecas* (1907), by Mr. Elías Amador, there appeared an article (p. 233) by Mr. Ramón A. Castañeda, in which he mentions in some detail several of the existing remains in the area. With regard to the identification of the dwellers in the region at the time of its subjugation by the Spaniards, as well as the customs which they had and the language they spoke at that time, there are data, although somewhat confused and sparse in number, in the following references, in addition to those found in the above-mentioned writings: Hervas, *Catálogo de las lenguas;* Mota Padilla, *Historia;* Torquemada, "Monarquía Indiana"; *Geografía,* by Orozco y Berra; "Observaciones" by Orozco y Berra and Hilarión Romero Gil, in the *Boletín de Geografía y Estadística,* and some others.

[2] Perhaps, as has been supposed, the circumstance that the veins of two nearby mines have, in their matrix, fluorite [*floruro de calcio*], with a beautiful green coloration, gives rise to the name of Chalchihuites being given the site.

[3] This assertion has been motivated in great part by the circumstance that the only and very few indigenous words by which some places are known are of Nahuatl derivation: Chalchihuites, Tonalan, Xalisco, Tlaxcalla, (these names designate the four old villages that later formed the town), Súchil (Xochitl), etc., etc. This does not mean anything, however, since we repeat that the *conquistadores* brought with them Nahuatl-speaking peoples for the purpose of colonizing the territory, and it is not known if they or the aborigines used such names, although it is more probable that it was the former, owing to the relatively correct structure of the words, which belong to Nahuatl and not to a dialect of it.

[4] Tepehuán, Tepecano, Huichol, etc., etc.

[5] Probably when the Spaniards arrived the monuments were already covered by the vegetation of years or centuries, since in no other way would the existence of important buildings have escaped the proverbial detailed descriptions of the *conquistadores* and friars (who describe tree by tree the land over which they walked). Among others [of the buildings] were those of Alta Vista, which is a very short distance from Chalchihuites, a mine continually being explored at that time owing to the rich silver-bearing veins which were, and are still in its soil.

[6] Chavero, *Mexico,* 1: 737.

[7] Lumholtz, *Mexico Desconocido,* Vol. 2, pl. 13.

[8] In one of the doorways closed off with rubble-masonry, this masonry is formed with rock fragments, bound with a very white and hard mortar,

which is constituted of carbonate of calcium hydrate [*carbonato de cal hidratado*], of very high quality, mixed with fine sand. I note this fact, because the primary dehydration of such a carbonate must have required an extremely high temperature, the production of which gives an idea of notable industrial advancement.

5   The Region of the Ancient "Chichimecs," with Notes on the Tepecanos and the Ruin of La Quemada, Mexico

[1] See Orozco y Berra, *Geografía*, map and text; Mota Padilla, *Historia*; Arlegui, *Crónica*; Bancroft, *Native Races*, Vol. 1; Icazbalceta, *Colección de Documentos*, t. 2; Herrera, *Hist. Gen.*, dec., lib. ii, cap. 12; Torquemada, *Monarquia Indiana*, t. 1, p. 81 et seq.; and other historians.

[2] Mota Padilla, *Historia*, p. 55.

[3] Principally Berghes, Tarayre, Nebel, and Batres.

[4] Originally San Juan Bautista de Mezquitic (see Mota Padilla, p. 354; also Arlegui), today a town of about twenty-five hundred inhabitants, situated in the northern expanded portion of the valley of the Rio de Bolaños, three days' horseback journey, or a little over one hundred miles, from Fresnillo or from Zacatecas.

[5] A small but old village ("Nastic" in Mota Padilla, p. 354) about four and a half miles south of Mezquitic, on the Rio de Bolaños.

[6] Such cliff formation is quite common about mesas or table-mountains in Mexico.

[7] *Mesa*, "table," "tableland"; *mesita*, a small mesa.

[8] Specimens 30–10661, 10662, 10681, in the American Museum of Natural History, New York City.

[9] These, as well as the majority of the specimens mentioned in this paper, are deposited in the American Museum of Natural History, New York City.

[10] Apparently exactly similar specimens of mortar have been reported by Guillemin Tarayre from La Quemada ruin. See *Archives de la Commission Scientifique du Mexique*, 3: 374–75.

[11] Almost exactly the same form of stone axe has been found at La Quemada. See Batres's original report, pl. 20.

[12] These stones were often found in pairs, and if superimposed the notches would form a central aperture.

[13] The name is probably derived from the Nahua, in which language there are several terms from which such a derivation would be possible, as *tepetl*, "hill or mountain"; *aco*, "above," "on the top of"; *iacath*, "point"; and there may be others. The Tepecanos call themselves also Hu-mā-kam or Hu-māt-kam, the meaning of which is close to "the ones," "the people."

[14] Bancroft, *Native Races*, 1: 617–44; direct reference, p. 628. See also 5: 347; reference to Herrera.

[15] Orozco y Berra, *Geografía* pp. 279, 284-85.

[16] "Mas los mismos teules chichimecos se subdividían en fracciones, con idiomas particulares. La primera familia que se presenta es la de los *cazcanes*, ocupada el terreno desde el Río Grande confinando con los tecuexes y los tepecanos."

[17] Lyon, *Journal*.

[18] Nahua *azcatl*, "ants"; *tlan*, "near," "nearby," "place of," containing many. The name appears as Azcatlan in the text and on the map of Jalisco by A. García Cubas in his *Atlas Metódico para la enseñanza de la geografía de la República Mexicana* (Mexico, 1874).

[19] From the latest description obtained, these figures must be similar to those of which I found the remnants in the ruins on the Cerro de Colotlan, a few miles north of Askeltan, above described.

[20] The Tepecano *chimáles* differ from those of the nearby Huichols in a number of particulars. They are mostly of larger size; the thick stick is not used by the Huichols; the use of cotton and especially of cotton-yarn badges is almost restricted to the Tepecanos; the shape of the badges among the Tepecanos is much more frequently hexagonal than among the Huichols, who generally make the diamond-shaped ones; the Huichol badges are rarely if ever plain white, those of the Tepecanos quite often; the beads are much more common in Tepecano badges; and, finally, among the Huichols the use of the badges is much more extended than it is among the Tepecanos.

[21] As I found later there is a river of this name near the northwestern boundary of Durango and Chihuahua. In a part of its valley lived (and a few remnants still live) the northern Tepehuanes.

[22] *Lengua Mexicana* among the natives invariably means the Nahua or "Axtec" language; the Spanish is known only as the "Castellano." On my last expedition to the region I found two old men, apparently pureblood survivors of the early Indian inhabitants of the country, one in Nostic and one in Huejucar (a day's journey northeastward), both of whom informed me that their forefathers spoke the "Mexicano." I should add that all the native names in this section are Nahuan.

[23] This was mentioned by Nestor in 1898. In May 1902, while revisiting Santa Catarina, which, so far as our knowledge goes, was a pure Huichol pueblo, I came across a number of old petroglyphs, such as are found in the ruins a little north of Askeltan, for which the Huichols could offer no explanation except that they were made by "other people." The term *mecos* is well known to the Tepecanos and to other natives in that part of Jalisco and in southern Zacatecas.

[24] Calentura is a form of malaria, usually with frequent attacks. The disease is common among other Mexican tribes and attacks also the whites. It is usually a chronic disease, against which the Indians employ the *palo amargo* (native quinia) and other herbs, but not always with success. The patients become very debilitated and are obliged to keep to bed. Anemia and emaciation follow, and may result in death. In most cases, however,

restoration to health, after the sixth or eighth week of the malady I was told, slowly takes place. The disease attacks people of all ages and may recur in the same patient.

[25] I have seen this on several occasions among the Mexican Indians as well as among the Indians of southern United States.

[26] A woolen belt, ordinarily two or three inches in width and from two to four yards long.

[27] The Southern Tepehuane equivalents follow the Tepecano words and are enclosed in parentheses.

[28] The Tepecanos themselves generally use the term *Kí-dagh-ra*, signifying "village."

[29] Most of the Tepecanos know the numerals only up to six; only a few old men know them up to ten; numerals higher than ten could not be obtained at all.

[30] Higher Tepehaune numerals are: 11, de-wan-ma^n; 12, de-man-gōk; 20, ma^n-ōp, ma^{n}ōm; 40, gōk-om; 50, gōk-om-de-mān-buš; 60, vajk-om; 100, šła-mām-om.

[31] No infinitive was obtainable.

[32] The terminal *ys* is ordinarily quite mute, and a similar condition is observable in other terminals.

[33] These parts of speech do not seem to have quite such sharp, definite meanings as with us. Some of the versions are undoubtedly not quite literal; they are equivalents, modified by the Indian mode of thought and usages of expression.

[34] *Hā-va* may be an adaptation from the Spanish *agua*, although the present Tepecanos believe it to be a word of their own language.

[35] "The water will now come from the sky."

[36] See Mota Padilla, *Historia*, p. 57.

[37] Batres, *Visita a los monumentos arqueológicos de La Quemada*.

[38] Average nasal index of Tepecanos = 83.6.

[39] Mota Padilla, *Historia*, p. 58.

[40] The local custom of giving the population of a place is to give the number of male adults.

[41] Mota Padilla, *Historia*, p. 55.

[42] "Mecatabasco" in Mota Padilla, *Historia*, p. 56.

[43] *Archives de la Commission Scientifique du Mexique*, Vol. 3.

[44] Batres, *Visita*.

[45] See Bancroft, *Native Races*, 4: 578–92.

[46] Ibid., 579–80.

[47] It is probable that some of the potsherds have been brought to the surface by rodents. The owner of the Hacienda de la Quemada has in his collection two or three imperfect pieces of this paint-inlaid pottery and several pieces, also imperfect, of painted ware exceedingly like the Totoate variety, all obtained from or near the ruins of La Quemada. Some of the pieces, as well as additional specimens, are illustrated in pls. 18, 22, and 23 of Batres's *Visita*.

[48] According to Tarayre. Batres's measurements give 16 to 18.2 meters.
[49] See Tarayre's plan in his pl. 5 or in Batres, *Visita.*
[50] See Berghe's plan in Tarayre's report.
[51] Tarayre (and also Batres, *Visita,* 24) mentions and pictures the face of a rock in the neighborhood with several upright serpent figures, and by other authors a slab with carved hand and foot is spoken of.

6 Late Archaeological Sites in Durango, Mexico, from Chalchihuites to Zape

[1] Manuel Gamio, "Los monumentos arqueológicos de las inmediaciones de Chalchihuites, Zacatecas," *Anales del Museo Nacional de Arqueología, Historia y Etnología,* 2 (México, 1910): 467–92.
[2] Noguera, *Ruinas arqueológicas.* A fuller bibliography is included in this work.
[3] Everardo Gamiz, *Geografía del Estado de Durango; Monografías de los municipalidades de Nombre de Dios, Poanas y Suchil* (Torreón, 1929). *La región sureste del Estado de Durango* (Torreón, 1936).
[4] Cf. the bibliography on La Quemada in Noguera's work above cited, especially Seler, Batres, Tarayre, Garcia, and Noguera. For further notes on the archaeology of this general region see Lumholtz, *Unknown Mexico* and Hrdlička, "The Chichimecs and Their Ancient Culture, with Notes on the Tepecanos, and the Ruin of La Quemada, Mexico," *American Anthropologist,* n., 5, 3 (1903): 384–440.
[5] Sayles, *An Archaeological Survey.*

9 The Opata: An Inland Tribe of Sonora

[1] Sauer, *Aboriginal Population,* p. 29.
[2] Sauer, *Road to Cíbola; Distribution of Aboriginal Tribes; Aboriginal Population.*
[3] Sauer, *Aboriginal Population.*
[4] Kroeber, *Uto-Aztecan Languages.*
[5] Ibid.; Johnson, Opata field notes, 1940.
[6] *Documentos,* p. 534.
[7] Sauer, *Road to Cíbola,* p. 27, et passim; *Aboriginal Population,* p. 27.
[8] Lombardo, *Arte,* p. 230.
[9] Beals, *Comparative Ethnology,* pp. 176–80.
[10] Smith, *Grammatical Sketch,* vocabulary.
[11] Beals, *Comparative Ethnology,* p. 183.
[12] Lombardo, *Arte,* p. 226.
[13] Ibid., pp. 37, 232, et passim. Hrdlička mentions a wooden hoe (*Notes,* p. 75).

[14] Lombardo, *Arte*, p. 235.

[15] Ibid., p. 226.

[16] Johnson, *El Idioma Yaqui*.

[17] *Fragmentary Manuscript*, p. 15.

[18] See Beals, *Comparative Ethnology*, p. 101.

[19] Lombardo, *Arte*, p. 226, and other early sources; Johnson, *El Idioma Yaqui*.

[20] Aztec *chil-tepi*, "small chili."

[21] Beals, *Comparative Ethnology*, p. 158; Sauer, *Aboriginal Population*, p. 26.

[22] *Documentos*, chap. 6.

[23] Ibid., p. 522.

[24] Ibid.

[25] *Documentos*, p. 522; Lombardo, *Arte: mah* "to roast mescal," *mai* "roasted mescal," p. 231, et passim.

[26] *Documentos*, p. 522.

[27] *Fragmentary Manuscript*, p. 19.

[28] *Documentos*, pp. 522, 527ff.; Smith, *Grammatical Sketch*.

[29] Lombardo, *Arte*, pp. 18, 238, et passim.

[30] Ibid., p. 226, et passim. Hrdlička (*Notes*, p. 75) mentions archaeological stone mortars in Opata country.

[31] Smith, *Grammatical Sketch*, vocabulary.

[32] Ibid., p. 595.

[33] *Documentos*, p. 516.

[34] Lombardo, *Arte*, p. 10.

[35] Ibid., pp. 233, 234, 241; *Fragmentary Manuscript*, pp. 9, 11; Johnson, *El Idioma Yaqui*.

[36] Lombardo, *Arte*, p. 240; Smith, *Grammatical Sketch*, vocabulary; *Fragmentary Manuscript*, p. 20.

[37] Lombardo, *Arte*, p. 8; Beals, *Comparative Ethnology*, p. 167; Obregón's *History*, p. 172; Johnson, *El Idioma Yaqui*.

[38] Smith, *Grammatical Sketch*, vocabulary; Beals, *Comparative Ethnology*, p. 187; Alegre, *Historia*, 2: 93.

[39] Lombardo, *Arte*, p. 9.

[40] Johnson, Opata field notes, 1940.

[41] *Documentos*, pp. 551–52.

[42] Lombardo, *Arte*, p. 67: nopi *"verbo; sacar lumbre con unos palitos."*

[43] Cf. Lombardo, *Arte*, passim for tanning vocabulary; Núñez, *Carta Edificante*, p. 3.

[44] See Lombardo, *Arte*, pp. 8, 87, 91, 149, 229; Johnson, Opata field notes, 1940.

[45] *Documentos*, pp. 551–52.

[46] Lombardo, *Arte*, p. 153 passim. *"La manta conque se cubren en lugar de calzones se llama* esat, este" (*Fragmentary Manuscript*, p. 17).

[47] Beals, *Comparative Ethnology*, p. 173; Obregón's *History*, p. 174.

[48] Lombardo, *Arte*, pp. 8, 18, 146, 154.

[49] *Documentos*, p. 550.

[50] *Documentos*, July 1730.

[51] Johnson, Opata field notes, 1940.

[52] Núñez, *Carta Edificante.*

[53] Lombardo, *Arte*, p. 2.

[54] Núñez, *Carta Edificante.*

[55] Possbly the dry ribs of the *sahuaro* (giant cactus)—utilized for arrows by Pima and Papago—is meant.

[56] Smith, *Grammatical Sketch*, vocabulary.

[57] Núñez, *Carta Edificante*, p. 3.

[58] Johnson, Yaqui field notes, 1939–40.

[59] Hrdlička, (*Notes*, p. 75) mentions stone axes as archaeological finds in the Opata region.

[60] Lombardo, *Arte*, pp. 7, 13; Smith, *Grammatical Sketch*, vocabulary.

[61] *Documentos*, p. 551.

[62] Ibid., pp. 628–29.

[63] Ibid., p. 544.

[64] Johnson, Yaqui field notes, 1939–40.

[65] Lombardo, *Arte*, pp. 165, 229.

[66] Zúñiga, *Rápida Ojeada*, p. 6.

[67] Ibid.

[68] Johnson, Yaqui field notes, 1939–40.

[69] *Documentos*, pp. 551–52.

[70] Ibid., p. 541.

[71] See *Documentos*, pp. 541, 544–48; Núñez, *Carta Edificante*, p. 3 passim.

[72] Hrdlička (*Notes*, pp. 75–76) refers to the occurrence of this dance in Tuape on the first Monday after Holy Week.

[73] *Documentos*, chap. 5, p. 534.

[74] Johnson, Yaqui field notes, 1939–40.

[75] *Documentos*, p. 541.

[76] Lombardo, *Arte*, p. 231.

[77] Johnson, Yaqui field notes, 1939–40.

[78] Lombardo, *Arte*, p. 238.

[79] *Documentos*, July 1730, p. 631.

[80] Ibid., p. 539. For a Pima parallel from Onavas in which women were also the protagonists, see Johnson, *Piman Foot Drum.*

[81] Hrdlička (*Notes*, p. 77) refers to a similar dance in Tuape called *La Cuelga.*

[82] Zúñiga, *Rápida Ojeada*, p. 6.

[83] *Documentos*, p. 542.

[84] Lombardo, *Arte*, pp. 149, 233.

[85] The forms *-gua, -guat* appear only in word-absolute; stem *mas-*, etc. The terms are taken from Lombardo, *Arte*, pp. 242–45, without change of orthography. See also Barcastro, *Sermones*; Radin, *Mexican Kinship Terms*; Smith, *Grammatical Sketch*; Pinart, *Vocabularies.*

[86] The element -ragua is the nominal abstractual suffix: see Lombardo, Arte, p. 142.

[87] Barcastro, Sermones, pp. 100–104.

[88] Lombardo, Arte, p. 220.

[89] Ibid., p. 20.

[90] See Lombardo, Arte; Smith, Grammatical Sketch, vocabulary; Johnson, El Idioma Yaqui.

[91] [As this statement stands it seems to mean that granduncle and grandaunt called their own grandnephews, as well as their own grandsons, by the term for grandson.]

[92] Lombardo, Arte, p. 245.

[93] Documentos, p. 543.

[94] Lombardo, Arte, p. 245.

[95] Baptismal godfather: common Catholic usage establishes the relationship between the true father and the godfather, who are called compadres, between the mother and the godmother, comadres.

[96] See Spicer, Pascua, chaps. 3 and 4.

[97] Lombardo, Arte, p. 142.

[98] See Documentos, chap. 6; Zúñiga, Rápida Ojeada, p. 4.

[99] Documentos, pp. 538–39.

[100] Ibid., pp. 547–48.

[101] See Documentos, p. 527, and Lombardo, Arte, for a full list of medicinal plants, their uses, and names in Opata and Spanish. See also Núñez's list (Carta Edificante).

[102] [Perhaps] Datura species; variously reported as marijuana, jimsonweed, etc.

[103] Hrdlička (Notes, pp. 78, 80) mentions menstrual seclusion and a forty-day period of special dietary restrictions after delivery.

[104] Núñez, Carta Edificante.

[105] Documentos, p. 512.

[106] Ibid., p. 517. Hrdlička (Notes, p. 82) states that dog excrement was applied to burns and scalds.

[107] Compare aquiguat, "daughter" (woman speaking).

[108] Documentos, July 1730, p. 626; Lombardo, Arte, pp. 202–3.

[109] Lombardo, Arte, pp. 202–3.

[110] Johnson, Opata field notes, 1940.

[111] Documentos, pp. 539–40.

[112] Idem, July 1730, p. 638.

[113] Núñez, Carta Edificante, p. 2.

[114] Documentos, p. 628.

[115] Lombardo, Arte, pp. 10, 18, 227.

[116] Documentos, p. 539.

[117] Ibid.

[118] Johnson, Opata field notes, 1940.

[119] Documentos, pp. 539–40.

[120] Ibid., p. 540.

121 Lombardo, *Arte*, p. 245.

122 Ibid., pp. 205, 245.

123 Ibid., pp. 201–3; Smith, *Grammatical Sketch*, vocabulary.

124 Smith, *Grammatical Sketch*, vocabulary.

125 Lombardo, *Arte*, pp. 194–200; also Smith, *Grammatical Sketch*, vocabulary.

126 Known as Santa María de los Dolores Tónichi when the Franciscans took over the Jesuit missions. The town was moved downriver perhaps two leagues in the eighteenth century.

127 *Documentos*, p. 494.

128 Bartlett, *Personal Narrative*, p. 240 passim.

129 *Documentos*, July 1730, p. 631.

130 Spicer, *Pascua*, chap. 5, et passim.

131 Johnson, Opata field notes, 1940.

132 Spicer, *Pascua*; Johnson, Yaqui field notes, 1939–40.

133 *Documentos*, p. 733.

134 Spicer, *Pascua*.

135 Now in the collections of the Museum of the American Indian, Heye Foundation.

136 Spicer, *Pascua*.

137 It would be out of place to cite here at length the controversy over masks in north Mexico and the Southwest and subsequently discovered archaeological and distributional data presented by Parsons, Beals, Eckholm, and others.

138 This within the memory of Sra. Estefana Tecolote de Bauza, the last speaker of Opata in Tónichi.

139 *Documentos*, chap. 7, pp. 566–89; July 1730, p. 632; Núñez, *Carta Edificante*; Johnson, Opata field notes, 1940.

140 Sauer, *Aboriginal Population*, pp. 26–27.

141 Bartlett, *Personal Narrative*.

142 *Documentos*, passim; Núñez, *Carta Edificante*.

143 Kroeber, *Cultural and Natural Areas*.

144 A possible identification is to be found in Ocaranza, *Los Franciscanos*, p. 128.

145 The writer is indebted to Dr. William Elmendorf and Prof. M. B. Emeneau respectively for the two references.

146 See also Beals, *Comparative Ethnology*, p. 110.

147 Limited couvade occurs among the Yaqui (Johnson, Yaqui field notes, 1939–40).

BIBLIOGRAPHY

Aguirre, Manuel
1765   Doctrina Cristiana y Pláticas Doctrinales traducidas en Lengua Opata. Mexico.

Alegre, Francisco Xavier
1841   Historia de la Compañía de Jesús en Nueva España. 3 vols. Mexico.

Arlegui, José
1937   Crónica de la Provincia de N.S.P.S. Francisco de Zacatecas. Mexico.

Armillas, Pedro
1963   Investigaciones arqueológicas en el Estado de Zacatecas. Boletín Inst. Nac. Antr. Hist.

Bancroft, H. H.
1882   The Native Races of the Pacific States. Vols. 1, 4, 5. A. L. Bancroft & Co.: San Francisco.
1884   History of the North Mexican States, 1: 319–26. San Francisco.

Barcastro, Antonio
1792   Sermones en la Lengua Opata. Ms. in the Pinart collection, Bancroft Library, University of California.

Bartlett, John R.
1854   Personal Narrative of Exploration . . . in Texas, New Mexico, California, Sonora and Chihuahua . . . with the United States and Mexican Boundary Commission in 1850–51–52–53. 2 vols. New York.

Beals, Ralph L.
1932   The Comparative Ethnology of Northern Mexico Before 1750. Ibero-Americana, No. 2. Berkeley.

Brand, Donald D.
1935   The Distribution of Pottery Types in Northwest Mexico. American Anthropologist, 37: 288, 294.

Chavero, Alfredo
1895   México á través de los siglos, Vol. 1. Barcelona.

Crane, H. R. and James B. Griffin
1958a   University of Michigan radiocarbon dates, 2. Science, 127: 1098–1105.
1958b   University of Michigan radiocarbon dates, 3. Science, 128: 1117–23.

Decorme, G.
1941   La Obra de los Jesuitas Mexicanos, Vol. 2. Las Misiones, Mexico.

DiPeso, Charles C.
1956   The Upper Pima of San Cayetano of Tumacacori. Amerind Foundation, Dragoon, Arizona.

Documentos para la Historia de México, 3a serie. Mexico.
1853–57 One of the principal sources, including information contained in the Rudo Ensayo. Parts 4, 5, and 6 supply most information. Titles include: Descripción Geográfica natural y curiosa de la Provincia de Sonora, por un amigo del servicio de Dios y el rey nuestro señor, año de 1764. Estado de la Provincia de Sonora, julio de 1730. Descripción y Noticia Individual de las Misiones de la Pimería Baja, 1772.

Fragmentary manuscript of an Opata vocabulary. Documento
n.d.   No. 333–41, Ramo de Temporalidades, Archivo de la Nación, Mexico, D. F.

Guillemin Tarayre, E.
1869   Exploration Mineralogique des Régions Mexicaines Suivie de Notes Archéologiques et Ethnographiques. Paris.

Hewett, Edgar L.
1902   Ancient Life in Mexico and Central America, 1: 448. New York.

Hinton, Thomas B.
1969   Remnant tribes of Sonora: Opata, Pima, Papago, and Seri. *In* Handbook of Middle American Indians, R. Wauchope (ed.), 8: 879–90.

Howard, Agnes McClain
1954   Cruciform artifacts of the Sierra Occidental. American Antiquity, 20, No. 2, 174–75.

1955   A paint palette and muller from Durango, Mexico. Newsletter, Missouri Archaeological Society, No. 88, February 15.

Hrdlička, Aleš
1903   The Chichimecs and Their Ancient Culture. American Anthropologist, 5: 431–32.

1904   Notes on the Indians of Sonora. American Anthropologist, 6: 51–89.

Johnson, A. S.
1958   Similarities in Hohokam and Chalchihuites artifacts. American Antiquity, 24: 126–30.

Johnson, J. B.
1940   El Idioma Yaqui (ms).
          The Piman Foot Drum and Fertility Rites. México Antiguo, 5: 140–41.

Jones, John A.
1962   Tepecano house types. Kiva, 27: 24–27.

Kelley, J. Charles
1954   Excavation and Reconnaissance in Durango, Mexico. Year Book
            of the American Philosophical Society, 1953, pp. 172–76. Phila-
            delphia.
1956   Settlement patterns in north-central Mexico. *In* Prehistoric set-
            tlement patterns in the New World, G. R. Willey (ed.).

Kelley, J. Charles and Ellen Abbott
1966   The cultural sequence on the north central frontier of Meso-
            america. *In* Actas y Memorias, 36 Congreso Internacional de
            Americanistas, España, 1: 325–44. Sevilla.

Kroeber, A. L.
1934   Uto-Aztecan Languages of Mexico. Ibero-Americana, No. 8.
            Berkeley.
1939   Cultural and Natural Areas of Native North America. University
            of California Publications in American Archaeology and Eth-
            nology, Vol. 38.

Lambert, Marjorie F.
1957   A rare stone humpbacked figurine from Pecos Pueblo, New
            Mexico. El Palacio, 64, Nos. 3–4, 93–109.

Lister, Robert H. and Agnes M. Howard
1955   The Chalchihuites culture of northwestern Mexico. American
            Antiquity, 21: 122–29.

Lombardo, Natal
1702   Arte de la Lengua Teguima, vulgarmente llamada Opata. Mexico.

Lumholtz, Carl
1902   Unknown Mexico, 1: 448. New York.
1904   El México Desconocido, Vol. 2. C. Scribner's & Sons: New York.

Lyon, G. T.
1828   Journal. London.

McGregor, John C.
1941   Southwestern Archaeology. John Wiley and Sons: New York.

Marquina, Ignacio
1951   Arquitectura prehispánica. Mem. Inst. Nac. Antr. Hist., Vol. 1.

Mason, J. A.
1936   Notes and News from the Middle American Area. American
            Antiquity, 2: 55–56, 150–51.

Mecham, J. L.
1927   Francisco de Ibarra and Nueva Vizcaya. Durham.

Mendizábal, Miguel O. de
1930   La Evolución del Noreste de México. Mexico.

Mota Padilla, Matías de la.
1843   Historia de la Conquista de la Nueva-Galicia, 3: 200.

Nebel, Carlos
1963   Viaje pintoresco y arqueológico sobre la parte más interesante de la República Mexicana. Mexico. Earlier editions 1836 (French), 1840.

Noguera, Eduardo
1930   Ruinas arqueológicas del norte de Mexico, Casas Grandes (Chihuahua), La Quemada, Chalchihuites (Zacatecas). Pub. Sec. Educ. Pública, Talleres Gráficos de la Nación, pp. 5–27.
1960   La Quemada, Chalchihuites. Guía oficial del Inst. Nac. Antro. Hist.

Núñez, Angel Antonio
1777   Carta Edificante Histórico-curiosa escrita desde la Misión de Sta. María de Baserac en los Fines de Sonora, 31 de diciembre de 1777. *In* Noticias de Varias Misiones, Vol. 76, Biblioteca Nacional de México.

Obregón, Balthasar de
1924   Historia de los descubrimientos antiguos y modernos de la Nueva España. Departamento editorial de la Secretaría de Educación Pública, Mexico.
1928   Obregón's History of the 16th Century Explorations in Western America, entitled Chronicle, Commentary, or Relation of Ancient and Modern Discoveries in New Spain and New Mexico, George P. Hammond and Agapito Rey (trs. and eds.). Los Angeles.

Ocaranza, R.
1933   Los Franciscanos en las Provincias de Sonora y Ostimuri, México.

Orozco y Berra, M.
1864   Geografía de las lenguas y carta etnográfica de México. Impr. de J. M. Andrade y F. Scalante, Mexico.

Parsons, Elsie Clews
1949   Pueblos Indian Religion. 2 vols. Chicago: University of Chicago Press.

Pennington, Campbell W.
1963   The Tarahumar of Mexico. Salt Lake City: University of Utah Press.
1969   The Tepehuan of Chihuahua: Their Material Culture. Salt Lake City: University of Utah Press.

Pérez de Ribas, Andrés
1645   Historia de los Triunfos de Nuestra Sta. Fé, en las Misiones de la Provincia de Nueva España. Madrid.

Pinart, A. L.
n.d.   Vocabularies of the Hehué Dialect of Opata. Ms. in the Pinart
            collection, Bancroft Library, University of California.
1880   Voyage en Sonora. Bulletin, Société de Géographie, pp. 193–
            244. Paris.

Porter, Muriel N.
1956   Excavations at Chupícuaro, Guanajuata, México. Trans. Amer.
            Phil. Soc., 46: pt. 5.

Radin, Paul
1931   Mexican Kinship Terms. University of California Publications in
            American Archaeology and Ethnology, 31: 1–14.

Riley, Carroll
1969   The Southern Tepehuan and Tepecano. In Handbook of Middle
            American Indians, R. Wauchope (ed.), 8: 814–21.

Riley, Carroll L. and John Hobgood
1959   A recent nativistic movement among the southern Tepehuan
            Indians. SW. Jour. Anthr., 15: 355–60.

Riley, Carroll L. and Howard D. Winters
1963   The prehistoric Tepehuan of northern Mexico. SW. Jour. Anthr.,
            19: 177–85.

Rouaix, Pastor
1929   Geografía del Estado de Durango. Dirección de Estudios Geo-
            gráficos y Climatológicos, Pub. No. 21. Mexico.

Sauer, C. O.
1932   The Road to Cíbola. Ibero-Americana, No. 3, Berkeley.
1934   The Distribution of Aboriginal Tribes and Languages in North-
            western Mexico. Ibero-Americana, No. 5. Berkeley.
1935   Aboriginal Population of Northwestern Mexico. Ibero-Americana,
            No. 10. Berkeley.

Sauer, C. O. and Donald Brand
1932   Aztatlán, Prehistoric Mexican Frontier on the Pacific Coast.
            Ibero-Americana, No. 1. Berkeley.
1935   Prehistoric Settlements of Sonora, with Special References to
            Cerros de Trincheras. Univ. of California Pub. in Geography, 5,
            No. 3. Berkeley.

Sayles, E. B.
1936   Some Southwestern Pottery Types, Series 5. Medallion Papers,
            No. 21. Globe.

1936   An Archaeological Survey of Chihuahua, Mexico. Medallion
            Papers, No. 22. Globe.

Service, Elman R.
1969   The Northern Tepehuan. In Handbook of Middle American In-
            dians, R. Wauchope (ed.), 8: 822–29.

Smith, Buckingham
1861   A Grammatical Sketch of the Heve Language. New York.
1863   Rudo Ensayo. Albany.
Spicer, E. H.
1940   Pascua, a Yaqui Village in Arizona. Chicago.
Suhm, Dee Ann, Alex D. Krieger, and Edward B. Jelks
1954   An Introductory Handbook of Texas Archeology. Bulletin, Texas
          Archeological Society, Vol. 25.
Tamarón y Romeral, Pedro
1937   Demostración del Vastísimo Obispado de la Nueva Viscaya—
          1765, pp. 85–92. Mexico.
Vaillant, G. C.
1932   Some Resemblances in the Ceramics of Central and North
          America. Medallion Papers, No. 12. Globe.
Wedel, Waldo R.
1941   Archeological Investigations at Buena Vista Lake, Kern County,
          California. Bur. Amer. Ethnol., Bull. 130.
Weigand, Phil C.
1968   The mines and mining techniques of the Chalchihuites Culture.
          American Antiquity, 33: 1, 45–61.
Zapata, Juan Ortiz
1678   Relación. Doc. Hist. Mex. 4th ser., 3: 310–14.
Zúñiga, Ignacio
1835   Rápida Ojeada al Estado de Sonora. Mexico.